RELIGION AND SOCIETY IN EARLY MODERN ENGLAND

'An excellent collection of prime sources for the study of religion in its social context, through and beyond the age of the Reformation in England.'

Patrick Collinson, *University of Cambridge*

'An unusually imaginative collection of readings on the religious life of England from the Reformation to the Restoration. There is a nice balance between documents which show what in fact happened and arguments for and against the many changes that marked these years, but what is perhaps most moving and memorable are the personal comments in memoirs and diaries that suddenly illuminate a time and an attitude.'

Paul S. Seaver, *Stanford University*

'Outstanding. There is a crying need for collections of primary source materials for courses in early modern history. Earlier documents collections have given us a very one-sided and top-down view. This is a breath of fresh air.'

Margo Todd, *Vanderbilt University*

'An invaluable classroom aid. There is nothing comparable to it currently in print.'

J. Sears McGee, *University of California, Santa Barbara*

'An excellent and imaginative collection. The coverage of documents chosen is admirably balanced.'

Diarmaid MacCulloch, *University of Oxford*

David Cressy is Professor of History at California State University, Long Beach. **Lori Anne Ferrell** is Associate Professor of History and Religion at the School of Theology at Claremont and the Claremont Graduate School.

RELIGION AND SOCIETY IN EARLY MODERN ENGLAND

A Sourcebook

edited by David Cressy and Lori Anne Ferrell

London and New York

First published 1996
by Routledge
11 New Fetter Lane, London EC4P 4EE

Simultaneously published in the USA and Canada
by Routledge
29 West 35th Street, New York, NY 10001

© 1996 David Cressy and Lori Anne Ferrell

Typeset in Garamond by
J&L Composition Ltd, Filey, North Yorkshire

Printed and bound in Great Britain by
Redwood Books, Trowbridge, Wiltshire

British Library Cataloguing in Publication Data
Religion and Society in Early Modern England: Sourcebook
I. Cressy, David   II. Ferrell, Lori Anne
274.206

Library of Congress Cataloguing in Publication Data
Religion and society in early modern England: a sourcebook/edited
by David Cressy and Lori Anne Ferrell.
p.   cm.
Includes bibliographical references and index.
1. England—Church history—16th century—Sources.   2. England—
Church history—17th century—Sources.   I. Cressy, David.
II. Ferrell, Lori Anne.
BR756.R445 1996
274.2′06—dc20   95–38690
CIP

ISBN 0–415–11848–4
0–415–11849–2 (pbk)

CONTENTS

Acknowledgements   viii

Introduction   1

1 TRADITION AND CHANGE:
  THE OLD RELIGION AND THE NEW
  The state of Melford church as I, Roger Martyn, did know it   11
  Hugh Latimer, Convocation sermon, 1536   13
  The Ten Articles, 1536   17
  Robert Parkyn's narrative of the reformation, 1532–54   24
  Rose Hickman's memoir of Protestant life under Mary   29
  John Foxe, *Acts and Monuments*   32
    The examination of Anne Askew, 1546   33
    The ordeal of Ridley and Latimer, 1555   34
  Accounts and inventories of St Edmund's parish,
    Salisbury, 1527-57   35

2 THE ESTABLISHED CHURCH
  The Book of Common Prayer, 1559   40
    Preface   40
    Of ceremonies, why some be abolished and some retained   42
    The order for the administration of the Lord's Supper,
      or holy communion   45
    The 'Black Rubric', 1552   47
    The ministration of baptism to be used in the church   48
    Public baptism   49
    The form of solemnization of matrimony   51
    The thanksgiving of women after childbirth   54
    The order for the burial of the dead   55
  An Act for the Uniformity of Common Prayer and Divine
    Service, 1559   56
  The Thirty-Nine Articles, 1563   59

The homily against contention and brawling   70
Thomas Becon's New Catechism, 1559   73
    Preface   74
    Of the duty of children toward their parents   75
Accounts and inventories of St Edmund's parish,
    Salisbury, 1579–1635   78

3 RELIGIOUS CULTURE AND RELIGIOUS
    CONTEST IN ELIZABETHAN ENGLAND
A view of popish abuses yet remaining in the English
    church, 1572   82
Archbishop Grindal's Injunctions for the laity in the
    province of York, 1571   90
Archbishop Grindal's letter to the queen, 1576   93
George Gifford's *Country Divinity*, 1582   99
Philip Stubbes, The manner of sanctifying the Sabbath, 1583   105
Oxfordshire archdeaconry court, 1584   107
William Allen's *Defence of English Catholics*, 1584   110
William Perkins, *A Golden Chain, or the Description of Theology*, 1590   114
Samuel Ward's diary, 1595   120

4 THE JACOBEAN CHURCH
Bishop Matthew's report on the Hampton Court
    Conference, 1604   123
Constitutions and Canons Ecclesiastical, 1604   127
Archbishop Bancroft's Letter regarding Catholic recusants, 1605   132
William Bradshaw's *English Puritanism*, 1605   135
Archbishop Abbot's letter regarding preaching, 1622   137
Samuel Gardiner, *The Foundation of the Faithful*, 1611   139
John Buckeridge, *A Sermon Touching Prostration and Kneeling*, 1618   141
Lancelot Andrewes, 'A Sermon Before the King', 1621   142
Richard Sheldon, *A Sermon Laying Open the Beast and His
    Marks*, 1622   143

5 CEREMONIALISM AND ITS DISCONTENTS
The King's Declaration of Sports, 1633   145
Bishop Piers's report on Somerset parish feasts, 1633   148
Henry Burton, *A Divine Tragedy Lately Acted*, 1636   151
Archbishop Laud's visitation of Leicestershire, 1634   155
Richard Montague's articles of enquiry for the diocese of
    Norwich, 1638   157

Christopher Dow's narrative of the rise and progress of
the 'Disciplinarians', 1637   168

Robert Skinner, A Sermon Preached before the King at
Whitehall, 1634   172

6 RELIGIOUS REVOLUTION

The Roots and Branches Petition, 1640   174

The Protestation Oath, 1641   180

The Solemn League and Covenant, 1643   180

William Dowsing's destructions in East Anglia, 1643–4   183

Directory for Public Worship, 1645   186

    Preface   187

    The Sacrament of Baptism   189

    The Solemnization of Marriage   190

    Concerning Burial of the Dead   191

    Of singing of psalms   192

Nicholas Proffet, *Englands Impenitencie under Smiting*, 1645   192

Thomas Edwards on the practices and errors of the sectaries,
1646   195

Richard Baxter's ministry at Kidderminster, 1647–60   199

Notes   204

Chronology   207

Glossary   209

Index   212

ACKNOWLEDGEMENTS

This book emerged from an intensive five-week workshop or 'institute' on society and religion in early modern England held in Claremont, California, in the summer of 1993. Hosted by the Claremont Graduate School and funded by the National Endowment for the Humanities, the institute brought together twenty-four college and university teachers and several of the leading scholars in the field to discuss the sources, texts, issues and problems represented here. As directors of the institute, we wish to thank the following visiting faculty for their lively and instructive contributions: Professor Patrick Collinson of Trinity College, Cambridge; Dr Christopher Haigh of Christ Church, Oxford; Professor Mark Kishlansky of Harvard University; Professor Peter Lake of Princeton University; Professor Sears McGee of the University of California, Santa Barbara; Dr John Morrill of Selwyn College, Cambridge; Professor Linda Pollock of Tulane University; Professor Margo Todd of Vanderbilt University; and Dr Keith Wrightson of Jesus College, Cambridge. As one participant remarked, 'it's like seeing one's favourite footnotes come to life'.

Members of the institute included teachers of English, history, philosophy and religion. We should like to thank them all for helping us to develop this collection: Dan Beaver, Edith Bershadsky, Jeannie Brink, John Coldewey, James Day, Stuart Dipple, James Forse, Gayle Gaskill, Tamara Goeglein, Michael Graham, James Hart, Jeff Hush, Norman Jones, Newton Key, Kathleen Noonan, Myron Noonkester, Debora Shugar, William Stockton, Elizabeth Van Beek, Henry Van Leeuwen, John Vidmar, Susan Wabuda, Timothy Wadkins, and Paul White.

INTRODUCTION

Religion permeated every aspect of English society in the sixteenth and seventeenth century. The pattern of the cosmos, the history and destiny of the world, and the ordering of social, political and domestic relations were all explained in biblical and theological terms. Christianity provided a system for understanding, a framework for discussion, and a vocabulary for the expression of complex notions, from the governance of the self to the governance of the state, from Christian dealing in the marketplace to proper conduct on the Sabbath. Faith and ritual affected people at many different levels, making spiritual, intellectual, emotional and visceral appeals. Public and private affairs alike were deeply infused by religion.

The shattering of the Roman Catholic church and the establishment of the Protestant church of England made religion a central arena of contest from the reign of Henry VIII to the time of the later Stuarts. The struggle to define and control 'true religion' affected everyone from the political centre to the provincial periphery. Nobody was immune from the claims of faith or the obligations of Christian duty. Everyone's life was affected by alterations in the structure and authority of the church, and by changes in religious values, beliefs, discipline and style. Monarchs and magistrates, university theologians and episcopal administrators, evangelical preachers and pastoral priests, all had a stake in the shaping and reshaping of English religious life. So too did earnest lay men and women of all social ranks, and troubled humble parishioners of every shade of conformity, irregularity and indifference.

Our purpose in gathering these documents is to expose the ligaments of English religious culture and to chart its transformation from the 1530s to the 1660s. The history of religion in this period is not just a history of theology, or of the organized church, or of worship, or of relations between church and state or dealings between the clergy and the laity, although each of those aspects is important. It is also a history of contest and negotiation, adjustment and accommodation, as diverse constituencies struggled to work out the consequences of religious change for social, political, and cultural life. Though many of our sources speak from the point of view of the bishop on the bench, the preacher in the pulpit or the celebrant at the altar, they also shed light on the social and cultural experience of the ordinary men and women who made up the Church of England's 10,000 local congregations. Many of our texts reveal diametrically opposed impulses: the search for a faith that convinced the intellect, and for a religion that satisfied the heart. They trace the tension between the complexities of convocation theology and the compromises of country divinity that foreshadow many of the divisions in modern historical scholarship.

Most historians now agree that traditional Roman Catholicism in early sixteenth-century England was lively, popular and robust. England belonged to the universal church of western Christendom, and its local religious activities satisfied most people's need for a faith that connected them to their locality, to their ancestors, and to God. The calendar was dense with communal religious observances and marked with seasonal bonfires and processions on saints' days that linked the festive and devotional elements of worship. The church porch and churchyard were sites of religious drama, and the interior of the church itself was a polychrome treasury of pious benefactions. Nostalgic reminiscences by Catholic laymen like Roger Martyn and partisan memoirs by priests like Robert Parkyn recall an idealized lost world of harmony, piety and tradition (ch. I, pp. 11, 24).

Most people appear to have believed in purgatory and in the efficacy of prayers for the dead. Most seemed comfortable with a eucharistic sacrament featuring the real presence of Christ. Ordinary people cared little for the authority of Rome, had faint understanding of papal supremacy, and were indifferent regarding the structure or polity of the church. Religion was a matter of routine, of faith, of duty, fellowship and familiarity, and its principal purpose was to lead the sinner to salvation.

This comfortable old religion suffered multiple blows in Henry VIII's reformations. Henry's desire for a male heir led him to seek divorce from Queen Katherine of Aragon, which in turn forced him to break from the Church of Rome. The 1533 Act in Restraint of Appeals made England jurisdictionally independent, and the 1534 Act of Supremacy put the king in the pope's place, as Supreme Head of the English church. The politics of the mid-1530s gave prominence and encouragement to protestant reformers, for whom German Lutheranism was a powerful influence, and their theological views can be traced in the Ten Articles of 1536 (ch. 1, p. 17), which reduced the holy sacraments from seven to three. Baptism, the eucharist and penance retained their sacramental status, while confirmation, matrimony, holy orders and extreme unction were de-emphasized. The government purged excess saints' days from the English liturgical calendar, sponsored attacks on shrines and religious images and launched a first wave of confiscations against the monasteries. At the same time it promoted the publication of the Bible in English, a project it had strenuously resisted just a few years earlier. This was an exhilarating time for the fiery preacher Hugh Latimer, Bishop of Worcester from 1535 (ch. 1, p. 13), and for his more cautious superior, Thomas Cranmer (Archbishop of Canterbury from 1533), but the period of officially sponsored reform was short-lived. Henry VIII turned violently against the reformers in 1538 and went some way towards restoring, or at least stabilizing, the old religion in the Six Articles of 1539. Archbishop Cranmer endured but Latimer resigned his see in protest. The period of protestant martyrdom began, ironically, in the reign of a king who had broken with Rome. Anne Askew, daughter of a Lincolnshire knight, was tortured and executed in 1546 for her protestant views on the mass (ch. 1, p. 33) while the king continued to think of himself as a dutiful defender of the faith.

Popular reactions to the Henrician changes are hard to discern. The Pilgrimage of Grace of 1536, a conservative revolt centred in Yorkshire and Lincolnshire, protested against the closure of monastic houses and rallied to a banner of the five wounds of Christ. Traditionalists elsewhere were not moved to militancy, perhaps because they could perceive no challenge to their fundamental beliefs or patterns of worship. Churchwardens' accounts, which chronicle the activities and economic transactions of parish churches, suggest that most devotional activities continued unchanged (ch. 1, p. 35). Zealous Protestants were few in number, even in the universities of Oxford and Cambridge and the city of London, places that were most hospitable to them. Acute observers at the end of Henry VIII's reign would notice some subtle but significant changes in the religious landscape, including the Bible in English in many churches and a few empty niches belonging to discredited saints. Church services were still in Latin, the priests still wore elaborate vestments, parishioners tended altar lights and prayed for the dead, and the community took part in a rich round of seasonal religious celebrations.

England acquired a protestant prayer book in the reign of Edward VI, but this act of state did not convert England into a protestant country. That would have to wait for another generation. Prostestants were a minority in 1547, but they held the reins of power. The Edwardian reformation couched a protestant form of worship within a hybrid catholic ecclesiastical polity. Bishops and archbishops still governed the church; indeed, prelates were its leading reformers. This was the heyday of Latimer's preaching and the peak of Cranmer's influence as a theologian, liturgist and administrator.

Archbishop Cranmer's two books of common prayer repay careful scrutiny. The first, in 1549, set forth an English vernacular version of the traditional Latin service, with some modest reforms in the conduct of worship. The directions, or 'rubrics', forbade priestly actions now deemed 'popish' or 'superstitious'. There would be no elevation of the sacrament to the people's gaze, for example, no more crossing of the baptismal child with spittle, salt or oil. These limited changes are nonetheless significant, for they reflect the reformation of the theology behind the worship, conveyed in a language the people could understand. They were enforced by a statute proclaiming the Book of Common Prayer service to be the only form of worship allowed throughout the land.

Like its predecessor, Cranmer's second prayer book of 1552 was designed to be 'common', that is, universal, standard and exclusive; it too laid out a programme of daily, weekly, seasonal and life-cycle religious services for everyone to follow. But the 1552 Book of Common Prayer reveals a rapid evolution in liturgical theology and religious politics. The transformation is most apparent in the sacrament of the eucharist, which suggests the influence of the controversial Swiss theologian Ulrich Zwingli. Whereas the 1549 rite could support the traditional Roman Catholic doctrine of transubstantiation, the 1552 ritual could be interpreted as a simple memorial service, and the word 'mass' was dropped. The 'Black Rubric' of 1552 pointedly warned parishioners not to mistake the bread and wine as transubstantiated elements worthy of 'adoration' (ch. 2, p. 48).

Sometimes reluctantly, parishes conformed to the new form of worship and began to dismantle their altars in favour of communion tables and to take down the rood screens that divided the chancel from the nave. But before much could be done to establish the reformed religion, the young King Edward died in 1553, and a Roman Catholic counter-reformation began under Queen Mary. Assisted by the energetic Bishop of London, Edmund Bonner, and by Cardinal Reginald Pole, Mary restored the old religion. Parish priests performed Latin masses, and parishioners set aside the heretical Book of Common Prayer. Traditionalist catholic churchwardens like Roger Martyn reinstated holy relics and sacred images that had been hidden to escape Edwardian iconoclasm. Married priests set aside their wives or gave up their ministry. Most people conformed to the restored Catholic worship, often with great enthusiasm. It appeared that the English apostasy was over.

Those who had embraced Protestantism faced several choices under Mary. They could conform, or accommodate themselves as best they could to the old religion, as Rose Hickman recounts in her memoir (ch. 1, p. 29). Staunch Protestants with sufficient resources and connections could slip into exile in Switzerland or the Low Countries. And those with the courage of martyrs could stand up for their faith and pay the consequences, as did Ridley and Latimer in 1555 and Cranmer the following year. Nearly three hundred Protestants faced the flames during Mary's reign. Their acts of faith were memorialized by the English martyrologist John Foxe, including Latimer's last words of comforting prophecy, 'we shall this day light such a candle, by God's grace, in England, as I trust shall never be put out' (ch. 1, p. 32).

England was a Roman Catholic country again, in communion with the Church of Rome, when Mary died in 1558 to be succeeded by her sister Elizabeth.

Proceeding with caution, the new Elizabethan regime set out once again to build a Protestant nation. Its success was due to the remarkable longevity of the queen, the disciplinary zeal of her bishops, the conservative pace of reform, and the rise of a foreign Catholic enemy, Spain, which the English could define as the agent of Antichrist. Evangelical preaching and the pastoral ministry of a rising generation of protestant priests created pockets of reformed religion, some of it more godly, advanced or nonconformist than the queen or her authorities would allow. At the same time, in areas reformers decried as the 'dark corners of the land', traditional religion and community practices persisted, virtually untouched by the new dispensation.

Elizabeth's church, like her brother's, blended a traditional episcopal structure, an anglicized semi-Catholic liturgy, and a thoroughly Protestant theology. Some of its architects and most of its critics regarded the Elizabethan church settlement as a flawed contraption, an interim arrangement obviously in need of further reformation. Apologists claimed that it was perfectly formed, congruent with the ancient church fathers, and uniquely pleasing to God. The Elizabethan Book of Common Prayer was modelled closely on that of 1552, with some revision or evasion of liturgical elements that could lead to more radical interpretations of the eucharist (ch. 2, p. 40).

Equipped with a revised Book of Common Prayer, backed by the statutory authority of the Act of Uniformity, armed theologically with the 1563 Articles of Religion, and buttressed by the disciplinary powers of the episcopate, the Church of England marshalled formidable powers to inculcate Protestant uniformity (ch. 2, pp. 40, 56, 59). Episcopal and archdeaconry courts, covering every part of England, exercised a wide jurisdiction, from regulating midwives to licensing schoolmasters, from judging matrimonial disputes to settling probates, and from enforcing church attendance to policing the liturgical requirements of the prayer book. Informed by churchwardens and other interested representatives of the parish community, the courts also passed judgement upon a steady stream of scolds, adulterers, fornicators and bastard bearers, so that some critics mocked these solemn judicial institutions as 'bawdy courts'. While its primary role entailed the ministration of sacraments and the performance of religious offices, the church may have been most visible to the laity through its various fees and exactions, admonitions and excommunications, and by its spectacle of public penance.

The theological leaders of the Elizabethan church were strongly attracted to Genevan Calvinism (ch. 3, p. 114). Some scholars discern a 'Calvinist consensus' amongst theologically sophisticated clergy and laity in late sixteenth-century and early seventeenth-century England. But some clerics were troubled by the most controversial of Calvinist doctrines, those relating to salvation. Article 17 of the Thirty-Nine Articles of 1563 describes the doctrine of predestination as

5

'comfortable', an adjective that seems apt only when we realize that the article defines predestination to salvation and conveniently overlooks Calvin's considerably less-soothing doctrine of predestination to damnation. For 'hotter' protestant reformers and convinced Calvinists, the reluctance of the English government to endorse the Genevan theology confirmed their view that England was in need of more reformation than the queen and her bishops would countenance.

The phenomenon of 'Puritanism' emerged in Elizabeth's reign. While many clergy and laity were contented with the status quo, a vociferous minority pressed for further change. Accepted, if disagreeable, members of the Church of England, Puritans pressed a developing agenda of criticism and renewal. By no means did all Puritans at all times agree on the items at issue, but a rough consensus linked many critics of the Elizabethan period with their Jacobean and Caroline successors. During Elizabeth's reign, the mainstream of the Puritan movement concerned itself with identifying and removing the 'popish remnants' that sullied the Book of Common Prayer (ch. 3, p. 82). A few demanded wholesale reorganization of the Church of England along Presbyterian lines. Especially vociferous in the 1570s, these Puritans saw no scriptural justification for episcopacy and regarded the ecclesiastical hierarchy as part of England's Roman legacy and as the oppressor of non-conforming brethren. Despite the fact that many Elizabethan bishops, like Edmund Grindal, were active promoters of Protestant reform, Presbyterians branded episcopacy as antithetical to the institution of a truly reformed English church (ch. 3, pp. 90, 93).

Personal reformation was another important aspect of early modern Puritanism. One could conform to the Church of England, accept its liturgy and discipline as a matter of expedience, and still espouse Puritan values. Even if one thought the established church but half reformed and society too prone to profanity, a Puritan could find a haven in a godly household. Lay men and women, especially of the gentry and middling sort, endeavoured to meet the demands of their faith through family prayer, discussion of sermons, and the keeping of spiritual diaries. Puritans, both lay and ecclesiastical, often berated their spiritual and social inferiors – the poor, the idle, the drunk and debauched – as 'reprobates' and called for a cultural revolution, a reformation of manners. Under the influence of evangelical preachers, parishes could strive to become models of puritan godliness without separating from the Church of England (ch. 3, pp. 99, 105, 120).

Catholics had not disappeared from the Elizabethan scene. Some of the clergy were wistful for the old religion, while many of the laity, perhaps more than is generally credited, remained deeply attached to traditional beliefs. Catholicism survived in England in an attenuated, underground form, despite the institutional overlay of the Church of England (ch. 3, p. 110). Catholic recusants were

assessed fines for non-attendance at church, while 'church papists' or occasional conformists met the minimum requirements of the law and kept their faith
in private. The English Catholic community was severely strained by the papal
excommunication of Queen Elizabeth in 1570 and by government rhetoric con-
demning popery as treason. In the second half of Elizabeth's reign, a new breed
of militant Catholics, English-born missionary priests trained in continental
seminaries, attempted to revitalize the Catholic remnant, but their daring enterprise often led them to their deaths. For English Protestants, the triumph over
the Spanish Armada in 1588 signalled defeat for the forces of Antichrist. Godly
preachers spoke of England as an elect nation and took heart from the providential message that the reformed religion would prevail.

Puritans and Catholics alike hoped that James VI of Scotland would lift con-
straints on their religious practice when he inherited the English throne in 1603.
But the new Stuart king proved to be a stalwart defender of the church as
established by law under the royal supremacy. James made it clear that he
considered the English episcopate the bulwark of a protestant monarchy. At
the Hampton Court Conference of 1604, the king rejected most of the Puritan
reform agenda, although he did authorize a new edition of the English Bible (ch.
4, pp. 123, 135). The position of popish recusants also worsened after the
discovery of the Gunpowder Plot in 1605 (ch. 4, p. 132). Most Protestant
ministers construed the escape from the Plot as a providential deliverance in
line with the defeat of the Spanish Armada.

Equipped with new canons and a reissued Book of Common Prayer, the
Jacobean church could well have become more rigidly conformist and more
tightly governed than its Elizabethan precursor (ch. 4, p. 127). In practice,
however, the king and his bishops allowed considerable latitude in the interest
of peace and harmony. James wanted a church that was unified and quiet, and
this was largely achieved by authorities overlooking minor infractions. Government often appeared to proceed by intemperate rhetoric rather than by stringent
prosecution of religious offences.

The second half of James's reign saw a shift in governmental policy and the
beginnings of a dangerous religious polarization. When the king favoured Sunday
frolics in his Book of Sports of 1618, he struck a blow against the severe
sabbatarianism of puritans in the north of England (ch. 5, p. 145). By doing
so, he sided simultaneously with village traditionalists and ceremonial church-
men, who shared an irritation with the moral demands, pious censures and
religious self-righteousness of the Jacobean godly. James's conciliatory atti-
tudes toward foreign Catholic powers and his toleration of increasingly high-
ceremonialist rhetoric signalled to many that the age of reformation was over
(ch. 4, p. 143). English delegates defended Calvinist orthodoxy at the synod of
Dort in 1618, but this did not lead to a strengthening of the Calvinist consensus

at home (ch. 4, p. 139). By the end of James's reign, anti-Calvinist clerics had gained ascendancy at court, and several bishops were espousing high-ceremonialist practices in their dioceses (ch. 4, pp. 137, 141, 142). James's son Charles exacerbated religious divisions after his accession in 1625 by favouring and promoting the supporters of this emergent style of churchmanship.

The new religious movement was identified with the controversial ecclesiastical efforts of William Laud, Archbishop of Canterbury from 1633. 'Laudian' theology emphasized human works as well as faith, and questioned Calvin's harsh doctrine of predestination. Laudians became notorious for their reverence for ceremony, and some were accused of teaching that divine grace was dependent upon proper performance of the sacraments. But while Laudianism was associated with anti-Calvinism and high-churchmanship, its salient characteristic was high-handedness. Puritans of the 1630s charged that Laudian ideas and practices were too reminiscent of the oppressions of popery. Some warned of a gradual return to Rome, while others, like Henry Burton, saw the growing religious and social turmoil as a providential sign that God was testing his elect and would punish those responsible for moral decay and ecclesiastical corruption (ch. 5, p. 151).

From its very inception the Church of England had been enmeshed in controversy over the meaning and conduct of religious ceremonies, especially the service of the eucharist. Problems relating to the naming and ornamenting of communion tables or altars, where they should be located, whether they should be railed or reverenced, and whether one should stand, sit, or kneel in front of them, continued to agitate the early seventeenth-century church. Depending on the local culture of worship and the disciplinary zeal of the bishops, the laity could approach the eucharist as participants or witnesses, and treat it as an expression of Christian fellowship, a holy sacrament, a parish picnic, or a mystical engagement with the body and blood of Christ. Much of this flexibility disappeared in the 1630s, as Laudians insisted upon sanctifying the sacramental setting of the altar.

Backed by Charles I, Laudian bishops worked hard to enforce earlier Jacobean canons. Some even went beyond them in the elaboration of religious ceremony (ch. 5, pp. 155, 157). Laudians took literally the psalmist's call to worship God 'in the beauty of holiness', and they were incensed at the material state of the church. Years of Protestant iconophobia and inattention to the visual apparatus of worship had left many of England's parish churches and cathedrals languishing in disrepair, and still others had been adapted to suit the austere tastes of Puritan congregations. Reversal of this neglect had actually begun in the later reign of Elizabeth I, and James I had done much to repair the fabric and restore the incomes of the church; but when Laudians continued this work, their sacerdotal and sacramental obsessions rendered suspect what had previously been uncontroversial. Parishioners balked at paying for the refurbishment of font covers and the installation of altar rails. For Puritans the Laudian agenda called up unwelcome resonances of past tyranny and superstition.

The Laudian confrontation with proponents of the 'Calvinist consensus' thus went beyond doctrinal disagreement to spark a cultural war. When Charles I reissued the Book of Sports in 1633 and insisted upon its application nation-wide, he inflamed an already incendiary political environment (ch. 5, pp. 145, 148, 151). Venerable Calvinist clerics, who had prided themselves on their ceaseless efforts against non-conformity, now found themselves labelled as Puritans. Christopher Dow's Laudian 'Narrative of the rise and progress of the "Disciplinarians"' exemplifies how partisan histories of religion (like those of Roger Martyn, John Foxe and William Allen) could be used to redraw the boundaries of 'mainstream' English Protestantism (ch. 5, p. 168).

When Charles and Laud attempted to impose a version of the Book of Common Prayer upon the Scottish church in 1637, the stage was set for a conflict that exploded into civil war. The Presbyterian Scots considered the prayer book popish in the extreme. Their rebellion led to the calling of parliament in 1640, and the unleashing of vituperative anti-episcopal energies. As the House of Commons debated the management of church and state, angry Londoners promulgated a petition, blaming the episcopate for intolerable innovations in doctrine and demanding its immediate extirpation with 'all its dependencies, roots and branches' (ch. 6, pp. 174, 180). The English revolution was fought over a variety of civil and ecclesiastical abuses, but the language of war was almost exclusively religious in nature. The army led by the future Protector of England, Oliver Cromwell, made a covenanting partnership amongst themselves and with God to bring down the enemies of 'true religion', enemies that included the king (ch. 6, pp. 180, 192). Charles's troops, on the other hand, went into battle for the royal supremacy and the Book of Common Prayer, both of which were swept away by the victorious revolutionary government. The prayer book was abro-gated and Archbishop Laud was executed in 1645, episcopacy was abolished in 1646, and monarchy itself was brought to an end with the execution of the king in 1649.

The revolution marked the end of the Tudor establishment of religion. The collapse of episcopal authority at the beginning of the 1640s released a flood of sectarian energy hitherto repressed in English society (ch. 6, p. 183). Presby-terianism, which from the time of Elizabeth had been identified with radical non-conformity, now functioned as a conservative force for order and uniformity, even producing a 'Directory for Public Worship' in 1645 (ch. 6, p. 186). Attempting to control religion, the government faced constant challenges from radical religious sects of all descriptions, including Anabaptists and Congregational Indepen-dents. Sectarian excesses in the name of religious freedom were exhaustively

9

catalogued by Thomas Edward's *Gangraena* (ch. 6, p. 195). The title bluntly conveys the author's opinion that the English religious commonwealth was rotting from within. The 1640s and 1650s were years of turmoil and distraction for the bulk of ordinary citizens, and there seems to have been a collective sigh of relief when church and crown were restored in 1660.

We have chosen to close with an extract from the diary of the Presbyterian minister Richard Baxter (ch. 6, p. 199). Baxter was a conservative during the period of the Cromwellian Protectorate and a dissenter under the restored King Charles II. His relation to the shifting religious politics of the mid-seventeenth century, though fascinating, is less important from our perspective than his enduring role as the leader of a parish community. Baxter's memoirs highlight a familiar round of pastoral service, as he christened, doctored, taught, married, counselled and buried his parishioners. His experiences remind us that many aspects of everyday life remained stable and secure despite the turbulence of religious change in early modern England.

1

TRADITION AND CHANGE: THE OLD RELIGION AND THE NEW

THE STATE OF MELFORD CHURCH AS I, ROGER MARTYN, DID KNOW IT

Roger Martyn (c.1527–1615) lovingly recalled the seasonal rituals, church decora-
tions, and devotional equipment that were lost from his parish church of Long Melford,
Suffolk, in the course of the reformation. His description evokes the vitality of late
medieval Catholicism before the Henrician, Edwardian and Elizabethan reforms. Martyn
came from a village gentry family and served as churchwarden under Queen Mary. From
the time of his childhood he relished the richness, festivity and community of the old
religion, with its saints' days, processions and bonfires. Writing this memoir later in
Elizabeth's reign, Martyn's nostalgia was tempered by hopes that Catholic worship
might one day again be restored. He even preserved remnants of the proscribed
religious equipment in case their use was sanctioned again.
Source: William Parker, *The History of Long Melford* (London, 1873), pp. 70–3.

At the back of the high altar in the said church there was a goodly mount,
made of one great tree, and set up to the foot of the window there, carved
very artificially with the story of Christ's passion, representing the horse-
men with their swords and the footmen, etc. as they used Christ on the
mount of Calvary, all being fair gilt, and lively and beautifully set forth. To
cover and keep clean all the which, there were very fair and painted boards,
made to shut to, which were opened upon high and solemn feast days,
which then was a very beautiful show. Which painted boards were set up
again in Queen Mary's time. At the north end of the same altar, there was a
goodly tilt tabernacle, reaching up to the roof of the chancel, in the which
there was one large fair gilt image of the Holy Trinity, being patron of the
church; besides other fair images. The like tabernacle was at the south end.

There was also in my aisle called 'Jesus aisle', at the back of the altar, a
table with a crucifix on it, with the two thieves hanging, on every side one,
which is in my house decayed; and the same I hope my heirs will repair and
restore again one day. There was also two fair tilt tabernacles from the
ground up to the roof, with a fair image of Jesus in the tabernacle at the
north end of the altar, holding a round ball in his hand, signifying I think

11

that he containeth the whole round world; and in the tabernacle at the south end there was a fair image of Our Blessed Lady having the afflicted body of her dear son, as he was taken down off the cross lying along on her lap, the tears as it were running down pitifully upon her beautiful cheeks, as it seemed bedewing the said sweet body of her son, and therefore named the image of Our Lady of Pity.

There was a fair rood loft with the rood; Mary and John of every side, and with a fair pair of organs standing thereby; which loft extended all the breadth of the church, and on Good Friday a priest then standing by the rood sang the Passion. The side thereof towards the body of the church, in twelve partitions in boards, was fair painted with the images of the twelve apostles. All the roof of the church was beautified with fair gilt stars. Finally, in the vestry where there were many rich copes and suits of vestments there was a fair press with fair large doors to shut to, wherein there were made devices to hang on all the copes, without folding or frumpling of them, with a convenient distance the one from the other. In the choir was a fair painted frame of timber, to be set up about Maundy Thursday, with holes for a number of fair tapers to stand in before the sepulchre, and to be lighted in service time. Sometimes it was set overthwart the choir before the altar. The sepulchre being always placed and finally garnished at the north end of the high altar, between that and Mr Clopton's little chapel there, in a vacant place of the wall, I think upon a tomb of one of his ancestors; the said frame with the tapers was set near the steps going up to the said altar. Lastly it was used to be set up, all along by Mr Clopton's aisle, with a door made to go out of the rood loft into it.

Upon Palm Sunday the blessed sacrament was carried in procession about the churchyard under a fair canopy borne by four yeomen. The procession coming to the church gate went westward, and they with the blessed sacrament went eastward; and when the procession came against the door of Mr Clopton's aisle, they with the blessed sacrament, and with a little bell and singing, approached at the east end of Our Lady's chapel, at which time a boy with a thing in his hand pointed to it, signifying a prophet as I think, sang standing on the turret, that is, on the said Mr Clopton's aisle door, *Ecce Rex tuus venit,* etc.,[1] and then all did kneel down, and then rising up went and met the sacrament, and so then went singing together into the church. And coming near the porch, a boy or one of the clerks did cast over among the boys flowers and singing cakes, etc.

On Corpus Christi day they went likewise with the blessed sacrament in procession about the church green in copes, and I think also they went in procession on St Mark's day about the said green, with hand-bells ringing before them, as they did about the bounds of the town in Rogation week, on the Monday one way, on the Tuesday another way, on the Wednesday another way, praying for rain or fair weather as the time required; having a drinking and a dinner there upon Monday, being fast day; and Tuesday being a fish day they had a breakfast with butter and cheese, etc. at the parsonage and a drinking at Mr Clopton's by Kentwell, at his manor of Lutons, near the ponds in the park, where there was a little chapel, I think of St Anne, for that was their longest perambulation. Upon Wednesday being fasting day they had a drinking at Melford Hall. All the choir dined there, three times in the year at least: viz. St Stephen's day, mid-Lent Sunday, and I think upon Easter Monday. On St James's day, mass being sung then by note, and the organs going in St James's chapel (which were brought into my house with the clock and bell that stood there, and the organs that stood upon the rood loft) that was then a little from the road, which chapel had been maintained by my ancestors; and therefore I will that my heirs, when time serve, shall repair, place there and maintain all these things again. There were also fair stools on either side, such as are in the church, which were had away by John King's means, who was Sir William Cordell's bailiff; about which chapel there was paled in round about a convenient piece of the green for one to walk in.

On St James's eve there was a bonfire, and a tub of ale and bread then given to the poor, and before my door there was made three other bonfires, viz. on Midsummer eve, on the eve of St Peter and St Paul, when they had the like drinkings, and on St Thomas's eve, on which, if it fell not on the fish day, they had some long pies of mutton, and pease cods, set out upon boards, with the aforesaid quantity of bread and ale. And in all these bonfires, some of the friends and more civil poor neighbours were called in, and sat at the board with my grandfather, who had at the lighting of the bonfires wax tapers with balls of wax, yellow and green, set up all the breadth of the hall, lighted then and burning there before the image of St John the Baptist. And after they were put out, a watch candle was lighted, and set in the midst of the said hall upon the pavement, burning all night.

HUGH LATIMER, CONVOCATION SERMON, 1536

Raised and educated as a Roman Catholic, Hugh Latimer (c.1485–1555) resigned the bishopric of Worcester in the reign of Henry VIII to protest against the religious conservatism of the Six Articles of 1539. He became a court preacher under Edward VI and a martyr under Mary. Latimer's preaching had a powerful impact on the early Protestant reformers and their followers. His life, memorialized by John Foxe, registers the fitful progress of the Protestant reformation in sixteenth-century England. This sermon, daringly delivered to an assembly of priests and bishops in 1536, contains a devastating critique of the clergy, a popular theme of the first century of the reformation. Source: *Sermons by Hugh Latimer*, ed. George Elwes Corrie, Parker Society (Cambridge, 1844), pp. 33–40.

The sermon that the Reverend Father in Christ, Mr Hugh Latimer, Bishop of Worcester, made to the Convocation of the clergy, before the parliament began, the 9th Day of June, the 28th year of the reign of our late King Henry the Eighth. Translated out of Latin into English, to the intent that things well said to a few may be understood of many, and do good to all them that desire to understand the truth. Filii hujus seculi, etc.[2]

Brethren, ye be come together this day, as far as I perceive, to hear of great and weighty matters. Ye be come together to entreat of things that most appertain to the commonwealth. This being thus, ye look, I am assured, to hear of me, which am commanded to make as a preface this exhortation (albeit I am unlearned and far unworthy) such things as shall be much meet for this your assembly. I therefore, not only very desirous to obey the commandment of our primate, but also right greatly coveting to serve and satisfy all your expectation; lo, briefly, and as plainly as I can, will speak of matters both worthy to be heard in your congregation, and also of such as best shall become mine office in this place. That I may do this the more commodiously, I have taken that notable sentence in which Our Lord was not afraid to pronounce 'the children of this world to be much more prudent and politic than the children of light in their generation'. Neither will I be afraid, trusting that he will aid and guide me to use this sentence, as a good ground and foundation of all such things as hereafter I shall speak of.

Now, I suppose that you see right well, being men of such learning, for what purpose the Lord said this, and that ye have no need to be holpen with any part of my labour in this thing. But yet, if ye will pardon me, I will wade somewhat deeper in this matter, and as nigh as I can, fetch it from the first original beginning. For undoubtedly, ye may much marvel at this saying, if ye well ponder both what is said and who saith it. Define me first these three things: what prudence is; what the world; what light; and who be the children of the world; who of the light: see what they signify in scripture. I marvel if by and by ye all agree, that the children of the world should be wiser than the children of the light. To come somewhat nigher the matter, thus the Lord beginneth: 'There was a certain rich man that had a steward, which was accused unto him that he had dissipated and wasted his goods. This rich man called his steward to him and said, What is this

14

that I hear of thee? Come, make me an account of thy stewardship; thou mayest no longer bear this office.'

Brethren, because these words are so spoken in a parable, and are so wrapped in wrinkles, that yet they seem to have a face and a similitude of a thing done indeed, and like an history, I think it much profitable to tarry somewhat in them. And though we may perchance find in our hearts to believe all that is there spoken to be true; yet I doubt whether we may abide it, that these words of Christ do pertain unto us, and admonish us of our duty, which do and live after such sort, as though Christ, when he spake any thing, had, as the time served him, served his turn, and not regarded the time that came after him, neither provided for us, or any matters of ours; as some of the philosophers thought, which said, that God walked up and down in heaven, and thinketh never a deal of our affairs. But, my good brethren, err not you so; stick not you to such your imaginations. For if ye inwardly behold these words, if ye diligently roll them in your minds, and after explicate and open them, ye shall see our time much touched in these mysteries. Ye shall perceive that God by this example shaketh us by the noses and pulleth us by the ears. Ye shall perceive very plain that God setteth before our eyes in this similitude what we ought most to flee, and what we ought soonest to follow. For Luke saith, 'The Lord spake these words to his disciples.' Wherefore let it be out of all doubt that he spake them to us, which even as we will be counted the successors and vicars of Christ's disciples, so we be, if we be good dispensers and do our duty. He said these things partly to us, which spake them partly of himself. For he is that rich man, which not only had, but hath, and shall have evermore, I say not one, but many stewards, even to the end of the world . . .

Who is a true and faithful steward? He is true, he is faithful, that coineth no new money, but taketh it ready coined of the good man of the house; and neither changeth it, ne clippeth it, after it is taken to him to spend, but spendeth even the selfsame that he had of his Lord, and spendeth it as his Lord's commandment is; neither to his own vantage uttering it, nor as the lewd servant did, hiding it in the ground. Brethren, if a faithful steward ought to do as I have said, I pray you, ponder and examine this well, whether our bishops and abbots, prelates and curates, have been hitherto faithful stewards or no? Ponder, whether yet many of them be as they should be or no? Go ye to, tell me now as your conscience leadeth you (I will let pass to speak of many other) was there not some, that despising the money of the Lord, as copper and not current, either coined new themselves, or else uttered abroad newly coined of the other; some time either adulterating the word of God, or else mingling it (as taverners do, which brew and utter the evil and good both in one pot), sometime in the stead of God's word blowing out the dreams of men, while they thus preached to the people the redemption that cometh by Christ's death to serve only them that died before his coming, that were in the time of the Old Testament; and that now since redemption and forgiveness of sins purchased by money, and devised by men, is of efficacy, and not redemption purchased by Christ? (They have a wonderful pretty example to persuade this thing, of a certain married woman, which, when her husband was in purgatory, in that fiery furnace that hath burned away so many of our pence, paid her husband's ransom, and so of duty claimed him to be set at liberty.)

While they thus preached to the people, that dead images (which at the first, as I think, were set up, only to represent things absent) not only ought to be covered with gold, but also ought of all faithful and Christian people (yea, in this scarceness and penury of all things) to be clad with silk garments, and those also laden with precious gems and jewels; and that beside all this, they are to be lighted with wax candles, both within the church and without the church, yea, and at noon days; as who should say, here no cost can be too great; whereas in the mean time we see Christ's faithful and lively images, bought with no less price than with his most precious blood (alas, alas!) to be an hungered, athirst, cold, and to lie in darkness, wrapped in all wretchedness, yea, to lie there till death take away their miseries, while they preached these will-works, that come but of our own devotion, although they be not so necessary as the works of mercy, and the precepts of God, yet they said, and in the pulpit, that will-works were more principal, more excellent, and (plainly to utter what they mean) more acceptable to God than works of mercy; as though now man's inventions and fancies could please God better than God's precepts, or strange things better than his own; while they thus preached that more fruit, more devotion cometh of the beholding of an image, though it be but a *Pater noster* while, than is gotten by reading and contemplation in scripture, though ye read and contemplate therein seven years' space; finally, while they preached thus, souls tormented in purgatory to have most need of our help, and that they can have no aid, but of us in this world; of the which two, if the one be not false, yet at the least it is ambiguous, uncertain, doubtful, and therefore rashly and arrogantly with such boldness affirmed in the audience of the people; the other, by all men's opinions, is manifestly false. I let pass to speak of much other such like counterfeit doctrine, which hath been blasted and blown out by some for the space of three hours together. Be these the Christian and divine mysteries, and not rather the dreams of men? Be these the faithful dispensers of God's mysteries, and not rather false dissipaters of them,

16

whom God never put in office, but rather the Devil set them over a miserable family, over an house miserably ordered and entreated? Happy were the people if such preached seldom.

And yet it is a wonder to see these, in their generation, to be much more prudent and politic than the faithful ministers are in their generation; while they go about more prudently to stablish men's dreams, than these do to hold up God's commandments . . .

But lest the length of my sermon offend you too sore, I will leave the rest of the parable and take me to the handling of the end of it; that is, I will declare unto you how the children of this world be more witty, crafty and subtle than are the children of light in their generation. Which sentence would God it lay in my poor tongue to explicate with such light of words, that I might seem rather to have painted it before your eyes, than to have spoken it; and that you might rather seem to see the thing, than to hear it! But I confess plainly this thing to be far above my power. Therefore this being only left to me, I wish for that I have not, and am sorry that that is not in me which I would so gladly have, that all that I say may turn to the glory of God, your souls' health, and the edifying of Christ's body. Wherefore I pray you all to pray with me unto God, and that in your petition you desire, that these two things he vouchsafe to grant us, first, a mouth for me to speak rightly; next, ears for you, that in hearing me ye may take profit at my hand: and that this may come to effect, you shall desire him, unto whom our master Christ bade we should pray, saying even the same prayer that he himself did institute. Wherein ye shall pray for our most gracious sovereign lord the king, chief and supreme head of the Church of England under Christ, and for the most excellent, gracious, and virtuous lady Queen Jane, his most lawful wife, and for all his, whether they be of the clergy or laity, whether they be of the nobility, or else other his grace's subjects, not forgetting those that being departed out of this transitory life, and now sleep in the sleep of peace, and rest from their labours in quietness and in peaceable sleep, faithfully, lovingly, and patiently looking for that that they clearly shall see when God shall be so pleased. For all these, and for grace necessary, ye shall say unto God God's prayer, *Pater noster.*

THE TEN ARTICLES, 1536

The Ten Articles of 1536, an intriguing mixture of reformed ideals and traditional beliefs, were the first articles of faith to be adopted by Convocation during the Henrician reformation. Note particularly the inclusion of penance as a sacrament, along with the eucharist and baptism; the attention paid to auricular confession, contrition and good works; the retention of images and the intercession of the saints; and the notion of the eucharistic presence as corporeal. All of these tenets have been re-examined in light of reformation theology and reformulated to indicate justification by faith and denial of the doctrine of transubstantiation. The reformism of 1536 would soon be halted by the conservative reaction of 1539.

Source: Charles Hardwick, *A History of the Articles of Religion, to Which is Added a Series of Documents from* AD *1536 to* AD *1615* (London, 1888), pp. 241–55 (appendix 1).

1 *The principal articles concerning our faith*

First, as touching the chief and principal articles of our faith, since it is thus agreed as hereafter followeth by the whole clergy of this our realm, we will that all bishops and preachers shall instruct and teach our people, by us committed to their spiritual charge, that they ought and must most constantly believe and defend all those things to be true, which be comprehended in the whole body and canon of the Bible, and also in the three creeds or symbols, whereof one was made by the apostles, and is the common creed, which every man useth; the second was made by the holy council of Nice, and is said daily in the mass; and the third was made by Athanasius, and is comprehended in the psalm *Quicunque vult*:[3] and that they ought and must take and interpret all the same things according to the selfsame sentence and interpretation, which the words of the selfsame creeds or symbols do purport, and the holy approved doctors of the church do entreat and defend the same . . .

2 *The sacrament of baptism*

Secondly, as touching the holy sacrament of baptism, we will that all bishops and preachers shall instruct and teach our people committed by us unto their spiritual charge, that they ought and must of necessity believe certainly all those things, which hath been always by the whole consent of the church approved, received, and used in the sacrament of baptism; that is to say, that the sacrament of baptism was instituted and ordained in the New Testament by our saviour Jesu Christ, as a thing necessary for the attaining of everlasting life, according to the saying of Christ . . . No man can enter into the kingdom of heaven, except he be born again of water and the Holy Ghost.

Item, that it is offered unto all men, as well infants as such as have the use of reason, that by baptism they shall have remission of sins, and the grace and favour of God, according to the saying of Christ . . . Whosoever believeth and is baptized shall be saved . . .

Item, that infants must needs be christened because they be born in original sin, which sin must needs be remitted; which cannot be done but by the sacrament of baptism, whereby they receive the Holy Ghost,

18

which exerciseth his grace and efficacy in them, and cleanseth and purifieth them from sin by his most secret virtue and operation.

Item, that children or men once baptized, can nor ought ever to be baptized again . . .

3 *The sacrament of penance*

Thirdly, Concerning the sacrament of penance, we will that all bishops and preachers shall instruct and teach our people committed by us unto their spiritual charge that they ought and must most constantly believe that that sacrament was institute of Christ in the New Testament as a thing so necessary for man's salvation that no man, which after his baptism is fallen again, and hath committed deadly sin, can, without the same, be saved, or attain everlasting life.

Item, that like as such men which after baptism do fall again into sin, if they do not penance in this life, shall undoubtedly be damned; even so whensoever the same men shall convert themselves from their naughty life, and do such penance for the same, as Christ requireth of them, they shall without doubt attain remission of their sins, and shall be saved.

Item, that the sacrament of perfect penance which Christ requireth of such manner persons consisteth of three parts, that is to say, contrition, confession and the amendment of the former life, and a new obedient reconciliation unto the laws and will of God, that is to say, exterior acts in works of charity according as they be commanded of God, which be called in scripture *fructus digni poenitentia,* the worthy fruits of penance . . .

Item, that in no wise they do contemn this auricular confession which is made unto ministers of the church, but that they ought to repute the same as a very expedient and necessary mean, whereby they may require and ask this absolution at the priest's hands, at such time as they shall find their consciences grieved with mortal sin, and have occasion so to do, to the intent they may thereby attain certain comfort and consolation of their consciences.

As touching the third part of penance, we will that all bishops and preachers shall instruct and teach our people committed by us to their spiritual charge, that although Christ and his death be the sufficient oblation, sacrifice, satisfaction, and recompence, for the which God the Father forgiveth and remitteth to all sinners not only their sin, but also eternal pain due for the same; yet all men truly penitent, contrite and confessed must needs also bring forth the fruits of penance, that is to say, prayer, fasting, almsdeeds, and must make restitution or satisfaction in will and deed to their neighbours, in such things as they have done them

19

wrong and injury in, and also must do all other good works of mercy and charity, and express their obedient will in the executing and fulfilling of God's commandments outwardly, when time, power, and occasion shall be ministered unto them, or else they shall never be saved; for this is the express precept and commandment of God . . .

4 The sacrament of the altar

Fourthly, as touching the sacrament of the altar, we will that all bishops and preachers shall instruct and teach our people committed by us unto their spiritual charge, that they ought and must constantly believe, that under the form and figure of bread and wine, which we there presently do see and perceive by outward senses, is verily, substantially and really contained and comprehended the very selfsame body and blood of Our Saviour Jesus Christ, which was born of the Virgin Mary, and suffered upon the cross for our redemption; and that under the same form and figure of bread and wine the very selfsame body and blood of Christ is corporally, really and in the very substance exhibited, distributed and received unto and of all them which receive the said sacrament; and that therefore the said sacrament is to be used with all due reverence and honour, and that every man ought first to prove and examine himself, and religiously to try and search his own conscience, before he shall receive the same . . .

5 Justification

Fifthly, as touching the order and cause of our justification, we will that all bishops and preachers shall instruct and teach our people committed by us to their spiritual charge that this word justification signifieth remission of our sins, and our acceptance or reconciliation into the grace and favour of God, that is to say, our perfect renovation in Christ.

Item, that sinners attain this justification by contrition and faith joined with charity, after such sort and manner as we before mentioned and declared; not as though our contrition, or faith, or any works proceeding thereof, can worthily merit or deserve to attain the said justification; for the only mercy and grace of the Father, promised freely unto us for his Son's sake, Jesu Christ, and the merits of his blood and passion, be the only sufficient and worthy causes thereof: and yet that notwithstanding, to the attaining of the same justification, God requireth to be in us not only inward contrition, perfect faith and charity, certain hope and confidence, with all other spiritual graces and motions, which, as we said before, must necessarily concur in remission of our sins, that is to say, our justification;

but also he requireth and commandeth us, that after we be justified we must also have good works of charity and obedience towards God, in the observing and fulfilling outwardly of his laws and commandments: for although acceptation to everlasting life be conjoined with justification, yet our good works be necessarily required to the attaining of everlasting life; and we being justified, be necessarily bound, and it is our necessary duty to do good works . . .

Articles concerning the laudable ceremonies used in the church

6 And first of images

As touching images, truth it is that the same have been used in the Old Testament, and also for the great abuses of them sometime destroyed and put down; and in the New Testament they have been also allowed, as good authors do declare. Wherefore we will that all bishops and preachers shall instruct and teach our people committed by us to their spiritual charge how they ought and may use them. And first, that there may be attributed unto them that they be representers of virtue and good example, and that they also be by occasion the kindlers and stirrers of men's minds, and make men oft to remember and lament their sins and offences, especially the images of Christ and Our Lady; and that therefore it is meet that they should stand in the churches, and none otherwise to be esteemed: and to the intent the rude people should not from henceforth take such superstition, as in time past it is thought that the same hath used to do, we will that our bishops and preachers diligently shall teach them, and according to this doctrine reform their abuses, for else there might fortune idolatry to ensue, which God forbid. And as for censing of them, and kneeling and offering unto them, with other like worshippings, although the same hath entered by devotion, and fallen to custom; yet the people ought to be diligently taught that they in no wise do it, nor think it meet to be done to the same images, but only to be done to God, and in his honour, although it be done before the images, whether it be of Christ, of the cross, of Our Lady, or of any other saint beside.

7 Of honouring of saints

As touching the honouring of saints, we will that all bishops and preachers shall instruct and teach our people, committed by us unto their spiritual charges, that saints, now being with Christ in heaven to be honoured of Christian people in earth; but not with that confidence and honour which are only due unto God, trusting to attain at their hands that which must be had only of God: but that they be thus to be honoured, because they be known the elect persons of Christ, because they be passed in godly life out of this transitory world, because they already do reign in glory with Christ; and most specially to laud and praise Christ in them for their excellent virtues which he planted in them, for example of and by them to such as yet are in this world to live in virtue and goodness, and also not to fear to die for Christ and his cause, as some of them did; and finally to take them, in that they may, to be advancers of our prayers and demands unto Christ. By these ways, and such like, be saints to be honoured and had in reverence, and by none other.

8 Of praying to saints

As touching praying to saints, we will that all bishops and preachers shall instruct and teach our people, committed by us unto their spiritual charge, that albeit grace, remission of sin and salvation cannot be obtained but of God only by the mediation of Our Saviour Christ, which is only sufficient mediator for our sins; yet it is very laudable to pray to saints in heaven everlastingly living, whose charity is ever permanent, to be intercessors, and to pray for us and with us, unto Almighty God . . . and in this manner we may pray to Our Blessed Lady, to St John Baptist, to all and every of the apostles or any other saint particularly, as our devotion doth serve us; so that it be done without any vain superstition, as to think that any saint is more merciful, or will hear us sooner than Christ, or that any saint doth serve for one thing more than another, or is patron of the same. And likewise we must keep holy days unto God, in memory of him and his saints, upon such days as the church hath ordained their memories to be celebrated; except they be mitigated and moderated by the assent and commandment of us, the supreme head, to the ordinaries, and then the subjects ought to obey it.

9 Of rites and ceremonies

As concerning the rites and ceremonies of Christ's church, as to have such vestments in doing God's service, as be and have been most part used, as sprinkling of holy water to put us in remembrance of our baptism and the blood of Christ sprinkled for our redemption upon the cross; giving of holy bread, to put us in remembrance of the sacrament of the altar, that all Christian men be one body mystical of Christ, as the bread is made of many grains, and yet but one loaf, and to put us in remembrance of the receiving of the holy sacrament and body of Christ, the which we ought to receive in right charity, which in the beginning of Christ's church men did more often receive than they use nowadays to do; bearing of candles on Candlemas day in memory of Christ the spiritual light, of whom Simeon did prophesy, as is read in the church that day: giving of ashes on Ash Wednesday, to put in remembrance every Christian man in the beginning of Lent and penance, that he is but ashes and earth, and thereto shall return, which is right necessary to be uttered from henceforth in our mother-tongue always on the same day; bearing of palms on Palm Sunday, in memory of the receiving of Christ into Jerusalem, a little before his death, that we may have the same desire to receive him into our hearts; creeping to the cross, and humbling ourselves to Christ on Good Friday before the cross, and there offering unto Christ before the same, and kissing of it in memory of our redemption by Christ made upon the cross; setting up the sepulture of Christ, whose body after his death was buried; the hallowing of the font, and other like exorcisms and benedictions by the ministers of Christ's church; and all other like laudable customs, rites, and ceremonies be not to be contemned and cast away, but to be used and continued as things good and laudable, to put us in remembrance of those spiritual things that they do signify; not suffering them to be forgot, or to be put in oblivion, but renewing them in our memories from time to time. But none of these ceremonies have power to remit sin, but only to stir and lift up our minds unto God, by whom only our sins be forgiven.

10 Of purgatory

Forasmuch as due order of charity requireth, and the book of Maccabees, and divers ancient doctors plainly show, that it is a very good and a charitable deed to pray for souls departed, and forasmuch also as such usage hath continued in the church so many years, even from the beginning, we will that all bishops and preachers shall instruct and teach our people committed by us unto their spiritual charge, that no man ought to be grieved with the continuance of the same, and that it standeth with the very due order of charity, a Christian man to pray for souls departed, and to commit them in our prayers to God's mercy, and also to cause other to pray for them in masses and exequies, and to give alms to other to pray for them, whereby they may be relieved and holpen of some part of their pain: but forasmuch as the place where they be, the name thereof, and kind of pains there, also be to us uncertain by scripture; therefore this with all other things we remit to Almighty God, unto whose mercy it is meet and convenient for us to commend them, trusting that God accepteth our prayers for them, referring the rest wholly to God, to whom is known their estate and condition. Wherefore it is much necessary that such abuses be clearly put away, which under the name of purgatory hath been advanced, as to make men believe that through the Bishop of Rome's pardons souls might clearly be delivered out of purgatory, and all the pains of it, or that masses said . . . in any place, or before any image, might likewise deliver them from all their pain, and send them straight to heaven; and other like abuses.

ROBERT PARKYN'S NARRATIVE OF THE REFORMATION, 1532–54

Robert Parkyn (d. 1570) was a Yorkshire priest who lamented the assault on traditional Roman Catholicism. He serves as a hostile witness to the break with Rome, the dissolution of the monasteries and the introduction of the Book of Common Prayer. Parkyn's chronicle traces the reform of the sacraments, the reduction of ceremony and the reconstitution of the Christian liturgical year. The reformation, in his view, came from the political centre and was cynically imposed on the parishes by the governments of Henry VIII and Edward VI. Parkyn lived to celebrate the restoration of Catholic worship under Mary and to accommodate himself to the Protestant regime of her successor.
Source: A. G. Dickens (ed.), 'Robert Parkyn's Narrative of the Reformation', *English Historical Review*, vol. 62 (1947), pp. 64–82.

Regnantibus impiis: ruina hominum[4]

Be it known to all men to whom this present writing shall come, see, hear, or read, that in the year of Our Lord God 1532 and in the 24th year of the reign of King Henry the Eighth, these grievous matters ensuing first began to take root; and after by process of time was accomplished and brought to pass in very deed within this realm of England, to the great discomfort of all such as was true Christians.

First, the king's majesty, viz. Henry the Eighth, in the 24th year of his reign was wrongly divorced from his lawful wife gracious Queen Katherine, and married Lady Anne Boleyn, which was crowned Queen of England on Whitsunday. But in the year following (*anno domini* 1533) the Pope of Rome with all his authority and power was abolished quite out of this realm, and then the king's majesty was proclaimed Supreme Head next and immediately under God of the Church of England and Ireland, through authority whereof he began to depose religious houses . . .

Then in the year following, viz. 1534, was granted to the king first fruits and tenths of all spiritual possessions. And because the good Bishop of Rochester and Sir Thomas More, two virtuous men and great clerks, would not consent to the king that he should be Supreme Head of holy church, therefore they were both beheaded in the month of June at London with three monks of the Charterhouse for the same, with many others in divers places.

The year following, viz. 1535, was the abovesaid Queen Anne beheaded for her wretched carnal living, and in September and October was great commotions (for maintenance of holy church) both in Lincolnshire and Yorkshire, but deceitfully they were brought down with treaty, without blood shedding, specially at a ground named Scawsby Lees not far from Doncaster.

This past then on St Edward's eve in October *anno domini* [1537] Prince Edward was born at Hampton Court. Continuing the said times, religious houses were nothing favoured, but yearly part dissolved, but *anno domini* 1539 all were suppressed furiously underfoot (even as the holy temple of Jerusalem was handled when the Chaldees had dominion thereof) and many abbots and other virtuous religious persons was shamefully put to death in divers places of this realm. And all this ungraciousness came through council of one wretch and heretic Thomas Cromwell, and such other of his affinity, which Cromwell was beheaded for high treason in the year after.

Then a proclamation went forth, *anno domini* 1540, that no holy day should be kept except feasts of Our Lady, the apostles, evangelists and Mary Magdalen. And that St Mark's day should not be taken as a fasting day, nor yet St Lawrence's eve, neither that children should be decked, nor go about upon St Nicholas, St Catherine, St Clement, St Edmund's eves or days, but all such childish fashions (as they named it) to cease. Thus in King Henry's days began holy church in England to be in great ruin as it appeared daily.

But when the said King Henry was departed to God's mercy in the 38th year of his reign and in the year of Our Lord God 1546, there did succeed his only son Prince Edward and was proclaimed through all his father's dominions King of England, France and Ireland, Defender of the Faith and of the Church of England and Ireland Supreme Head next and immediately under God. And in the first year of his reign was straight injunctions given to all the spirituality of England, wherein specially was deposed all processions and that none should be used, but only to kneel in the mid aisle of the church unto certain suffrages in English were sung or said on holy days.

Also in the beginning of the second year of his reign, *anno domini* 1547, on the Purification day of Our Lady (viz. Candlemas day), there was no candles sanctified, borne or held in men's hands, as before times laudably was accustomed, but utterly omitted.

In the beginning of Lent all such suffrages as pertained to the sanctifying of the ashes was omitted and left undone, and so no ashes was given to any persons. In the same Lent all images, pictures, tables, crucifixes, tabernacles, was utterly abolished and taken away forth of churches within this realm of England, and all serges of wax (except two standing upon high altars).

Item, on Palm Sunday, being Our Lady day Annunciation, no palms were sanctified nor borne in men's hands, no procession, no passion read in Latin at mass, but in English only in the pulpit.

Item, on Sheer Thursday at even (*anno domini* 1548) no altars was washed nor Maundy given. And on Good Friday, no sepulchre was prepared, nor any mention made that day in holy church of Christ Jesus's bitter passion, death and burial (as of long time before was used), the passion only excepted, which was read in English. All other ceremonies, as creeping before the cross, twenty-four candles, and discipline, was utterly omitted.

On Easter eve, no fire was sanctified, no paschal candle, no procession unto the font, no candle present at sanctifying thereof, no words sung nor said from the font unto the choir (as laudably was used beforetime), but immediately did proceed unto the holy mass, at which mass the people were communicant with both kinds, viz. they received Christ's blessed body under form of bread, and his blessed blood under form of wine, and that consequently after the priest himself had received the said blessed sacrament. And thus they used other days, when the people were well minded to be communicate or partakers of that holy mystery.

Item, on Easter day at morrow (being the first day of April), no mention was made of Jesus Christ's mighty Resurrection, nor any procession that day before mass nor at evensong about the font, nor any other day in the week. And within two weeks after, all prebendaries, hospitals, chantries, and free chapels within Yorkshire and other the king's dominions was given up by compulsion into his majesty's hands, with all manner of jewels, chalices, books, bells, vestments, with all other ornaments pertaining thereto.

Item, St Mark's day was not kept as a day of abstinence, but every man to be at liberty and eat all kinds of meat at his pleasure.

Item, Rogation days no procession was made about the fields, but cruel tyrants did cast down all crosses standing in open ways dispitefully.

Item, in many places of this realm (but specially in the south parts, as Suffolk, Norfolk, Kent and Wales, etc.) neither bread nor water was sanctified or distributed among Christian people on Sundays, but clearly omitted as things tending to idolatry. Yea, and also the pyxes hanging over the altars (wherein was remaining Christ's blessed body under form of bread) was spitefully cast away as things most abominable, and did not pass of the blessed hosts therein contained, but villainously despised them, uttering such words thereby as it did abhor true Christian ears for to hear; but only that Christ's mercy is so much, it was marvel that the earth did not open and swallow up such villainous persons, as it did Dathan and Abiram. The said villainous persons denied that most blessed sacrament and so would have had no mass used within this realm; yea, and stiffly affirmed that Messiah was not yet born, and so finally denied all sacraments, except matrimony, because it was first institute in paradise terrestrial, affirming also that it was lawful for priests to marry women, using them as their wives, which was very pleasant to many, for they were married in very deed both bishops and other inferiors, being so blinded with carnal concupiscence that they preached and taught the people openly, that it was lawful so to do by God's law, and enacted the same. Which priests so married when they did celebrate would make no elevation at mass after consecration, but all other honest priests did according to the old laudable fashion in remembrance how Our Saviour Jesus Christ was elevated upon a cross of tree for mankind's redemption. Thus was this realm of England in great division and unquietness, sore plagued with enemies in the north parts by sword and in the south by pestilence.

Of All Souls' day (*anno ubi supra*) was the pyx with the most blessed sacrament therein taken down in York Minster and set upon the high altar; likewise did all parish churches in York and divers deaneries within the shire.

Then was there a great parliament holden at Westminster at London the same winter, beginning the 4th day of November and there continued and kept to the 14th day of March in the third year of the reign of King Edward the Sixth, wherein the holy mass was subdued and deposed by act of parliament, and none to be used, but only a communion . . .

After the feast of the Annunciation of Our Lady (*anno domini* 1549), the king's majesty's acts was proclaimed, declaring how it was lawful by God's law priests to marry women, and so many was married indeed . . .

Consequently, followed straight monition, yea, and commandment (according to the king's majesty's acts) at visitations after Easter, that no priest should celebrate or say mass in Latin, or minister any sacrament in Latin words after the feast of Pentecost then next following, but only in English (as they would avoid the king's high displeasure and such penalties as was manifest in the said acts). And so the holy mass was utterly deposed throughout all this realm of England and other of the king's dominions at the said Pentecost, and in place thereof a communion to be said in English without any elevation of Christ's body and blood under form of bread and wine, or adoration, or reservation in the pyx, for a certain English book was set forth in print, containing all such service as should be used in the church of God, and no other (entitled the Book of Common Prayer) . . .

A great parliament held at Westminster and begun the 23rd day of January and then continued and kept unto the 15th day of April in the sixth year of the king's majesty's reign, and in the year of Our Lord God 1552, wherein no goodness towards holy church proceeded, but all things contrary. For in the parliament was deposed by act these three holy days before accustomed to have been kept holy, viz. Conversion of St Paul, St Barnabas and Mary Magdalen; and that a new communion book in English (called the Book of Common Prayer) should take effect at All Hallows day next ensuing date hereof (viz. first day of November), and so the communion book in English (which is above mentioned) to be of none effect. Oh, note the great instability and newfangledness of the heretic Warwick (alias Duke of Northumberland) with his adherents, viz. carnal bishops of this realm and very traitors to God. For consequently after that Robert Holgate, Archbishop of York, was come from the said parliament, he sent straight commandment in beginning of June through all his diocese that the table in the choir whereupon the holy communion was ministered, it standing with the ends toward south and north, should be used contrary, viz. to be set in the choir beneath the lowest stair or grace, having the ends thereof towards the east and west, and the priest his face towards the north all the communion time, which was nothing seeming nor after any good order.

Item, it was commanded that no organs should be used in the church, whereby any melody should be made to God his honour, laud and praise, but utterly forbidden. . .

The virtuous lady Mary . . . was proclaimed on the 19th of July (1553) . . . at which proclamation all good people there being present highly rejoiced, giving thanks, honour and praise unto Almighty God, and so went singing *Te Deum laudamus* into Paul's church . . .

In the meantime in many places of the realm, priests were commanded by lords and knights Catholic to say mass in Latin with consecration and elevation of the body and blood of Christ under form of bread and wine with a decent order as hath been used beforetime, but such as was of heretical opinions might not away therewith but spake evil thereof, for as then there was no act, statute, proclamation or commandment set forth for the same; therefore, many one dared not be bold to celebrate in Latin, though their hearts were wholly inclined that way. Howbeit, in August there was a proclamation set forth declaring how the gracious Queen Mary did license priests to say mass in Latin after the old ancient custom, as was used in her father's days . . .

28

Thus through grace of the Holy Ghost, the straight of holy church something began to amend and to arise from the old heresies before used in this realm, for the holy mass in Latin was put down totally from the feast of Pentecost *anno domini* 1549 unto the beginning of August *anno domini* 1553, but then in many places of Yorkshire priests unmarried was very glad to celebrate and say mass in Latin with matins and evensong thereto, according for very fervent zeal and love that they had unto God and his laws. And so in the beginning of September there were very few parish churches in Yorkshire but mass was sung or said in Latin on the first Sunday of the said month or at furthest, on the feast day of the Nativity of Our Blessed Lady.

Holy bread and holy water was given, altars was reedified, pictures or images set up, the cross with the crucifix thereon ready to be borne in procession, and with the same went procession. And in conclusion, all the English service of laity used in the church of God was voluntarily laid away and the Latin taken up again (not only with matins, mass and evensong, but also in ministration of sacraments), and yet all these came to pass without compulsion of any act, statute, proclamation or law, but only that the gracious Queen Mary in her proclamation did utter these words: viz. her majesty did wish and much desire that the same religion which ever she professed from her infancy hitherto, and still was aminded to observe and maintain the same for herself (through God's grace, enduring her time) were of all her subjects quietly and charitably embraced . . .

So to be brief, all old ceremonies laudably used beforetime in holy church was then revived, daily frequented, and used, after that the right reverend Father in God, the Lord Cardinal Pole, legate *a latere*, was entered this realm in the month of November (1554) bringing with him the pope's power and authority.

ROSE HICKMAN'S MEMOIR OF PROTESTANT LIFE UNDER MARY

Rose Hickman (1526–1613), the daughter and wife of London merchants, was an early adherent of Protestantism. Her memoir, written in her old age, recalls the difficulties she encountered and the ingenuity with which she overcame them during the Catholic counter-reformation of Queen Mary. Hickman's account of her response to the popish ceremony of baptism and her adventures as a Protestant mother in exile formed a self-flattering portrait written to inspire a younger generation.
Source: Maria Dowling and Joy Shakespeare, 'Religion and Politics in Mid Tudor England through the Eyes of an English Protestant Woman: The Recollections of Rose Hickman,' *Bulletin of the Institute of Historical Research*, vol. 55 (1982), pp. 94–102.

My mother in the days of King Henry VIII came to some light of the gospel by means of some English books sent privately to her by my father's factors from beyond sea; whereupon she used to call me with my two sisters into her chamber to read to us out of the same good books very privately, for fear of trouble, because those good books were then accounted heretical; and a merchant named Paginton who used to bring English bibles from beyond sea was slain with a gun as he went in the street. Therefore my mother charged us to say nothing of her reading to us for fear of trouble.

Then there was a plague in London, and my father and mother removed seven miles off into the country, where she was delivered of a child, fell sick and died. In time of her sickness she fell asleep, and being awaked she smiled, saying that she saw God the Father and Christ at his right hand stretching forth his hands to receive her, and so died comfortably in the faith.

How my husband and I spent our time in the reign of Queen Mary: As in token of my most bounden duty and thankfulness to the Almighty, I do use often in the day time but especially in the night as I lie waking in my bed, to meditate on his most merciful deliverances which he hath given to my good husband, Master Anthony Hickman, and me in the days of Queen Mary when the cruel Papists persecuted the people of God. So I now being above eighty-four years old and looking continually when the Lord will call me forth of this life, have thought good to set down the same in writing and to leave it to my children to move them to continue that thankfulness to Almighty God which I, their old mother, cannot acknowledge too much nor too often to his glory and praise, and to stand fast in that faith and service of God unto which their father and mother did stand so firmly, and manifest such zeal and affection as in this little treatise appeareth . . .

When Queen Mary came to the crown the idolatrous mass was set up with public profession of popery throughout this realm, and cruel persecution of those good Christians that in a good conscience refused to yield themselves to that idolatry. At which time we did receive into our house in the city of London divers godly and well disposed Christians that were desirous to shelter themselves from the cruel persecution of those times. And we and they did table together in a chamber, keeping the doors close shut for fear of the promoters, as we read in the gospel the disciples of Christ did for fear of the Jews. And thus we kept our house in London in the beginning of Queen Mary's days. But then there came forth a very strict proclamation, enjoining all to come to church and receive the sacrament after the popish fashion; after which proclamation we durst no longer keep our house, but my husband used means to convey away the preachers and other good Christians, that were in our house, beyond sea, giving them money to supply their wants . . .

Then my good husband was accused to the high commissioners for the conveying away and relieving those good Christians, whom the high commissioners called the queen's enemies, and for not conforming himself to popery according to the queen's Injunctions, and for the same my husband and my brother, who was also accused with him, were committed to close prison in the Fleet. And during the time of their imprisonment they could not be suffered to have any private correspondence together, neither could any other be suffered to have conference with either of them. . .

Afterwards my husband, to drive away the wicked days, went to Antwerp,[5] where he had a fair house which he rented for £40 a year, and I being with child went into Oxfordshire to a gentleman's house that was a lodge and stood far off from any church or town, the name whereof was Chiswell, and there I was delivered. And from thence I sent to Oxford to the bishops, who were then and there in prison and did afterwards suffer martyrdom there,[6] to be advised by them whether I might suffer my child to be baptized after the popish manner; who answered me that the sacrament of baptism, as it was used by the Papists, was the least corrupted, and therefore I might. But therewithall they said that I might have been gone out of England before that time if I had done well. And so my child was there baptized by a popish priest; but because I would avoid the popish stuff as much as I could, I did not put salt into the handkerchief that was to be delivered to the priest at the baptism, but put sugar in it instead of salt. Afterwards I prepared to go to Antwerp to my husband's house there, and although my husband had two fair houses in England, the one in London the other in Essex at Romford, both of them well furnished with household stuff, yet I accounted all nothing in comparison to liberty of conscience for the profession of Christ . . .

The reason why we did think ourselves safer in Antwerp than in England was not for any more liberty of the gospel given there, but because there were not parish churches but only [a] cathedral; wherein though the popish service was used, yet it could not be easily known who came to church and who not. But there was a chapel for the English merchants and thereunto all of them were compellable to go upon solemn feast days to wait upon their governor. And the night before that day my good husband would lie mourning in his bed and could not sleep for grief to think that he was on the morrow to go with the governor to that idolatrous service. But the governor though he was a Papist yet he was no persecutor nor cruel Papist, for he was contented to bear with my husband so far as he might without being seen to do it, and would say to him that though he did bark yet he did not bite.

Whilst I was in Antwerp I had another child and had great care to keep it from the baptism of the Papists; for in hatred that the inhabitants there do bear to the Anabaptists the magistrates used to enter at midnight into houses where any children were suspected to be kept unbaptized, and if he found any such, he used to put them in a sack and cast them into the water and so drown them. From which cruelty to save my child I did as followeth: viz., whereas it is the custom there to hang at the street door where a woman lieth in, a little piece of lawn, it was so that our house opened into two streets, therefore I hanged forth a piece of lawn upon either side or door, to the end that the neighbours on either side might suppose that it went out at the other door to be baptized. And it so pleased God that there was a secret congregation of Protestants, unto which congregation by the help of some godly women there I procured my child to be secretly carried, and there to be baptized by a Protestant minister, I not knowing godfather nor godmother.

And thus I continued in Antwerp till the death of Queen Mary, which was not a little joyful to me to hear of; for during the time of her tyrannous reign I had often prayed earnestly to God to take either her or me forth of the world. In all which time I never was present at any of the popish masses, or any other of their idolatrous service. For all which blessings and deliverances sent to me from my good God I most humbly beseech his majesty that I and mine may never forget to be thankful, not seeking our own vain glory thereby, but giving all praise and glory to his goodness who so graciously preserved, blessed and delivered me.

JOHN FOXE, *ACTS AND MONUMENTS*

In his popular 'Book of Martyrs', John Foxe (1516–87) presents the ordeals of early English Protestants in the context of the persecution and martyrdom of early Christians under the Romans, and contributes to the formation of England's national Protestant identity. Foxe's *Actes and Monuments of these Latter and Perillous Dayes* (1563), soon retitled *Actes and Monuments of Matters Most Speciall and Memorable*, was printed in dozens of editions in the sixteenth and seventeenth centuries. Its influence can be discerned in the works of such writers as Spenser, Milton and Bunyan. The following selections recount the inquisition by London officials and churchmen of Anne Askew (1521–46), who was executed in the reign of Henry VIII for denying the doctrine of transubstantiation; and the incidents preceding the executions of Hugh Latimer (c.1485–1555) and Nicholas Ridley (c.1500–55), two of the famous 'Oxford martyrs' burned at the stake in the reign of Mary I.
Source: John Foxe, *Actes and Monuments* (1576) (*STC* 11224), pp. 1205, 1661.

The examination of Anne Askew, 1546

To satisfy your expectation, good people (sayeth she), this was my first examination in the year of Our Lord 1545 and in the month of March.

First, Christopher Dare examined me at Sadlers Hall, being one of the Quest, and asked if I did not believe that the sacrament hanging over the altar was the very body of Christ really. Then I demanded this question of him: wherefore St Stephen was stoned to death? and he said, he could not tell. Then I answered, that no more would I assoil his vain question.

Secondly, he said that there was a woman, which did testify, that I should read how God was not in temples made with hands. Then I showed him the 7th and 17th chapters of the Acts of the Apostles, what Stephen and Paul had said therein. Whereupon he asked me how I took those sentences. I answered I would not throw pearls among swine, for acorns were good enough.

Thirdly, he asked wherefore I said I had rather to read five lines in the Bible, than to hear five masses in the temple? I confessed, that I said no less: not for the dispraise of either the epistle or the gospel, but because the one did greatly edify me, and the other nothing at all. As St Paul doth witness in the 14th chapter of his first epistle to the Corinthians where as he sayeth: if the trumpet giveth an uncertain sound, who will prepare himself to the battle?

Fourthly, he laid unto my charge that I should say: if an ill priest ministered, it was the Devil and not God. My answer was that I never spake any such thing. But this was my saying: that whosoever he were that ministered unto me, his ill conditions could not hurt my faith, but in spirit I received nevertheless the body and blood of Christ.

He asked me what I said concerning confession? I answered him by meaning, which was as St James sayeth, that every man ought to knowledge his faults to other, and the one to pray for the other.

Sixthly, he asked me what I said to the King's Book? And I answered him, that I could say nothing to it, because I never saw it.

Seventhly, he asked me if I had the spirit of God in me? I answered, if I had not, I was but a reprobate or cast away. Then he said he had sent for a priest to examine me, which was here at hand.

The priest asked me what I said to the sacrament of the altar, and required much to know therein my meaning. But I desired him again to hold me excused concerning that matter. None other answer would I make him, because I perceived him to be a Papist.

Eighthly he asked me if I did not think that private masses did help souls departed. I said it was great idolatry to believe more in them than in the death which Christ died for us.

Then they had me thence unto my lord mayor, and he examined me, as they had before, and I answered him directly in all things, as I answered the Quest before. Besides this, my lord mayor laid one thing unto my charge, which was never spoken of me, but of them: and that was whether a mouse eating the host received God or no? This question did I never ask, but indeed they asked it of me. Whereunto I made them no answer, but smiled.

Then the bishop's chancellor rebuked me, and said, that I was much to blame for uttering the scriptures. For St Paul (he said) forbode women to speak or talk of the word of God. I answered him that I knew Paul's meaning as well as he, which is in I Corinthians 14, that a woman ought not to speak in the congregation by the way of teaching. And then I asked him, how many women he had seen go into the pulpit and preach? He said he never saw none. Then I said, he ought to find no fault in poor women, except they had offended the law.

The ordeal of Ridley and Latimer, 1555

Ridley went to the stake, kneeled down by it, kissed it, most effectiously prayed, and behind him Master Latimer kneeled, as earnestly calling upon God as he. After they arose, the one talked with the other a little while, till they which were appointed to see the execution, removed themselves out of the sun. What they said I can learn of no man.

Then Dr Smith, of whose recantation in King Edward's time you heard before, began his sermon to them, upon this text of St Paul, in the thirteenth chapter of the first epistle to the Corinthians: *Si corpus meum tradam ignim, charitatem autem non habeo, nihil in de utilitatis capio.*[7] That is: if I yield my body to the fire to be burnt, and have not charity, I shall gain nothing thereby. Wherein he alleged that the goodness of the cause, and not the order of death, maketh the holiness of the person: which he confirmed by the examples of Judas, and of a woman in Oxford that of late hanged herself, for that they and suchlike as he recited might then be adjudged righteous, which desperately sundered their lives from their bodies, as he feared that those men that stood before him would do. But he cried still to the people to beware of them, for they were heretics, and died out of the church. And on the other side, he declared their diversity in opinions, as Lutherans, Oecolampadians, Zwinglians, of which sect they were (he said) and that was the worst: but the old church of Christ and the Catholic faith believed far otherwise. At which place they lifted up both their hands and eyes to heaven, as it were calling God to witness of the truth. The which countenance they made in many other places of his sermon, whereas they thought he spake amiss. He ended with a very short

34

exhortation to them to recant and come home again to the church, and save their lives and souls, which else were condemned. His sermon was scant in all a quarter of an hour.

Doctor Ridley said to Master Latimer: Will you begin to answer the sermon, or shall I? Master Latimer said: Begin you first, I pray you. I will, said Master Ridley.

Then the wicked sermon being ended, Doctor Ridley and Master Latimer kneeled down upon their knees towards my Lord Williams of Thame, the vice-chancellor of Oxford, and divers other commissioners appointed for that purpose, which sat upon a form thereby. Unto whom Master Ridley said: I beseech you my lord, even for Christ's sake that I may speak but two or three words; and whilst my lord bent his head to the mayor and vice-chancellor, to know (as it appeared) whether he might give him leave to speak, the bailiffs and Doctor Marshall, vice-chancellor, ran hastily unto him, and with their hands stopped his mouth and said: Master Ridley, if you will revoke your erroneous opinions, and recant the same, you shall not only have liberty so to do, but also the benefit of a subject, that is, have your life. Not otherwise? said Master Ridley. No, quoth Doctor Marshall, therefore if you will not do so, then there is no remedy but you must suffer for your deserts. Well, quoth Master Ridley, so long as the breath is in my body, I will never deny my Lord Christ and his known truth: God's will be done in me. And with that he rose up, and said with a loud voice: Well, then I commit my cause to Almighty God, which shall indifferently judge all.

ACCOUNTS AND INVENTORIES OF ST EDMUND'S PARISH, SALISBURY, 1527–57

Churchwardens' accounts record parochial expenditure on religious activity, devotional equipment and the routine maintenance of the structure and fabric of the church. Recording payments for banner processions and rood lights in the reign of Henry VIII, the substitution of tables for altars under Edward VI, and the restoration of Catholic worship under Mary, they serve as a guide to changing religious styles and beliefs. Inventories of parish goods similarly point to shifting spiritual emphases and changing liturgical needs. These extracts from St Edmund's parish in the cathedral town of Salisbury may be compared with later entries from the reigns of Elizabeth, James I and Charles I.
Source: Henry James Fowle Swayne (ed.), *Churchwardens' Accounts of S. Edmund & S. Thomas, Sarum 1443–1702* (Salisbury, 1896), pp. 68–9, 91–2, 101–2, 373.

1527–8 (total disbursements £14 18s 4d)

To the parish priest for reading of the bede roll, 12d.
For ringing the Monday in the Rogation week, for bread, ale and banners-bearing, 7d.

35

Three days following in likewise, 19d.

A carpenter for mending of a pew and for nails, 5d.

For ringing on Whit Sunday, 4d.

To a labourer a whole week to serve a plumber and making clean of gutters, 15d.

To a plumber and his man for five days and a half at 10d a day, 4s 7d . . .

For ringing the Thursday and bearing of banners, 4d.

For ringing on Corpus Christi day, 2d . . .

To Mother Rose for sewing over of albs, 4d.

To Thomas Prince for a pound of visitation light, 6d.

To making of the torches and eight pound of new wax, 5s 4d . . .

To Sir Humphrey . . . for keeping of Jesus mass, 4s . . .

To Thomas Prince for making of the rood light, 9s.

To Petty the smith for making of the iron to hang the canopy on, 5d . . .

To Father Roose for lighting of the rood light, 12d.

To Dorothy Wulfe for four baldricks, 5s 4d.

To Roger Smith for a key and for mending of a pew, 4d . . .

Inventory, 1531–2

A cross of silver and gilt with Mary and John; a pair of candlesticks of silver and all gilt; a pair of candlesticks of silver and parcels gilt; a monstrance all gilt; a pax of silver with a crucifix with Mary and John which standeth in a gospel book; a bell of silver parcel gilt; five chalices; a pax of copper; two cross staves covered with silver; a little oil vat of silver; two censers of silver with a sheep all parcel gilt; two cruets of silver parcel gilt; a relic of St Wolfrise set in silver parcel gilt; an oil vat parcel gilt; a little chain of silver for the sacrament; a foot of silver that was set upon St Edmund's foot and so taken off and resteth in the church; two cruets and a pax of silver of the gift of Sir William Young, priest.

1550–1 (total disbursements £36 17s 5d)

To Cox for helping us to fold the copes and other gear, 2d.

For mending of the lock of the coffer wherein the book of christenings and buryings lieth, 2d.

Oil for the bells, 3d.

Ringing on four holy day eves, 4d.

Paper and ink, 6d.

Ringing in the procession week, 10d . . .

Oil for christening and kneeling oil, 2d . . .

Mending of a surplice for one of the boys and for washing of the same, 2d . . .

To five labourers for pulling down of the altars, 13s 8d.

Trussing of five bells, 6d.

Washing of an altar cloth, 1d.

Candles to ring seven o'clock and five o'clock, and for the masons to work by, 20d.

Two masons and one labourer, for carrying out of the stones of the altar, and for lime to [whitewash] the walls . . . 5s 2d.

The making of a surplice for the sexton, and the washing, 18d . . .

Making a copy of the Injunctions, 8d . . .

To Cox and another man for carrying of stones and rubble out of the church, 2d . . .

To masons for pulling down of the high altar, 10s 4d . . .

Sack of lime to white lime the church, 12d . . .

Mending of a glass window in the north side of the church, 12d . . .

An homily book set out in parts, 16d . . .

A glass to serve the communion, 1d . . .

Washing of a surplice and an altar cloth and a towel, 3d.

Making of the tables for the communion, 2s . . .

The legging of a form to serve for people when they do receive the communion, 1d . . .

Cox and another man for making clean of the church and the pews after Easter, 8d.

Inventory, 1554–5

A chalice all gilt with his patten weighing 23 ounces; another chalice with his patten parcel gilt weighing 13 ounces; a cross of latten gilt; a latten pax gilt; a suit of vestments of red damask; a cope of red dasmask; a suit of vestments of blue damask; a cope of blue damask; two altar cloths of white damask; two silk curtains of white; three palls of dornix; three towels; two silk curtains of red; four altar cloths; two white curtains; three albs; a sheet with a Jesus; three surplices for men; two altar cloths of silk with a crucifix; two surplices for children; one cushion of silk; a black altar cloth of silk; two censers of brass; an altar cloth of diverse colours; three stoles, two white and one red; three pair of candlesticks of brass; a cloth for the rood loft of canvas; two old half antiphoners; three processionals; a manual; two graduals and a mass book; a towel wrought with silk; another of Sendal; a chasuble of crimson velvet; a pax of Mary and John gilt; five candlesticks of brass; nine candlesticks of brass to put tapers in; two torches of wax; nine tapers; a chasuble of satin of Bruges; a holy water pot of brass; a canopy cloth painted with a fringe; nine banner cloths; two silk cushions, one of green and another of red; a towel wrought with silk; another of Sendal; a box to put hosts in.

1556–7 (total £9 10s 1d)

Paid the Monday in Rogation week to the bell-ringers, 4d.
Bell-ringers on Holy Thursday, 6d.
Drink for the banner-bearers, 3d.
To the priests of St Thomas and to the clerks the Thursday in the Whitsun week, 12d.
Drink for them that did bear up the copes, 4d . . .
Robert Aunsell, for two stones for the rood, 4d.
Nails for the lamp, 1d.
Making of the new canopy, 9d.
A copy of the articles, 6d . . .
Upon Corpus Christi day to the bell-ringers, 4d.
To them that did wear copes, 3d.
Banner-bearers, 4d . . .
Mending of the tablement upon the first mass altar, 2d.
Painting of the wall behind the rood, 6s 8d.
Oil for the lamp, 2d . . .
A bushel of coals to melt lead to solder the iron clamps for the rood loft, 1d . . .
John Atkins for tending of the wives' light, 4d.
Bearing of the wives' light to church, 2d.
The minstrels for bringing the light to the church, 8d.
Our clerk for mending of the organs, 11s . . .
Oil against All Hallows tide for the bells, 3d.
Ringing on All Hallows eve, 2d . . .
Candles against Christmas, 6d.
Two skins of white leather to mend the organs, 12d . . .
Mending of two copes, which one of them was lined through, 10s . . .
Mending of the bier, 8d.
The first Friday in Lent, to make the singing men drink, 12d.
Oil for the bells, 2d.
For a cloth and for painting of it to hang afore the rood, 6s 8d . . .
Joiner for setting two posts under the rood loft, 3s . . .
Colouring the two posts that was set to bear up the rood loft, 3d . . .
Drink for them that did dress the sepulchre, 2d . . .

Nicholas Burgess for watching the sepulchre, 6d . . .

Seven pounds of tallow candles, 10d . . .

Charges for meat and drink for the women and men that did gather at Hocktide, 7s.

2

THE ESTABLISHED CHURCH

THE BOOK OF COMMON PRAYER, 1559

Under Edward VI, Archbishop of Canterbury Thomas Cranmer and other scholars transformed the Roman missal, breviary, graduale and ordinale into an English liturgy. The prayer book of 1549 was a cautiously reformed document, printed under the aegis of parliament and enforced by the first Act of Uniformity. A more radically Protestant prayer book followed in 1552, but was soon repealed by Queen Mary upon her accession. The Elizabethan prayer book of 1559 was essentially the version of 1552 , with some notable exceptions that rendered it more conservative. The Book of Common Prayer familiarized generations of English worshippers to an idiosyncratic form of Protestantism that was reformed in doctrine but traditional in liturgy.
Source: *Liturgical Services: Liturgies and Occasional Forms of Prayer Set Forth in the Reign of Queen Elizabeth*, ed. William Keatinge Clay, Parker Society (Cambridge, 1868), pp. 33–8, 180–238; 'Black Rubric' from *The Two Liturgies*, A.D. 1549, and A.D. 1552, ed. Joseph Ketley, Parker Society (Cambridge, 1864), p. 283.

Preface

There was never any thing by the wit of man so well devised, or so sure established, which in continuance of time hath not been corrupted, as (among other things) it may plainly appear by the common prayers in the church, commonly called divine service. The first original and ground whereof, if a man would search out by the ancient fathers, he shall find that the same was not ordained but of a good purpose and for a great advancement of godliness. For they so ordered the matter that all the whole Bible, or the greatest part thereof, should be read over once in the year, intending thereby that the clergy, and specially such as were ministers of the congregation, should, by often reading and meditation of God's word, be stirred up to godliness themselves, and be more able to exhort other by wholesome doctrine, and to confute them that were adversaries to the truth. And further, that the people by daily hearing of holy scripture read in the church should continually profit more and more in the knowledge of God and be the more inflamed with the love of his true religion. But these

40

many years past this godly and decent order of the ancient fathers hath been so altered, broken, and neglected by planting in uncertain stories, legends, responds, verses, vain repetitions, commemorations and synodals that commonly when any book of the Bible was begun, before three or four chapters were read out, all the rest are unread. And in this sort the book of Isaiah was begun in Advent and the book of Genesis in Septuagesima, but they were only begun and never read through. After a like sort were other books of Holy Scripture used. And moreover, whereas St Paul would have such language spoken to the people in the church as they might understand and have profit by hearing the same, the service in this Church of England these many years hath been read in Latin to the people, which they understood not, so that they have heard with their ears only, and their hearts, spirit, and mind have not been edified thereby. And furthermore, notwithstanding that the ancient fathers have divided the psalms into seven portions whereof every one was called a nocturn, now of late time a few of them have been daily said and oft repeated, and the rest utterly omitted. Moreover, the number and hardness of the rules called the pie and the manifold changings of the service was the cause that to turn the book only was so hard and intricate a matter that many times there was more business to find out what should be read than to read it when it was found out.

These inconveniences therefore considered, here is set forth such an order whereby the same shall be redressed. And for a readiness in this matter, here is drawn out a calendar for that purpose, which is plain and easy to be understanden, wherein, so much as may be, the reading of Holy Scriptures is so set forth that all things shall be done in order without breaking one piece thereof from another. For this cause be cut off anthems, responds, invitatories, and such like things as did break the continual course of the reading of the scripture. Yet because there is no remedy but that of necessity there must be some rules, therefore certain rules are here set forth, which as they be few in number so they be plain and easy to be understanden. So that here you have an order for prayer, as touching the reading of Holy Scripture, much agreeable to the mind and purpose of the old fathers, and a great deal more profitable and commodious than that which of late was used. It is more profitable because here are left out many things whereof some be untrue, some uncertain, some vain and super-stitious, and is ordained nothing to be read but the very pure word of God, the Holy Scriptures, or that which is evidently grounded upon the same, and that in such a language and order as is most easy and plain for the understanding, both of the readers and hearers. It is also more commo-dious, both for the shortness thereof and for the plainness of the order, and for that the rules be few and easy. Furthermore, by this order the curates shall need none other books for their public service but this book and the Bible, by the means whereof the people shall not be at so great charge for books as in time past they have been.

And where heretofore there hath been great diversity in saying and singing in churches within this realm, some following Salisbury use, some Hereford use, some the use of Bangor, some of York, and some of Lincoln, now from henceforth all the whole realm shall have but one use. And if any would judge this way more painful because that all things must be read upon the book whereas before by the reason of so often repetition they could say many things by heart, if those men will weigh their labour with the profit and knowledge which daily they shall obtain by reading upon the book, they will not refuse the pain in consideration of the great profit that shall ensue thereof.

And for as much as nothing can almost be so plainly set forth but doubts may rise in the use and practicing of the same, to appease all such diversity (if any arise) and for the resolution of all doubts concerning the manner how to understand, do, and execute the things contained in this book, the parties that so doubt, or diversely take anything shall alway resort to the bishop of the diocese, who by his discretion shall take order for the quieting and appeasing of the same so that the same order be not contrary to anything contained in this book. And if the bishop of the diocese be in any doubt, then may he send for the resolution thereof unto the archbishop.

Though it be appointed in the afore written preface that all things shall be read and sung in the church in the English tongue, to the end that the congregation may be thereby edified, yet it is not meant but when men say morning and evening prayer privately, they may say the same in any language that they themselves do understand.

And all priests and deacons shall be bound to say daily the morning and evening prayer, either privately or openly, except they be letted by preaching, studying of divinity, or by some other urgent cause.

And the curate that ministereth in every parish church, or chapel, being at home and not being otherwise reasonably letted, shall say the same in the parish church or chapel where he ministereth and shall toll a bell thereto a convenient time before he begin, that such as be disposed may come to hear God's word and to pray with him.

Of ceremonies, why some be abolished and some retained

The word 'ceremonies' refers to the liturgical practices (as distinguished from theological beliefs) outlined in The Book of Common Prayer. This section remained virtually unaltered from 1549, but changes in the religious temperament of Protestant England meant that widely varying interpretations of its meaning were possible. Controversies under Elizabeth and the early Stuarts thus revolved around what practices and beliefs could be defined as *essential* (commanded by God), or *adiaphoric* (matters of theological indifference, subject to the authority of the monarch).

Of such ceremonies as be used in the church and have had their beginning by the institution of man, some at the first were of godly intent and purpose devised and yet at length turned to vanity and superstition, some entered into the church by undiscreet devotion and such a zeal as was without knowledge. And forbecause they were winked at in the beginning, they grew daily to more and more abuses, which not only for their unprofitableness but also because they have much blinded the people and obscured the glory of God are worthy to be cut away and clean rejected. Other there be which although they have been devised by man, yet it is thought good to reserve them still, as well for a decent order in the church, for the which they were first devised, as because they pertain to edification, whereunto all things done in the church, as the apostle teacheth, ought to be referred. And although the keeping or omitting of a ceremony in itself considered is but a small thing, yet the willful and contemptuous transgression and breaking of a common order and discipline is no small offence before God.

Let all things be done among you, saith St Paul, in a seemly and due order. The appointment of the which order pertaineth not to private men, therefore no man ought to take in hand nor presume to appoint or alter any public or common order in Christ's church, except he be lawfully called and authorized thereunto.

And whereas in this our time the minds of men are so diverse that some think it a great matter of conscience to depart from a piece of the least of their ceremonies, they be so addicted to their old customs, and again on the other side, some be so newfangled that they would innovate all thing, and so do despise the old, that nothing can like them but that is new, it was thought expedient not so much to have respect how to please and satisfy either of these parties, as how to please God and profit them both. And yet lest any man should be offended whom good reason might satisfy, here be certain causes rendered why some of the accustomed ceremonies be put away and some retained and kept still.

Some are put away because the great excess and multitude of them hath so increased in these latter days that the burden of them was intolerable, whereof St Augustine in his time complained that they were grown to such a number that the state of Christian people was in worse case concerning that matter than were the Jews. And he counselled that such yoke and burden should be taken away, as time would serve quietly to do it.

But what would St Augustine have said if he had seen the ceremonies of late days used among us, whereunto the multitude used in his time was not to be compared? This our excessive multitude of ceremonies was so great and many of them so dark that they did more confound and darken than declare and set forth Christ's benefits unto us.

And besides this, Christ's gospel is not a ceremonial law, as much of Moses' law was, but it is a religion to serve God, not in bondage of the figure or shadow, but in the freedom of spirit, being content only with those ceremonies which do serve to a decent order and godly discipline, and such as be apt to stir up the dull mind of man to the remembrance of his duty to God by some notable and special signification whereby he might be edified.

Furthermore, the most weighty cause of the abolishment of certain ceremonies was that they were so far abused, partly by the superstitious blindness of the rude and unlearned and partly by the unsatiable avarice of such as sought more their own lucre than the glory of God, that the abuses could not well be taken away, the thing remaining still. But now, as concerning those persons which peradventure will be offended for that some of the old ceremonies are retained still, if they consider that without some ceremonies it is not possible to keep any order or quiet discipline in the church, they shall easily perceive just cause to reform their judgements. And if they think much that any of the old do remain and would rather have all devised anew, then such men granting some ceremonies convenient to be had, surely where the old may be well used there they cannot reasonably reprove the old only for their age without bewraying of their own folly. For in such a case they ought rather to have reverence unto them for their antiquity, if they will declare themselves to be more studious of unity and concord than of innovations and newfangleness, which, as much as may be with the true setting forth of Christ's religion, is always to be eschewed. Furthermore, such shall have no just cause with the ceremonies reserved, to be offended. For as those be taken away which were most abused and did burden men's consciences without any cause, so the other that remain are retained for a discipline and order, which upon just causes may be altered and changed, and therefore are not to be esteemed equal with God's law. And moreover, they be neither dark nor dumb ceremonies, but are so set forth that every man may understand what they do mean and to what use they do serve. So that it is not like that they in time to come should be abused as the other have been. And in these our doings, we condemn no other nations, nor prescribe anything but to our own people only. For we think it convenient that every country should use such ceremonies as they shall think best to the setting forth of God's honour or glory and to the reducing of the people to a most perfect and godly living, without error or superstition. And that they should put away other things which from time to time they perceive to be most abused, as in men's ordinances it often chanceth diversely in diverse countries.

The order for the administration of the Lord's Supper, or holy communion

According to Protestant doctrine, communion was one of the two sacraments of the church (the other being baptism). According to the Elizabethan theologian John Jewel, the communion bread and wine provided an 'evident token of the body and blood of Jesus Christ', and in sharing these elements communicants were 'joined, united and [made] incorporate unto Christ'. In order to pacify both the reformed and conservative factions of the Church of England, the 1559 liturgy combined the 1549 and 1552 words of administration, resulting in an ambiguous formulation that neither denied nor endorsed the idea of a corporeal presence of Christ in the eucharistic elements. Note the requirement that participants in communion ought to be in charity with their neighbours.

So many as do intend to be partakers of the holy communion, shall signify their names to the curate overnight, or else in the morning, afore the beginning of morning prayer, or immediately after. And if any of those be an open and notorious evil liver, so that the congregation by him is offended, or have done any wrong to his neighbours by word or deed, the curate having knowledge thereof, shall call him, and advertise him, in any wise not to presume to the Lord's table, until he have openly declared himself to have truly repented and amended his former naughty life, that the congregation may thereby be satisfied, which afore were offended; and that he have recompensed the parties whom he hath done wrong unto, or at the least declare himself to be in full purpose so to do, as soon as he conveniently may.

The same order shall the curate use with those betwixt whom he perceiveth malice and hatred to reign, not suffering them to be partakers of the Lord's table until he know them to be reconciled. And if one of the parties so at variance be content to forgive from the bottom of his heart all that the other hath trespassed against him, and to make amends for that he himself hath offended, and the other party will not be persuaded to a godly unity, but remain still in his frowardness and malice: the minister in that case ought to admit the penitent person to the holy communion, and not him that is obstinate.

The table having at the communion time a fair white linen cloth upon it, shall stand in the body of the church, or in the chancel, where morning prayer and evening prayer be appointed to be said. And the priest standing at the north side of the table shall say the Lord's Prayer with this collect following:

Almighty God, unto whom all hearts be open, all desires known, and from whom no secrets are hid: cleanse the thoughts of our hearts by the inspiration of thy Holy Spirit, that we may perfectly love thee, and worthily magnify thy holy name; through Christ Our Lord. Amen.

Then shall the priest rehearse distinctly all the Ten Commandments, and the people, kneeling, shall after every commandment ask God's mercy for their transgression of the same . . .

And the Epistle and gospel being ended, shall be said the Creed:

I believe in one God, the Father almighty, maker of heaven and earth, and of all things visible and invisible. And in one Lord Jesus Christ, the only begotten Son of God, begotten of his father before all worlds: God of God, light of light, very God of very God: begotten, not made, being of one substance with the Father, by whom all things were made. Who for us men and for our salvation came down from heaven, and was incarnate by the Holy Ghost of the virgin Mary, and was made man; and was crucified also for us, under Pontius Pilate. He suffered and was buried, And the third day he rose again according to the scriptures, and ascended into heaven, and sitteth at the right hand of the Father. And he shall come again with glory, to judge both the quick and the dead, whose kingdom shall have no end.

And I believe in the Holy Ghost, the lord and giver of life, who proceedeth from the Father and the Son; who with the Father and the Son together is worshipped and glorified, who spake by the prophets. And I believe one Catholic and apostolic church. I acknowledge one baptism for the remission of sins. And I look for the resurrection of the dead, and the life of the world to come, Amen.

Then shall the priest say to them that come to receive the holy communion:

You that do truly and earnestly repent you of your sins, and be in love and charity with your neighbours, and intend to lead a new life, following the commandments of God, and walking from henceforth in his holy ways: draw near, and take this holy sacrament to your comfort; make your humble confession to Almighty God before this congregation here gathered together in his holy name, meekly kneeling upon your knees.

Then shall this general confession be made . . .

Almighty God, Father of Our Lord Jesus Christ, maker of all things, judge of all men: we acknowledge and bewail our manifold sins and wickedness, which we from time to time most grievously have committed, by thought, word and deed, against thy divine majesty; provoking most justly thy wrath and indignation against us: we do earnestly repent, and be heartily sorry for these our misdoings: the remembrance of them is grievous unto us, the burden of them is intolerable: have mercy upon us, have mercy upon us, most merciful Father, for thy Son Our Lord Jesus Christ's sake: forgive us all that is past, and grant that we may ever hereafter serve and please thee, in newness of life, to the honour and glory of thy name; through Jesus Christ Our Lord. Amen . . .

Then shall the priest kneeling down at God's board, say in the name of all them that shall receive the communion, this prayer following:

We do not presume to come to this thy table (O merciful Lord) trusting in our own righteousness, but in thy manifold and great mercies. We be not worthy so much as to gather the crumbs under thy table, but thou art the same Lord, whose property is always to have mercy. Grant us therefore (gracious Lord) so to eat the flesh of thy dear Son Jesus Christ, and to drink his blood, that our sinful bodies may be made clean by his body, and our souls washed through his most precious blood, and that we may evermore dwell in him, and he in us. Amen.

Then the priest standing up shall say as followeth:

Almighty God our heavenly Father, which of thy tender mercy didst give thine only Son Jesus Christ, to suffer death upon the cross for our redemption; who made there (by his one oblation of himself once offered) a full, perfect, and sufficient sacrifice, oblation, and satisfaction for the sins of the whole world; and did institute, and in his holy gospel command us to continue, a perpetual memory of that his precious death, until his coming again. Hear us, O merciful Father, we beseech thee; and grant that we receiving these thy creatures of bread and wine, according to thy Son Our Saviour Jesu Christ's holy institution, in remembrance of his death and passion, may be partakers of his most blessed body and blood: who in the same night that he was betrayed, took bread, and when he had given thanks, he brake it, and gave it to his disciples, saying, Take, eat, this is my body which is given for you. Do this in remembrance of me. Likewise after supper he took the cup, and when he had given thanks, he gave it to them, saying, Drink ye all of this, for this is my blood of the new testament, which is shed for you and for many, for remission of sins: do this as oft as ye shall drink it in remembrance of me.

Then shall the minister first receive the communion in both kinds himself, and next deliver it to other ministers, if any be there present (that they may help the chief minister) and after to the people in their hands kneeling. And when he delivereth the bread, he shall say: The body of Our Lord Jesus Christ which was given for thee, preserve thy body and soul into everlasting life: and take and eat this, in remembrance that Christ died for thee, and feed on him in thy heart by faith, with thanksgiving.

And the minister that delivereth the cup, shall say: The blood of Our Lord Jesus Christ which was shed for thee, preserve thy body and soul into everlasting life: and drink this in remembrance that Christ's blood was shed for thee, and be thankful.

The 'Black Rubric', 1552

A rubric is a direction for the conduct of a liturgical service, usually written in red, as the name implies. This particular rubric was printed in black in the 1552 Prayer Book as a last-minute inclusion, in response to the fiery Scots preacher John Knox who preached at the court of Edward VI decrying the retention of 'superstitious' ceremonies. While this rubric does not condemn kneeling at communion, it reinterprets it, focusing more on order and uniformity than on reverence to the sacred elements. Perhaps because of its radical associations, the 'Black Rubric' did not appear in the 1559 Book of Common Prayer.

Although no order can be so perfectly devised, but it may be of some, either for their ignorance and infirmity, or else of malice and obstinacy, misconstrued, depraved, and interpreted in a wrong part; and yet because brotherly charity willeth that so much as conveniently may be, offences should be taken away, therefore are we willing to do the same. Whereas it is ordained in the book of common prayer, in the administration of the Lord's Supper, that the communicants kneeling should receive the holy communion; which thing being well meant, for a signification of the humble and grateful acknowledging of the benefits of Christ, given unto the worthy receiver, and to avoid the profanation and disorder, which about the holy communion might else ensue; lest yet the same kneeling might be thought or taken otherwise, we do declare that it is not meant thereby, that any adoration is done, or ought to be done, either unto the sacramental bread or wine there bodily received, or to any real and essential presence there being of Christ's natural flesh and blood. For as concerning the sacramental bread and wine, they remain still in their very natural substances, and therefore may not be adored, for that were idolatry to be abhorred of all faithful Christians. And as concerning the natural body and blood of Our Saviour Christ, they are in heaven and not here. For it is against the truth of Christ's true natural body to be in more places than in one at one time.

The ministration of baptism to be used in the church

The sacrament of baptism was a mystical ceremony that signified cleansing from original sin. It was also a naming ceremony and a ritual of initiation marking entrance into the visible church and incorporation into the community of Christians. The minister usually performed this ceremony in church within a few days of the birth, but if the child seemed likely to die baptism could be done at home. Traditionally midwives fulfilled this emergency function, but by the early Stuart period baptism by women was rare. Controversies flared over the efficacy of the sacrament, whether it actually removed original sin or merely signified Christ's redemption; over the sign of the cross, which some Puritans protested as a popish remnant; and over the role of godparents and the powerful promises they made on behalf of the child. The orthodox position was restated in the Thirty-Nine Articles and in the Canons of 1604.

It appeareth by ancient writers that the sacrament of baptism in the old time was not commonly ministered but at two times in the year: at Easter and Whitsuntide. At which times it was openly ministered in the presence of all the congregation: which custom (now being grown out of use) although it cannot for many considerations be well restored again, yet it is thought good to follow the same as near as conveniently may be. Wherefore the people are to be admonished that it is most convenient that baptism should not be ministered but upon Sundays and other holy days when the most number of people may come together, as well for that the congregation there present may testify the receiving of them that be newly baptized into the number of Christ's church, as also because in the baptism of infants every man present may be put in remembrance of his own profession made to God in his baptism. For which cause also, it is expedient that baptism be ministered in the English tongue. Nevertheless (if necessity so require) children may at all times be baptized at home.

Public baptism

When there are children to be baptized upon the Sunday or holy day, the parents shall give knowledge overnight, or in the morning afore the beginning of morning prayer, to the curate. And then the godfathers, godmothers and people with the children must be ready at the font either immediately after the last lesson at morning prayer, or else immediately after the last lesson at evening prayer, as the curate by his discretion shall appoint. And then standing there, the priest shall ask whether the children be baptized or no. If they answer, No: then shall the priest say thus:

Dearly beloved, forasmuch as all men be conceived and born in sin, and that Our Saviour Christ saith, None can enter into the kingdom of God, except he be regenerate and born anew of water and the Holy Ghost: I beseech you to call upon God the Father, through Our Lord Jesus Christ, that of his bounteous mercy he will grant to these children that thing which by nature they cannot have, that they may be baptized with water and the Holy Ghost, and received into Christ's holy church, and be made lively members of the same.

Then the priest shall say:

Let us pray. Almighty and everlasting God, which of thy great mercy didst save Noah and his family in the ark from perishing by water, and also didst safely lead the children of Israel thy people through the Red Sea, figuring thereby thy holy baptism, and by the baptism of thy well-beloved Son Jesus Christ, didst sanctify the flood Jordan and all other waters to the mystical washing away of sin: We beseech thee for thy infinite mercies, that thou wilt mercifully look upon these children, sanctify them and wash them with thy Holy Ghost, that they being delivered from thy wrath may be received into the ark of Christ's church, and being steadfast in faith, joyful through hope, and rooted in charity, may so pass the waves of this troublesome world, that finally they may come to the land of everlasting life, there to reign with thee, world without end; through Jesus Christ Our Lord. Amen . . .

Then the priest shall speak unto the godfathers and godmothers on this wise:

Well-beloved friends, ye have brought these children here to be baptized; ye have prayed that Our Lord Jesus Christ would vouchsafe to receive them, to lay his hands upon them, to bless them, to release them of their sins, to give them the kingdom of heaven, and everlasting life. Ye have heard also that Our Lord Jesus Christ hath promised in his gospel to grant all these things that ye have prayed for; which promise he for his part will most surely keep and perform. Wherefore after this promise made by Christ, these infants must also faithfully for their part promise by you that be their sureties, that they will forsake the Devil and all his works, and constantly believe God's holy word, and obediently keep his commandments.

Then shall the priest demand of the godfathers and godmothers these questions following:

Dost thou forsake the Devil and all his works, the vain pomp, and glory of the world, with all covetous desires of the same, the carnal desires of the flesh, so that thou wilt not follow, nor be led by them?

Answer. I forsake them all.

Minister. Dost thou believe in God the Father Almighty, maker of heaven and earth? And in Jesus Christ his only begotten Son Our Lord, and that he was conceived by the Holy Ghost, born of the Virgin Mary, that he suffered under Pontius Pilate, was crucified, dead, and buried, that he went down into hell, and also did rise again the third day, that he ascended into heaven and sitteth at the right hand of God the Father Almighty, and from thence shall come again at the end of the world, to judge the quick and the dead? And dost thou believe in the Holy Ghost, the holy Catholic church, the communion of saints, the remission of sins, the resurrection of the flesh, and everlasting life after death?

Answer. All this I steadfastly believe.

Minister. Wilt thou be baptized in this faith?

Answer. That is my desire.

Then shall the priest say:

O Merciful God, grant that the old Adam in these children may be so buried, that the new man may be raised up in them. Amen. Grant that all carnal affections may die in them, and that all things belonging to the Spirit may live and grow in them. Amen. Grant that they may have power and strength to have victory, and to triumph against the Devil, the world, and the flesh. Amen. Grant that whosoever is here dedicated to thee by our office and ministry, may also be endued with heavenly virtues, and everlastingly rewarded through thy mercy, O blessed Lord God, who dost live and govern all things world without end. Amen . . .

Then the priest shall take the child in his hands, and ask the name, and naming the child, shall dip it in the water, so it be discreetly and warily done, saying: N., I baptize thee in the name of the Father, and of the Son, and of the Holy Ghost. Amen. *And if the child be weak, it shall suffice to pour water upon it, saying the foresaid words* . . .

Then the priest shall make a cross upon the child's forehead, saying: We receive this child into the congregation of Christ's flock, and do sign him with the sign of the cross, in token that hereafter he shall not be ashamed to confess the faith of Christ crucified, and manfully to fight under his banner against sin, the world, and the Devil, and to continue Christ's faithful soldier and servant unto his life's end. Amen . . .

At the last end, the priest calling the godfathers and godmothers together, shall say this short exhortation following:

Forasmuch as these children have promised by you to forsake the Devil and all his works, to believe in God, and to serve him: you must remember that it is your parts and duties to see that these infants be taught so soon as they shall be able to learn what a solemn vow, promise, and profession they have made by you. And that they may know these things the better, ye shall call upon them to hear sermons. And chiefly ye shall provide that they may learn the Creed, the Lord's Prayer, and the Ten Commandments in the English tongue, and all other things which a Christian man ought to know and believe to his soul's health; and that these children may be virtuously brought up to lead a godly and a Christian life, remembering alway that baptism doth represent unto us our profession, which is to follow the example of Our Saviour Christ, and to be made like unto him, that as he died and rose again for us, so should we which are baptized die from sin, and rise again unto righteousness, continually mortifying all our evil and corrupt affections, and daily proceeding in all virtue and godliness of living.

The minister shall command that the children be brought to the bishop to be confirmed of him, so soon as they can say in their vulgar tongue the articles of the faith, the Lord's Prayer, and the Ten Commandments, and be further instructed in the Catechism set forth for that purpose, accordingly as it is there expressed.

The form of solemnization of matrimony

The ritual solemnization of matrimony joined a man and a woman together as husband and wife. The ceremony marked the beginning of full adult responsibilities. Although in law a couple could be married by a private exchange of vows, the church insisted that the wedding be performed in public following the form in the Book of Common Prayer. The open ecclesiastical ceremony ensured that the parties were not prohibited from marrying each other by reason of close kinship, prior contract, or bigamy. Most couples partook of this ceremony, but problems of clandestine marriage continued.

Puritans objected that the ring in marriage was yet another remnant of popery, and some radicals argued that matrimony should not be an ecclesiastical ceremony at all.

First the banns must be asked three several Sundays or holy days, in the time of service, the people being present after the accustomed manner. And if the persons that would be married dwell in divers parishes, the banns must be asked in both parishes, and the curate of the one parish shall not solemnize matrimony betwixt them without a certificate of the banns being thrice asked from the curate of the other parish. At the day appointed for solemnization of matrimony, the persons to be married shall come into the body of the church, with their friends and neighbours. And there the priest shall thus say:

Dearly beloved friends, we are gathered together here in the sight of God, and in the face of his congregation, to join together this man and this woman in holy matrimony, which is an honourable estate, instituted of God in paradise in the time of man's innocency, signifying unto us the mystical union, that is betwixt Christ and his church: which holy estate Christ adorned and beautified with his presence and first miracle that he wrought in Cana of Galilee, and is commended of St Paul to be honourable among all men, and therefore is not to be enterprised nor taken in hand unadvisedly, lightly, or wantonly, to satisfy men's carnal lusts and appetites, like brute beasts that have no understanding, but reverently, discreetly, advisedly, soberly, and in the fear of God, duly considering the causes for which matrimony was ordained. One was, the procreation of children to be brought up in the fear and nurture of the Lord, and praise of God. Secondly, it was ordained for a remedy against sin, and to avoid fornication, that such persons as have not the gift of continency might marry, and keep themselves undefiled members of Christ's body. Thirdly, for the mutual society, help, and comfort, that the one ought to have of the other, both in prosperity and adversity: into the which holy estate these two persons present come now to be joined. Therefore, if any man can show any just cause why they may not lawfully be joined together, let him now speak, or else hereafter forever hold his peace.

And also speaking to the persons that shall be married, he shall say:

I require and charge you (as you will answer at the dreadful day of judgement, when the secrets of all hearts shall be disclosed) that if either of you do know any impediment why ye may not be lawfully joined together in matrimony, that ye confess it. For be ye well assured, that so many as be coupled together otherwise than God's word doth allow, are not joined together by God, neither is their matrimony lawful.

At which day of marriage, if any man do allege and declare any impediment why they may not be coupled together in matrimony, by God's law or the laws of this realm, and will be bound, and sufficient sureties with him, to the parties, or else put in a caution to the full value of such charges as the persons to be married doth sustain to prove his allegation: then the solemnization must be deferred unto such time as the truth be tried. If no impediment be alleged, then shall the curate say unto the man: N., Wilt thou have this woman to thy wedded wife, to live together after God's ordinance in the holy estate of matrimony? Wilt thou love her, comfort her, honour and keep her, in sickness, and in health? And forsaking all other, keep thee only to her, so long as you both shall live? *The man shall answer*: I will.

Then shall the priest say to the woman: N., Wilt thou have this man to thy wedded husband, to live together after God's ordinance in the holy estate of matrimony? Wilt thou obey him and serve him, love, honour, and keep him, in sickness, and in health? And forsaking all other, keep thee only unto him, so long as you both shall live? *The woman shall answer*: I will.

Then shall the minister say: Who giveth this woman to be married unto this man?

And the minister receiving the woman at her father or friend's hands, shall cause the man to take the woman by the right hand, and so either to give their troth to other. The man first saying: I, N. take thee N. to my wedded wife, to have and to hold from this day forward, for better, for worse, for richer, for poorer, in sickness, and in health, to love and to cherish, till death us depart, according to God's holy ordinance: And thereto I plight thee my troth.

Then shall they loose their hands, and the woman taking again the man by the right hand shall say: I, N. take thee N. to my wedded husband, to have and to hold from this day forward, for better, for worse, for richer, for poorer, in sickness, and in health, to love, cherish, and to obey, till death us depart, according to God's holy ordinance: And thereto I give thee my troth.

Then shall they again loose their hands, and the man shall give unto the woman a ring, laying the same upon the book with the accustomed duty to the priest and clerk. And the priest taking the ring, shall deliver it unto the man, to put it upon the fourth finger of the woman's left hand. And the man taught by the priest shall say: With this ring I thee wed: with my body I thee worship: and with all my worldly goods I thee endow. In the name of the Father, and of the Son, and of the Holy Ghost. Amen.

Then the man leaving the ring upon the fourth finger of the woman's left hand, the minister shall say: O eternal God, creator and preserver of all mankind, giver of all spiritual grace, the author of everlasting life: Send thy blessing upon these thy servants, this man and this woman, whom we bless in thy name, that as Isaac and Rebecca lived faithfully together, so these persons may surely perform and keep the vow and covenant betwixt them made, whereof this ring given and received is a token and pledge, and may ever remain in perfect love and peace together, and live according unto thy laws; through Jesus Christ Our Lord. Amen.

Then shall the priest join their right hands together, and say: Those whom God hath joined together, let no man put asunder.

Then shall the minister speak unto the people: Forasmuch as N. and N. have consented together in holy wedlock, and have witnessed the same before God and this company, and thereto have given and pledged their troth either to other, and have declared the same by giving and receiving of a ring, and by joining of hands: I pronounce that they be man and wife together. In the name of the Father, and of the Son, and of the Holy Ghost. Amen.

The thanksgiving of women after childbirth, commonly called the churching of women

The brief ceremony of churching, required of all women a month after they had given birth, generated an enormous amount of controversy. Although the Church of England insisted that the primary purpose of the service was thanksgiving, many still associated it with the old Catholic ceremony of purification. Although no rubric or canon required special costume or accompaniment, custom dictated that the woman to be churched should wear a veil and be attended to church by the women who had helped her in childbirth. The service focused on the woman's deliverance from the pain and the peril of childbearing, not on her delivery of a child.

The woman shall come into the church, and there shall kneel down in some convenient place nigh unto the place where the table standeth. And the priest standing by her shall say these words, or such like as the case shall require. Forasmuch as it hath pleased Almighty God of his goodness to give you safe deliverance, and hath preserved you in the great danger of childbirth: ye shall therefore give hearty thanks unto God and pray.

Then shall the priest say this Psalm.

I have lifted up mine eyes unto the hills, from whence cometh my help.

My help cometh even from the Lord, which hath made heaven and earth.

He will not suffer thy foot to be moved, and he that keepeth thee will not sleep.

Behold, he that keepeth Israel, shall neither slumber nor sleep.

The Lord himself is thy keeper, the Lord is thy defence upon thy right hand.

So that the sun shall not burn thee by day, neither the moon by night.

The Lord shall preserve thee from evil, yea it is even he that shall keep thy soul.

The Lord shall preserve thy going out, and thy coming in, from this time forth for evermore.

Glory be to the Father, and to the Son, etc. As it was in the beginning, is now and is ever, etc.[1]

Lord have mercy upon us.
Christ have mercy upon us.
Lord have mercy upon us.

Our Father which, etc.

Answer. But deliver us from evil. Amen.
Priest. O Lord save this woman thy servant.
Answer. Which putteth her trust in thee.
Priest. Be thou to her a strong tower.
Answer. From the face of her enemy.
Priest. Lord hear our prayer.
Answer. And let my cry come unto thee.
Priest. Let us pray.

O Almighty God, which hast delivered this woman thy servant from the great pain and peril of childbirth: Grant, we beseech thee (most merciful Father) that she through thy help, may both faithfully live and walk in her vocation, according to thy will in this life present) and also may be partaker of everlasting glory in the life to come; through Jesus Christ Our Lord. Amen.

The woman that cometh to give her thanks must offer accustomed offerings. And if there be a communion, it is convenient that she receive the holy communion.

The order for the burial of the dead

At the moment of death, in Protestant belief, the soul left the body to meet its maker, leaving behind a corpse in need of Christian burial. Whether the corpse was carried to church in a grand funeral procession or quietly brought in a simple shroud, it would be set in the earth to the accompaniment of these words from the Book of Common Prayer. Thereafter the body would lie in consecrated ground within the churchyard or inside the parish church until the trumpet and call of resurrection. This dignified service offered comfort to mourners and survivors, but some hard-line Calvinists criticized the concept of 'sure and certain hope of resurrection'.

The priest meeting the corpse at the church stile, shall say or else the priests and clerks shall sing, and so go either unto the church, or toward the grave . . . When they come at the grave, whilst the corpse is made ready to be laid into the earth, the priest shall say, or the priest and clerks shall sing: Man that is born of a woman hath but a short time to live and is full of misery. He cometh up and is cut down like a flower; he flieth as it were a shadow, and never continueth in one stay. In the midst of life we be in death. Of whom may we seek for succour but of thee, O Lord,

55

which for our sins justly are displeased? Yet, O Lord God most holy, O Lord most mighty, O holy and most merciful saviour, deliver us not into the bitter pains of eternal death. Thou knowest, Lord, the secrets of our hearts, shut not up thy merciful eyes to our prayers: but spare us Lord most holy, O God most mighty, O holy and merciful saviour, thou most worthy judge eternal, suffer us not at our last hour for any pains of death to fall from thee.

Then while the earth shall be cast upon the body by some standing by, the priest shall say: Forasmuch as it hath pleased Almighty God of his great mercy to take unto himself the soul of our dear brother here departed: we therefore commit his body to the ground, earth to earth, ashes to ashes, dust to dust, in sure and certain hope of resurrection to eternal life, through Our Lord Jesus Christ, who shall change our vile body that it may be like to his glorious body, according to the mighty working, whereby he is able to subdue all things to himself . . .

The priest shall say: Almighty God, with whom do live the spirits of them that depart hence in the Lord, and in whom the souls of them that be elected, after they be delivered from the burden of the flesh, be in joy and felicity: we give thee hearty thanks, for that it hath pleased thee to deliver this, N., our brother, out of the miseries of this sinful world: beseeching thee, that it may please thee of thy gracious goodness, shortly to accomplish the number of thine elect, and to haste thy kingdom, that we with this our brother, and all other departed in the true faith of thy holy name, may have our perfect consummation and bliss, both in body and soul, in thy eternal and everlasting glory. Amen.

AN ACT FOR THE UNIFORMITY OF COMMON PRAYER AND DIVINE SERVICE, 1559

This parliamentary statute established the disciplinary framework for the Church of England and lent the force of the state to the regulation of religious uniformity. Printed at the beginning of the Elizabethan prayer book and in all subsequent editions, it became the most widely disseminated of all Tudor statutes. A product of intensive debate in Elizabeth's first parliament, the Act of Uniformity required strict church attendance and rigid adherence to the Book of Common Prayer. A tantalizing final clause offered hope to godly activists that the work of reform might yet continue, a hope that was eventually disappointed.
Source: *Statutes of the Realm*, 1 Eliz. cap. 2.

Where at the death of our late sovereign Lord King Edward the Sixth there remained one uniform order of common service and prayer and of the administration of sacraments, rites, and ceremonies in the Church of England, which was set forth in one book entitled *The Book of Common*

Prayer and Administration of Sacraments and other Rites and Ceremonies in the Church of England, authorized by act of parliament holden in the fifth and sixth years of our said late sovereign lord King Edward the Sixth entitled *An Act for the Uniformity of Common Prayer and Administration of the Sacraments;* the which was repealed and taken away by act of parliament in the first year of the reign of our late sovereign lady Queen Mary, to the great decay of the due honour of God and discomfort to the professors of the truth of Christ's religion.

Be it therefore enacted by the authority of this present parliament that the said statute of repeal and everything therein contained only concerning the said book and the service, administration of sacraments, rites, and ceremonies contained or appointed in or by the said book shall be void and of none effect from and after the feast of the Nativity of St John Baptist next coming. And that the said book with the order of service and of the administration of sacraments, rites, and ceremonies, with the alteration and additions therein added and appointed by this statute, shall stand and be from and after the said feast of the Nativity of St John Baptist in full force and effect according to the tenor and effect of this statute; anything in the aforesaid statute of repeal to the contrary notwithstanding.

And further be it enacted by the queen's highness, with the assent of the lords and commons in this present parliament assembled and by authority of the same, that all and singular ministers in any cathedral or parish church or other place within this realm of England, Wales, and the marches of the same, or other the queen's dominions, shall, from and after the feast of the Nativity of St John Baptist next coming, be bounden to say and use the matins, evensong, celebration of the Lord's Supper, and administration of each of the sacraments, and all their common and open prayer, in such order and form as is mentioned in the said book so authorized by parliament in the said fifth and sixth year of the reign of King Edward the Sixth, with one alteration or addition of certain lessons to be used on every Sunday in the year, and the form of the litany altered and corrected, and two sentences only added in the delivery of the sacrament to the communicants, and none other or otherwise. And that if any manner of parson, vicar, or other whatsoever minister that ought or should sing or say common prayer mentioned in the said book, or minister the sacraments, from and after the feast of the Nativity of St John Baptist next coming, refuse to use the said common prayers or to minister the sacraments in such cathedral or parish church or other places as he should use to minister the same, in such order and form as they be mentioned and set forth in the said book, or shall willfully or obstinately standing in the same use any other rite, ceremony, order, form, or manner of celebrating of the Lord's

57

Supper openly or privily, or matins, evensong, administration of the sacraments, or other open prayers than is mentioned and set forth in the said book (open prayer in and throughout this act is meant that prayer which is for other to come unto or hear, either in common churches or privy chapels or oratories, commonly called the service of the church) or shall preach, declare, or speak anything in the derogation or depraving of the said book or anything therein contained, or of any part thereof, and shall be thereof lawfully convicted according to the laws of this realm by verdict of twelve men, or by his own confession, or by the notorious evidence of the fact: shall lose and forfeit to the queen's highness, her heirs and successors, for his first offence the profit of all his spiritual benefices or promotions coming or arising in one whole year next after this conviction. And also that the person so convicted shall for the same offence suffer imprisonment by the space of six months without bail or mainprise. And if any such person once convict of any offence concerning the premises shall after his first conviction eftsoons offend and be thereof in form aforesaid lawfully convict, that then the same person shall for his second offence suffer imprisonment by the space of one whole year and also shall therefore be deprived, *ipso facto,* of all his spiritual promotions . . .

And it is ordained and enacted by the authority abovesaid, that if any person or persons whatsoever after the said feast of the Nativity of St John Baptist next coming, shall in any interludes, plays, songs, rhymes, or by other open words, declare or speak anything in the derogation, depraving, or despising of the same book or of anything therein contained or any part thereof, or shall by open fact, deed, or by open threatenings compel or cause or otherwise procure or maintain any parson, vicar, or other minister in any cathedral or parish church or in chapel or in any other place to sing or say any common and open prayer or to minister any sacrament otherwise or in any other manner and form than is mentioned in the said book, or that by any of the said means shall unlawfully interrupt or let any parson, vicar, or other minister in any cathedral or parish church, chapel, or any other place to sing or say common and open prayer or to minister the sacraments or any of them in such manner and form as is mentioned in the said book, that then every such person being thereof lawfully convicted in form abovesaid shall forfeit to the queen our sovereign lady, her heirs and successors, for the first offence a hundred marks. And if any parson or parsons being once convict of any such offence eftsoons offend against any of the last recited offences and shall in form aforesaid be thereof lawfully convict, that then the same parson so offending and convict shall for the second offence forfeit to the queen our sovereign lady, her heirs and successors, four hundred marks . . .

And that from and after the said feast of the Nativity of St John Baptist next coming, all and every person and persons inhabiting within this realm, or any other the queen's majesty's dominions, shall diligently and faithfully, having no lawful or reasonable excuse to be absent, endeavour themselves to resort to their parish church or chapel accustomed, or upon reasonable let thereof to some usual place where common prayer and such service of God shall be used in such time of let upon every Sunday and other days ordained and used to be kept as holy days. And then and there to abide orderly and soberly during the time of the common prayer, preachings, or other service of God there to be used and ministered, upon pain of punishment by the censures of the church. And also upon pain that every person so offending shall forfeit for every such offence twelve pence to be levied by the churchwardens of the parish where such offence shall be done, to the use of the poor of the same parish, of the goods, lands, and tenements of such offender, by way of distress . . .

Provided always, and be it enacted, that such ornaments of the church and of the ministers thereof shall be retained and be in use as was in this Church of England by authority of parliament in the second year of the reign of King Edward the Sixth until other order shall be therein taken by the authority of the queen's majesty, with the advice of her commissioners appointed and authorized under the great seal of England for causes ecclesiastical or of the metropolitan of this realm. And also that if there shall happen any contempt or irreverence to be used in the ceremonies or rites of the church by the misusing of the orders appointed in this book, the queen's majesty may, by the like advice of the said commissioners or metropolitan, ordain and publish such further ceremonies or rites as may be most for the advancement of God's glory, the edifying of his church, and the due reverence of Christ's holy mysteries and sacraments.

THE THIRTY-NINE ARTICLES, 1563

This set of articles, or basic beliefs, represents the culmination of a series of attempts, beginning with the Ten Articles of 1536, to define the reformed faith of the church. Subscription to the Thirty-nine Articles was required of all clergy in the Church of England. The articles fall into four categories: the first (nos 1–8) deal with doctrines necessary to the Christian faith; the second (nos 9–18) deal with Protestant doctrines of salvation; the third (nos 19–31) deal with doctrines of the visible church; and the fourth (nos 32–7) deal with matters specific to the discipline of the Church of England. The theological controversies of the sixteenth century led to calls for a more authoritative doctrinal statement, but the articles are anything but definitive. They resist restrictive interpretation, a quality best discerned in Article 17, which manages to present the Calvinist doctrine of predestination in such a way as to render it practicably ambiguous.
Source: *Articles Whereupon it was Agreed by the Archbishoppes and Bishoppes* (London, 1571) (*STC* 10039).

1 Of faith in the Holy Trinity

There is but one living and true God, everlasting, without body, parts, or passions; of infinite power, wisdom, and goodness; the maker and preserver of all things both visible and invisible. And in unity of this Godhead there be three persons, of one substance, power, and eternity; the Father, the Son, and the Holy Ghost.

2 Of the word or Son of God, which was made very man

The Son, which is the word of the Father, begotten from everlasting of the Father, the very and eternal God, of one substance with the Father, took man's nature in the womb of the Blessed Virgin, of her substance: so that two whole and perfect natures, that is to say, the godhead and manhood, were joined together in one person, never to be divided, whereof is one Christ, very God and very man; who truly suffered, was crucified, dead, and buried, to reconcile his Father to us, and to be a sacrifice, not only for original guilt, but also for all actual sins of men.

3 Of the going down of Christ into hell

As Christ died for us, and was buried, so also it is to be believed that he went down into hell.

4 Of the resurrection of Christ

Christ did truly arise again from death, and took again his body, with flesh, bones, and all things appertaining to the perfection of man's nature; wherewith he ascended into heaven, and there sitteth, until he return to judge all men at the last day.

5 Of the Holy Ghost

The Holy Ghost, proceeding from the Father and the Son, is of one substance, majesty, and glory, with the Father and the Son, very and eternal God.

6 Of the sufficiency of the Holy Scriptures for salvation

Holy Scripture containeth all things necessary to salvation: so that whatsoever is not read therein, nor may be proved thereby, is not to be required of any man, that it should be believed as an article of the faith, or be thought requisite or necessary to salvation. In the name of the Holy Scripture we do understand those canonical books of the Old and New Testament, of whose authority was never any doubt in the church.

Of the names and number of the canonical books: *Genesis, Exodus, Leviticus, Numbers, Deuteronomy, Joshua, Judges, Ruth, the First Book of Samuel, the Second Book of Samuel, the First Book of Kings, the Second Book of Kings, the First Book of Chronicles, the Second Book of Chronicles, the First Book of Esdras, the Second Book of Esdras, the Book of Esther, the Book of Job, the Psalms, the Proverbs, Ecclesiastes or Preacher, Cantica or Songs of Solomon, Four Prophets the greater, Twelve Prophets the less.*

And the other books (as Jerome saith) the church doth read for example of life and instruction of manners; but yet doth it not apply them to establish any doctrine; such are these following: *the Third Book of Esdras, the Fourth Book of Esdras, the Book of Tobias, the Book of Judith, the rest of the Book of Esther, the Book of Wisdom, Jesus the Son of Sirach, Baruch the Prophet, the Song of the Three Children, the Story of Susanna, Of Bel and the Dragon, the Prayer of Manasses, the First Book of Maccabees, the Second Book of Maccabees.*

All the books of the New Testament, as they are commonly received, we do receive and account them canonical.

7 Of the Old Testament

The Old Testament is not contrary to the New: for both in the Old and New Testament everlasting life is offered to mankind by Christ, who is the only mediator between God and man, being both God and man. Wherefore they are not to be heard which feign that the old fathers did look only for transitory promises. Although the law given from God by Moses, as touching ceremonies and rites, do not bind Christian men, nor the civil precepts thereof ought of necessity to be received in any commonwealth; yet notwithstanding, no Christian man whatsoever is free from the obedience of the commandments which are called moral.

8 Of the three Creeds

The three creeds, Nicene Creed, Athanasius's Creed, and that which is commonly called the Apostles' Creed, ought thoroughly to be received and believed: for they may be proved by most certain warrants of Holy Scripture.

9 *Of original or birth-sin*

Original sin standeth not in the following of Adam (as the Pelagians do vainly talk), but it is the fault and corruption of the nature of every man, that naturally is engendered of the offspring of Adam; whereby man is very far gone from original righteousness, and is of his own nature inclined to evil, so that the flesh lusteth always contrary to the spirit; and therefore in every person born into this world, it deserveth God's wrath and damnation. And this infection of nature doth remain, yea in them that are regenerated; whereby the lust of the flesh . . . is not subject to the law of God. And although there is no condemnation for them that believe and are baptized, yet the apostle doth confess, that concupiscence and lust hath of itself the nature of sin.

10 *Of Free-Will*

The condition of man after the fall of Adam is such that he cannot turn and prepare himself, by his own natural strength and good works, to faith and calling upon God: Wherefore we have no power to do good works pleasant and acceptable to God, without the grace of God by Christ preventing us, that we may have a good will, and working with us, when we have that good will.

11 *Of the justification of man*

We are accounted righteous before God, only for the merit of Our Lord and Saviour Jesus Christ, by faith, and not for our own works or deservings: Wherefore, that we are justified by faith only is a most wholesome doctrine, and very full of comfort, as more largely is expressed in the Homily of Justification.

12 *Of good works*

Albeit that good works, which are the fruits of faith, and follow after justification, cannot put away our sins, and endure the severity of God's judgement; yet are they pleasing and acceptable to God in Christ, and do spring out necessarily of a true and lively faith; insomuch that by them a lively faith may be as evidently known as a tree discerned by the fruit.

13 Of works before justification

Works done before the grace of Christ, and the inspiration of his Spirit, are not pleasant to God, forasmuch as they spring not of faith in Jesus Christ, neither do they make men meet to receive grace, or (as the school-authors say) deserve grace of congruity: yea rather, for that they are not done as God hath willed and commanded them to be done, we doubt not but they have the nature of sin.

14 Of works of supererogation

Voluntary works besides, over and above God's commandments, which they call works of supererogation, cannot be taught without arrogancy and impiety: for by them men do declare, that they do not only render unto God as much as they are bound to do, but that they do more for his sake than of bounden duty is required: whereas Christ saith plainly, When ye have done all that are commanded to you, say, We are unprofitable servants.

15 Of Christ alone without sin

Christ in the truth of our nature was made like unto us in all things, sin only except, from which he was clearly void, both in his flesh, and in his spirit. He came to be the Lamb without spot, who, by sacrifice of himself once made, should take away the sins of the world, and sin (as St John saith) was not in him. But all we the rest (although baptized, and born again in Christ) yet offend in many things; and if we say we have no sin, we deceive ourselves and the truth is not in us.

16 Of sin after baptism

Not every deadly sin willingly committed after baptism is sin against the Holy Ghost, and unpardonable. Wherefore the grant of repentance is not to be denied to such as fall into sin after baptism. After we have received the Holy Ghost, we may depart from grace given, and fall into sin, and by the grace of God we may arise again, and amend our lives. And therefore they are to be condemned, which say, they can no more sin as long as they live here, or deny the place of forgiveness to such as truly repent.

17 Of predestination and election

Predestination to life is the everlasting purpose of God, whereby (before the foundations of the world were laid) he hath constantly decreed by his counsel secret to us, to deliver from curse and damnation those whom he hath chosen in Christ out of mankind, and to bring them by Christ to everlasting salvation, as vessels made to honour. Wherefore, they which be endued with so excellent a benefit of God be called according to God's purpose by his Spirit working in due season: they through grace obey the calling: they be justified freely: they be made sons of God by adoption: they be made like the image of his only-begotten Son Jesus Christ: they walk religiously in good works, and at length, by God's mercy, they attain to everlasting felicity.

As the godly consideration of predestination, and our election in Christ, is full of sweet, pleasant, and unspeakable comfort to godly persons, and such as feel in themselves the working of the spirit of Christ, mortifying the works of the flesh, and their earthly members, and drawing up their mind to high and heavenly things, as well because it doth greatly establish and confirm their faith of eternal salvation to be enjoyed through Christ, as because it doth fervently kindle their love towards God: So, for curious and carnal persons, lacking the spirit of Christ, to have continually before their eyes the sentence of God's predestination, is a most dangerous downfall, whereby the Devil doth thrust them either into desperation, or into wretchlessness of most unclean living, no less perilous than desperation.

Furthermore, we must receive God's promises in such wise, as they be generally set forth to us in Holy Scripture: and, in our doings, that will of God is to be followed, which we have expressly declared unto us in the word of God.

18 Of obtaining eternal salvation only by the name of Christ

They also are to be had accursed that presume to say, That every man shall be saved by the law or sect which he professeth, so that he be diligent to frame his life according to that law, and the light of nature. For Holy scripture doth set out unto us only the name of Jesus Christ, whereby men must be saved.

19 Of the church

The visible church of Christ is a congregation of faithful men, in the which the pure word of God is preached, and the sacraments be duly ministered according to Christ's ordinance in all those things that of necessity are requisite to the same. As the church of Jerusalem, Alexandria, and Antioch, have erred; so also the church of Rome hath erred, not only in their living and manner of ceremonies, but also in matters of faith.

20 Of the authority of the church

The church hath power to decree rites or ceremonies, and authority in controversies of faith: And yet it is not lawful for the church to ordain any thing that is contrary to God's word written, neither may it so expound one place of scripture, that it be repugnant to another. Wherefore, although the church be a witness and a keeper of holy writ, yet, as it ought not to decree any thing against the same, so besides the same ought it not to enforce any thing to be believed for necessity of salvation.

21 Of the authority of general councils

General councils may not be gathered together without the commandment and will of princes. And when they be gathered together (forasmuch as they be an assembly of men, whereof all be not governed with the spirit and word of God), they may err, and sometimes have erred, even in things pertaining unto God. Wherefore things ordained by them as necessary to salvation have neither strength nor authority, unless it may be declared that they be taken out of Holy Scripture.

22 Of purgatory

The Romish doctrine concerning purgatory, pardons, worshipping and adoration as well of images as of relics, and also invocation of saints, is a fond thing, vainly invented, and grounded upon no warranty of scripture, but rather repugnant to the word of God.

23 Of ministering in the congregation

It is not lawful for any man to take upon him the office of public preaching, or ministering the sacraments in the congregation, before he be lawfully called and sent to execute the same. And those we ought to judge lawfully called and sent, which be chosen and called to this work by men who have public authority given unto them in the congregation, to call and send ministers into the Lord's vineyard.

24 Of speaking in the congregation in such a tongue as the people understandeth

It is a thing plainly repugnant to the word of God, and the custom of the primitive church, to have public prayer in the church, or to minister the sacraments in a tongue not understanded of the people.

65

25 Of the sacraments

Sacraments ordained of Christ be not only badges or tokens of Christian men's profession, but rather they be certain sure witnesses and effectual signs of grace and God's good will towards us, by the which he doth work invisibly in us, and doth not only quicken, but also strengthen and confirm our faith in him.

There are two sacraments ordained of Christ Our Lord in the gospel, that is to say, baptism, and the supper of the Lord. Those five commonly called sacraments, that is to say, confirmation, penance, orders, matrimony, and extreme unction, are not to be counted for sacraments of the gospel, being such as have grown partly of the corrupt following of the apostles, partly are states of life allowed in the scriptures; but yet have not like nature of sacraments with baptism and the Lord's Supper, for that they have not any visible sign or ceremony ordained of God.

The sacraments were not ordained of Christ to be gazed upon, or to be carried about, but that we should duly use them. And in such only as worthily receive the same they have a wholesome effect or operation: but they that receive them unworthily, purchase to themselves damnation, as St Paul saith.

26 Of the unworthiness of the ministers, which hinders not the effect of the sacrament

Although in the visible church the evil be ever mingled with the good, and sometime the evil have chief authority in the ministration of the word and sacraments, yet forasmuch as they do not the same in their own name, but in Christ's, and do minister by his commission and authority, we may use their ministry, both in hearing the word of God, and in the receiving of the sacraments. Neither is the effect of Christ's ordinance taken away by their wickedness, nor the grace of God's gifts diminished from such as by faith and rightly do receive the sacraments ministered unto them; which be effectual, because of Christ's institution and promise, although they be ministered by evil men.

Nevertheless, it apperaineth to the discipline of the church, that enquiry be made of evil ministers, and that they be accused by those that have knowledge of their offences; and finally being found guilty, by just judgement be deposed.

27 Of baptism

Baptism is not only a sign of profession, and mark of difference, whereby Christian men are discerned from others that be not christened, but it is also a sign of regeneration or new birth, whereby, as by an instrument, they that receive baptism rightly are grafted into the church; the promises of forgiveness of sin, and of our adoption to be the sons of God by the Holy Ghost, are visibly signed and sealed; faith is confirmed, and grace increased by virtue of prayer unto God. The baptism of young children is in any wise to be retained in the church, as most agreeable with the institution of Christ.

28 Of the Lord's Supper

The supper of the Lord is not only a sign of the love that Christians ought to have among themselves one to another; but rather it is a sacrament of our redemption by Christ's death: insomuch that to such as rightly, worthily, and with faith, receive the same, the bread which we break is a partaking of the body of Christ; and likewise the cup of blessing is a partaking of the blood of Christ.

Transubstantiation (or the change of the substance of bread and wine) in the supper of the Lord, cannot be proved by holy writ, but is repugnant to the plain words of scripture, overthroweth the nature of a sacrament, and hath given occasion to many superstitions. The body of Christ is given, taken, and eaten, in the supper, only after an heavenly and spiritual manner. And the mean whereby the body of Christ is received and eaten in the supper is faith.

The sacrament of the Lord's supper was not by Christ's ordinance reserved, carried about, lifted up, or worshipped.

29 Of the wicked which do not eat the body of Christ in the use of the Lord's Supper

The wicked, and such as be void of a lively faith, although they do carnally and visibly press with their teeth (as St Augustine saith) the sacrament of the body and blood of Christ, yet in no wise are they partakers of Christ: but rather, to their condemnation, do eat and drink the sign or sacrament of so great a thing.

30 Of both kinds

The cup of the Lord is not to be denied to the lay-people: for both the parts of the Lord's sacrament, by Christ's ordinance and commandment, ought to be ministered to all Christian men alike.

31 Of the one oblation of Christ finished upon the cross

The offering of Christ once made is the perfect redemption, propitiation, and satisfaction, for all the sins of the whole world, both original and actual; and there is none other satisfaction for sin, but that alone. Wherefore the sacrifices of masses, in the which it was commonly said, that the priest did offer Christ for the quick and the dead, to have remission of pain or guilt, were blasphemous fables, and dangerous deceits.

32 Of the marriage of priests

Bishops, priests, and deacons, are not commanded by God's law, either to vow the estate of single life, or to abstain from marriage: therefore it is lawful also for them, as for all other Christian men, to marry at their own discretion, as they shall judge the same to serve better to godliness.

33 Of excommunicate persons, how they are to be avoided

That person which by open denunciation of the church is rightly cut off from the unity of the church, and excommunicated, ought to be taken of the whole multitude of the faithful, as an heathen and publican, until he be openly reconciled by penance, and received into the church by a judge that hath authority thereunto.

34 Of the traditions of the church

It is not necessary that traditions and ceremonies be in all places one, or utterly like; for at all times they have been divers, and may be changed according to the diversity of countries, times, and men's manners, so that nothing be ordained against God's word. Whosoever through his private judgement, willingly and purposely, doth openly break the traditions and ceremonies of the church, which be not repugnant to the word of God, and be ordained and approved by common authority, ought to be rebuked openly (that other may fear to do the like) as he that offendeth against the common order of the church, and hurteth the authority of the magistrate, and woundeth the consciences of the weak brethren.

Every particular or national church hath authority to ordain, change, and abolish ceremonies or rites of the church ordained only by man's authority, so that all things be done to edifying.

35 Of homilies

The second Book of Homilies . . . doth contain a godly and wholesome doctrine, and necessary for these times, as doth the former Book of Homilies, which were set forth in the time of Edward the Sixth; and therefore we judge them to be read in churches by the ministers, diligently and distinctly, that they may be understanded of the people. [Names of the Homilies follow.]

36 Of Consecration of bishops and ministers

The Book of Consecration of Archbishops and Bishops, and Ordering of Priests and Deacons, lately set forth in the time of Edward the Sixth, and confirmed at the same time by authority of parliament, doth contain all things necessary to such consecration and ordering: neither hath it any thing, that of itself is superstitious or ungodly. And therefore, whosoever are consecrate or ordered according to the rites of that book, since the second year of the aforenamed King Edward unto this time, or hereafter shall be consecrated or ordered according to the same rites; we decree all such to be rightly, orderly, and lawfully consecrated and ordered.

37 Of the civil magistrates

The queen's majesty hath the chief power in this realm of England and other her dominions, unto whom the chief government of all estates of this realm, whether they be ecclesiastical or civil, in all causes doth appertain, and is not, nor ought to be, subject to any foreign jurisdiction.

Where we attribute to the queen's majesty the chief government, by which titles we understand the minds of some slanderous folks to be offended, we give not to our princes the ministering either of God's word, or of the sacraments, the which thing the Injunctions also lately set forth by Elizabeth our queen do most plainly testify; but that only prerogative, which we see to have been given always to all godly princes in Holy Scriptures by God himself; that is, that they should rule all estates and degrees committed to their charge by God, whether they be ecclesiastical or temporal, and restrain with the civil sword the stubborn and evil-doers.

The Bishop of Rome hath no jurisdiction in this realm of England. The laws of the realm may punish Christian men with death, for heinous and grievous offences. It is lawful for Christian men, at the commandment of the magistrate, to wear weapons, and serve in the wars.

38 Of Christian men's goods which are not common

The riches and goods of Christians are not common, as touching the right, title, and possession of the same, as certain Anabaptists do falsely boast. Notwithstanding, every man ought, of such things as he possesseth, liberally to give alms to the poor, according to his ability.

39 Of a Christian man's oath

As we confess that vain and rash swearing is forbidden Christian men by Our Lord Jesus Christ, and James his apostle, so we judge, that Christian religion doth not prohibit, but that a man may swear when the magistrate requireth, in a cause of faith and charity, so it be done according to the prophet's teaching, in justice, judgement, and truth.

THE HOMILY AGAINST CONTENTION AND BRAWLING

Every parish was required to have a copy of the Homilies, simple sermons on Christian duty to be read to the assembled congregation several times a year. The Homilies dated from the reign of Edward VI and were frequently reprinted. More homilies were added under Elizabeth I. This homily warns of the dangers of division, and stresses the principles of charity and harmony that were supposed to unite parishioners in their social and religious life.
Source: *Certaine Sermons or Homilies Appointed to be Read in Churches* (London, 1623) (*STC* 13659), pp. 89–92.

This day (good Christian people) shall be declared unto you, the unprofitableness and shameful unhonesty of contention, strife and debate, to the intent, that when you shall see as it were in a table painted before your eyes, the evilfavouredness and deformity of this most detestable vice, your stomachs may be moved to rise against it, and to detest and abhor that sin, which is so much to be hated, and pernicious, and hurtful to all men. But among all kinds of contention, none is more hurtful than is contention in matters of religion. Eschew (saith St Paul) foolish and unlearned questions, knowing that they breed strife. It becometh not the servant of God to fight, or strive, but to be meek toward all men. This contention and strife was in St Paul's time among the Corinthians, and is at this time among us English men. For too many there be which upon the ale-benches or other places delight to set forth certain questions, not so much pertaining to edification, as to vain glory, and showing forth of their cunning, and so unsoberly to reason and dispute, that when neither part will give place to other, they fall to chiding and contention, and sometime from hot words, to further inconvenience.

70

St Paul could not abide to hear among the Corinthians, their words of discord or dissention: I hold of Paul, I of Cephas, and I of Apollo. What would he then say, if he heard these words of contention (which be now almost in every man's mouth.) He is a pharisee, he is a gospeller, he is of the new sort, he is of the old faith, he is a new-broached brother, he is a good Catholic father, he is a Papist, he is an heretic. O how the church is divided. O how the cities be cut and mangled. O how the coat of Christ, that was without seam, is all to rent and torn. O body mystical of Christ, where is that holy and happy unity, out of the which whosoever is, he is not in Christ? If one member be pulled from another, where is the body? If the body be drawn from the head, where is the life of the body? We cannot be joined to Christ our head, except we be glued with concord and charity one to another. For he that is not of this unity is not of the church of Christ, which is a congregation of unity together, and not a division. St Paul saith, that as long as emulation or envying, contention, and factions or sects be among us, we be carnal, and walk according to the fleshly man. And St James saith, If ye have bitter emulation or envying, and contention in your hearts, glory not of it: for where as contention is, there is unsteadfastness, and all evil deeds.

And why do we not hear St Paul, which prayeth us, where as he might command us, saying, I beseech you in the name of Our Lord Jesus Christ, that you will speak all one thing, and that there be no dissention among you, but that you will be one whole body, of one mind, and of one opinion in the truth. If his desire be reasonable and honest, why do we not grant it? If his request be for our profit, why do we refuse it? And if we list not to hear his petition of prayer, yet let us hear his exhortation, where he saith, I exhort you that you walk as it becometh the vocation in which you be called, with all submission and meekness, with lenity and softness of mind, bearing one another by charity, studying to keep the unity of the spirit by the bond of peace: for there is one body, one spirit, one faith, one baptism. There is (saith he) but one body, of the which he can be no lively member, that is at variance with the other members. There is one spirit, which joineth and knitteth all things in one. And how can this one spirit reign in us, when we among ourselves be divided? There is but one faith, and how can we say, he is of the old faith, and he is of the new faith? There is but one baptism and then shall not all they which be baptized be one? Contention causeth division, wherefore it ought not to be among Christians, whom one faith and baptism joineth in an unity.

But if we contemn St Paul's request and exhortation, yet at the least let us regard his earnest entreating, in the which he doth very earnestly charge us and (as I may so speak) conjure us in this form and manner, If there be any

71

consolation in Christ, if there be any comfort of love, if you have any fellowship of the spirit, if you have any bowels of pity and compassion, fulfil my joy, being all like affected, having one charity, being of one mind, of one opinion, that nothing be done by contention, or vainglory. Who is he, that hath any bowels of pity, that will not be moved with these words so pithy? Whose heart is so stony, that the sword of these words (which be more sharp than any two edged sword) may not cut and break asunder? Wherefore let us endeavour our selves to fulfil St Paul's joy here in this place, which shall be at length to our great joy in another place. Let us so read the scripture, that by reading thereof, we may be made the better livers, rather than the more contentious disputers. If any thing be necessary to be taught, reasoned, or disputed, let us do it with all meekness, softness, and lenity. If any thing shall chance to be spoken uncomely, let one bear another's frailty. He that is faulty, let him rather amend, then defend that which he hath spoken amiss, lest he fall by contention from a foolish error into an obstinate heresy. For it is better to give place meekly, than to win the victory with the breach of charity, which chanceth when every man will defend his opinion obstinately. If we be the Christian men, why do we not follow Christ, which saith, Learn of me, for I am meek and lowly in heart? A disciple must learn the lesson of his schoolmaster, and a servant must obey the commandment of his master.

He that is wise and learned (saith St James), let him show his goodness by his good conversation, and soberness of his wisdom. For where there is envy and contention, that wisdom cometh not from God, but is worldly wisdom, man's wisdom and devilish wisdom. For the wisdom that cometh from above from the spirit of God, is chaste and pure, corrupted with no evil affections: it is quiet, meek, and peaceable, abhorring all desire and contention: it is tractable, obedient, not grudging to learn, and to give place to them that teach better for the reformation. For there shall never be an end of striving and contention, if we contend who in contention shall be master, and have the over hand: if we shall heap error upon error, if we continue to defend that obstinately, which was spoken unadvisedly. For truth it is, that stiffness in maintaining an opinion, breedeth contention, brawling, and chiding, which is a vice among all other most pernicious and pestilent to common peace and quietness. And it standeth betwixt two persons and parties (for no man commonly doth chide with himself) so it comprehendeth two most detestable vices: the one is picking of quarrels, with sharp and contentious words: the other standeth in froward answering, and multiplying evil words again. The first is so abominable, that St Paul saith, if any that is called a brother, be a worshipper of idols, a brawler, a picker of quarrels, a thief, or an extortioner, with him that is such a man, see that ye eat not.

Now here consider that St Paul numbereth a scolder, a brawler, or a picker of quarrels, among thieves and idolaters, and many times there cometh less hurt of a thief, than of a railing tongue: for the one taketh away a man's good name, the other taketh but his riches, which is of much less value and estimation than is his good name. And a thief hurteth but him from whom he stealeth: but he that hath an evil tongue, troubleth all the town, where he dwelleth, and sometime the whole country. And a railing tongue is a pestilence so full of contagiousness, that St Paul willeth Christian men to forbear the company of such, and neither to eat nor drink with them. And whereas he will not that a Christian woman should forsake her husband, although he be an infidel, or that a Christian servant should depart from his master, which is an infidel and heathen, and to suffer a Christian man to keep company with an infidel: yet he forbiddeth us to eat or drink with a scolder, or quarrelpicker. And also in the first chapter to the Corinthians, he saith thus, Be not deceived, for neither fornicators, neither worshippers of fools, neither thieves, nor drunkards, nor cursed speakers shall dwell in the kingdom of heaven.

It must needs be a great fault, that doth move and cause the father to disinherit his natural son. And how can it otherwise be, but that this cursed speaking must needs be a most damnable sin, the which doth cause God our most merciful and loving Father, to deprive us of his most blessed kingdom of heaven? Against the other sin that standeth in requiting taunt for taunt, speaketh Christ himself, saying: I say unto you, resist not evil, but love your enemies, and say well by them, that say evil by you, do well unto them that do evil unto you, and pray for them that do hurt and persecute you, that you may be the children of your Father which is in heaven, who suffereth his sun to rise both upon good and evil, and sendeth his rain both upon the just and unjust. To this doctrine of Christ agreeth very well the teaching of St Paul, that chosen vessel of God, who ceaseth not to exhort and call upon us, saying, Bless them that curse you, bless I say, and curse not, recompense to no man evil for evil, if it be possible (as much as lieth in you) live peaceably with all men.

THOMAS BECON'S NEW CATECHISM, 1559

Catechisms, or manuals of Christian instruction, were extremely popular in this period, reflecting the emphasis on education that underpinned the ideals of both Protestant and Catholic reformations. Thomas Becon (1512–67), a priest who became an evangelical in the 1530s and married, was a prolific writer and homilist of the mid-sixteenth century. He published his early works under the pseudonym Theodore Basil, names he later gave to his children. The form of Becon's catechism is dialogic and private. It

shows that catechetical activity was not confined to public and official instruction in the church, but was also a necessary duty for parents and children in the home.
Source: *The Catechism of Thomas Becon, STP, with other pieces by him*, ed. John Ayer (Parker Society, Cambridge, 1844), pp. 4–5.

Preface

The preface of the author unto his children, Theodore and Basil, his two sons, and Rachel, his only daughter: Grace, mercy and peace, from God the Father, and from the Lord Jesus Christ Our Lord and alone Saviour, through the mighty operation of the Holy Ghost, be with you, my dear children, both now and ever. Amen.

After that it pleased the Lord my God to call me unto the holy state of honourable matrimony, and to bless me with the increase of you, not of you only, but also of two more your brethren, named Theodore and Christophile, which now rest in glory with our head Christ, I thought no charge more straightly to be laid upon me of the Lord our God, than with all diligence to provide and aforesee, that you, my most dear and sweet children, may be brought up, even from your very cradles (as they use to say) in the knowledge and doctrine of the one alone true and everlasting God, and of his Son Christ Jesus, our most mighty Lord and alone sufficient Saviour: which knowledge, learned out of the holy scriptures, bringeth to the faithful believers everlasting life.

And as I judged this to be my duty and office committed unto me of God, if I would in any point answer his good will and pleasure, and satisfy my vocation or calling; so likewise to the uttermost of my power I have ever travailed godly and virtuously to bring you up in the knowledge of God and of his holy word, even from your tender years, that at the last you, being now young children, may wax ancient in Christ, and through him obtain everlasting life.

For in mine opinion, howsoever the wicked world judgeth in this behalf, those fathers, which only study to enrich their children with worldly possessions, and neglect their duty in the virtuous education and godly bringing up of their youth, are rather to be counted fathers of the body than of the mind, of the flesh than of the soul, and may right well be resembled, likened, and compared to unreasonable and brute beasts, which are also led with this care, and so affected toward their younglings, that with all diligence they travail and labour for the fostering and feeding of them, by this means providing that they lack nothing concerning the safe state and harmless conservation of the body. These parents are beastly parents: these fathers and mothers are ungodly fathers and mothers, and altogether unworthy of this great blessing of God, I mean the gift of children, whom God hath given unto them for this purpose and end, that they in this world should be godly and virtuously brought up in the doctrine and knowledge of his holy word, lead a good life, call on his holy name, be thankful for his benefits, study to profit the commonweal, and to do good to all men; that, when they shall be called out from this vale of misery, they may be made citizens of the heavenly kingdom, and there for ever reign and remain with their head Christ, in the glory of his Father. And would God we had not too too many of these ungodly parents in this our age! Verily unto such corruption of manners and lewd disposition of life are we come nowadays, that all parents almost seek rather how to advance their children in worldly than in godly things; how to beautify them rather with the vain and flitting goods of the corruptible body, than with the true, constant, and immortal goods of the uncorruptible mind; how to get them rather the favour of men, than the good will of God; how they may increase rather in worldly studies, than in the knowledge of God; and in fine, how they may rather become in this world men of great renown and of innumerable possessions, than after this life glorious and well-accepted citizens of that most glorious and heavenly kingdom. Certes the greatest multitude of our parents at this day, although they profess Christ, and glory to be called Christians, are much inferior to the heathen, which knew not God nor any point of godliness rightly, if we should respect the good and virtuous bringing up of youth.

Of the duty of children toward their parents

SON.   As concerning the duty of children toward their parents, we talked of that matter in the declaration of the fifth commandment; so that it may seem now almost superfluous any more to speak of it; notwithstanding, forasmuch as the place and order requireth that we speak somewhat also now of the office and duty of children, and it is your pleasure that I should so do, I will gladly express unto you whatsoever I have to say in this behalf.

FATHER.   I allow thy diligence.

SON.   The most worthy apostle St Paul describeth the office and duty of children toward their parents on this manner: 'Children, obey your fathers and mothers in the Lord; for that is right. Honour thy father and mother (the same is the first commandment in the promise), that thou mayest prosper, and live long on the earth'.[2] Again he saith: 'Ye children, obey your fathers and mothers in all things; for that is well-pleasing to the Lord'.[3] Here see we, that the office and duty of children toward their parents consisteth in two things.

FATHER.   What two things are they?

SON.   Honour and obedience. That child, which will do his office truly and faithfully according to the commandment of God, must both honour and obey his father and mother.

FATHER.   In what points doth the honour of parents consist?

SON.   First of all, in having a reverent opinion of them, of their prudence and wisdom, of their state and vocation, of their regiment and governance; being persuaded that they are our parents, not by fortune and chance, but by the singular providence and good will of God, given unto us of God for our great commodity, profit, and wealth.

Secondly, in loving them, yea, and that not feignedly, but from the very bottom of the heart; and in wishing unto them all good things from God, as unto persons which, next unto God, have and do best deserve of us.

Thirdly, in giving them that reverence and honour outwardly, which by the commandment of God is due from children to their parents; as to bow the knee unto them, to ask them blessing, to put off their cap, to give them place, reverently and meekly to speak unto them, and with all outward gestures to show a reverent honour and honourable reverence toward them, as persons representing the majesty of God.

Fourthly, in labouring to the uttermost of their power to be thankful, and to requite their parents for such and so great benefits as they have received of God by them and their labours. As for an example, if their parents be aged and fallen into poverty, so that they are not able to live of themselves, nor to get their living by their own industry and labour, then ought the children, if they will truly honour their parents, to labour for them, to see unto their necessity, to provide necessaries for them, and by no means, so much as in them is, to suffer them for to lack any good thing; forasmuch as their parents cared and provided for them, when they were not able to care and provide for themselves.

Fifthly and finally, in concealing, hiding, covering, and in interpreting all their parents' faults, vices, and incommodities unto the best, never objecting nor upbraiding them by any thing done amiss; but quietly and patiently to bear all things at their hands, considering that in thus doing they greatly please God, and offer unto him an acceptable sacrifice; and by no means to follow the wicked manners of the most wicked Ham, which, when Noah his father was drunken and lay uncovered in the tent, went and told his two brethren without; but rather to practice the godly behaviour of Shem and Japheth, which, taking a garment, laid it upon their shoulders, and, coming backward, covered the nakedness of their father, namely, their faces being turned away, lest they should see their father's nakedness. By this means were they blessed, and Ham cursed.[4]

It becometh a good and godly child, not to display, but to conceal the faults of his father, even as he wisheth that God should cover his own offences, as the wise man saith: 'Rejoice not when thy father is reproved; for it is not honour unto thee, but shame. For the worship of a man's father is his own worship; and where the father is without honour, it is the dishonesty of the son. My son, make much of thy father in his age, and grieve him not as long as he liveth. And if his understanding fail, have patience with him, and despise him not in thy strength. For the good deed that thou showest to thy father shall not be forgotten; and when thou thyself wantest, it shall be rewarded thee', etc.[5]

FATHER.   Wherein consisteth the obedience of a child toward his father?

SON.   In two things principally. First, in showing himself obedient, not feignedly, but from the very heart, to the will and commandment of his father in executing, performing, and accomplishing the same with all diligence, evermore seeking to do that which may please him, and eschewing again at all times whatsoever in any point may displease him.

FATHER.   But what if the father command the child to do that thing which is contrary to the word of God?

SON.   Here the child oweth unto the father no obedience. For 'we must obey God more than men'.[6] But of this matter we spake when we talked of the fifth commandment. Secondly, in attempting no grave or weighty matter without the counsel of his father, but to desire and crave his father's advice and judgement in all things; as not to enterprise marriage without his consent, nor to entangle himself with any weighty cause without the counsel and consent of his father; always preferring his father's judgement before his own, as one of more experience, larger wisdom, and greater knowledge, yea, as one that tendereth his commodity and profit no less than his own.

FATHER.   What ought to move children to show this honour and obedience unto their parents?

SON.   First, the commandment of God, which saith: 'Honour thy father and thy mother'. Again: 'Ye children, obey your fathers and mothers in the Lord'. Secondly, the promise which is annexed to the commandment; even this, that they which honour and obey their parents shall prosper and live long on the earth. Thirdly, the commination or threatening of God's anger and vengeance against all disobedient children. 'Whoso laugheth his father to scorn, and setteth his mother's commandment at nought,' saith the wise man, 'the ravens pick out his eyes in the valley, and devoured be he of the young eagles'.[7] How miserably perished Absalom for his disobedience against his father! Is not the commandment of God, that such children as are stubborn and disobedient to their parents should be stoned unto death? Fourthly, the great labours and pains which the parents take, and the infinite charges and costs which they also bestow, in bringing up of them. These and such like things, diligently considered, shall easily move the heart of any natural and well-disposed child to show true honour and unfeigned obedience unto his parents, and cause him to seek all means possible to gratify his parents again, and to answer kindness for kindness.

FATHER. God for his mercy work this good disposition in the hearts of all children toward their parents!

SON.   Amen.

ACCOUNTS AND INVENTORIES OF ST EDMUND'S PARISH, SALISBURY, 1579–1635

Routine payments for the maintenance of the church and special provisions for liturgical activity point to the vitality and development of religious practice in Elizabethan and Stuart parishes. The bells marked the major festivities of the Christian year and the royal and commemorative holidays of the new Protestant calendar. These accounts and inventories from Salisbury suggest the relative importance of the pulpit and the altar, and emphasize the material accoutrements of the sacrament of holy communion. The construction of an altar rail in 1633 was part of the controversial Laudian programme to beautify and resanctify the churches.

Source: Henry James Fowle Swayne (ed.), *Churchwardens' Accounts of S. Edmund & S. Thomas, Sarum 1443–1702* (Salisbury, 1896), pp. 129, 158, 199–201, 374–5.

1579–80 (total disbursements £13 19s 9d)

Laid out for the 17th day of November for ringing for the queen's majesty, 9s . . .

Coals and frankincense against Christmas, 14d.

Ringing against Christmas, 6d.
Ringers for ringing upon Candlemas day, 3d.
Fourteen pounds of candles for the whole year, 3s . . .
John Jones for six hundred slates, 12s.
Carrying them to the church, 12d . . .
Lath nails and tile pins, 3d . . .
Plumbers for five days, 9s . . .
Ringers at Easter, 4d.
The organ player for a week's service, 5d.
Bread and wine, 23s.

Inventory, 1597–8

A chalice with the patten and all gilt weighing 23 ounces; a communion cup of silver with a cover; two cushions of silk, one green, another red; an altar cloth of green silk lined with white; the best pall of damask; the second pall with branches of silver; two communion towels; a new cloth of damask diaper for the communion table; a red velvet cushion for the pulpit with stars, given by Mr John Robins; a latten candlestick given by Walter Burgess this year; the cope was translated by William Parsons to a pulpit cloth and a cushion this year; a new towel of diaper and two napkins to wrap the communion cups in; one cloth of red silk damask fringed with gold and lined with blue for the communion table.

1608–9 (total disbursements £32 7s 9d)

Paid the clerk for one year's wages, £8.
Paid the sexton for one years's wages, 53s 4d . . .
Ringing upon the king's Coronation day, 8s . . .
Mending all the glass in the aisle, 13s 4d . . .
Ringers on the king's birthday, 8s . . .
For receiving our presentment at my lord's visitation, 2s 8d.
Twelve bushels of lime for repairing the sexton's house and the church porch, 4s.
Mason for seven days' work, 7s.
Labourer for six days, 4s.
Ringing on the day of Gowry's treason, 8s . . .
Ringing on the day of the Papists' conspiracy, 8s . . .
Ringers on the king's proclamation day, 8s.
Mending our organs, 50s . . .
Washing the surplice three times, 18d . . .

For writing the register and for parchment, 3s.
For writing the book of the names of the communicants, 2s 6d.

Inventory, 1618–19

Two silver cups with covers all whole gilt; one silver plate for the communion all whole gilt; four Tyning flagons serving for the communion table; one cloth for the communion table, embroidered with silk and gold; one embroidered pulpit cloth; one communion cloth of diaper; two diaper napkins; three towels for the forms at the communion, two of diaper, one of dowlas; two cushions, one for the pulpit, one for Mr Mayor's pew; one new bible of the new translation; one old bible; one new Book of Common Prayer and two old books; two surplices; one lamp in the church; one great brass candlestick; a frame for the hour-glass in the church, with three sockets for candles standing in the frame; one little bell which was for the jack of the clock house.

1633–4 (total disbursements £52 3s 7d)

Ringing coronation and Gunpowder Treason day, 16s . . .
Bread and wine, £8 13s 9d.
Oil and besoms, 3s 6d.
Washing of the church clothes, 4s.
Candles, £1 5s 6d.
Writing of the book of communicants, 2s 6d.
Parchment and writing the register, 3s . . .
At the visitation, when we deliver our presentments and the register, 5s 4d . . .
Mending of all the glass windows in the church with painted glass, £2 8s . . .
For six bell ropes . . . £1 1s 2d . . .
Fifty-five foot of plank to make forms for the church, 9s 3d . . .
A hundred tiles to mend the large window by the ringing loft, 2s 3d . . .
Pair of gemmels for the midwife's seat, 1s.
For making the rail in the chancel, for two short forms, for a piece of wainscot to lie upon the communion table to save the cloth, and for other work, £4 . . .
For repairing the organs, £10.

Inventory, 1634–5

One chalice silver and gilt; one cup silver and gilt with a cover; two small dishes silver and gilt; four flagons pewter; one great church bible in folio; two common prayer books in folio; one book of prayers for the 5th of November; one carpet of silk and gold for the communion table; one pulpit cloth of silk and embroidered work; one pulpit cushion and one cushion of velvet for the mayor's pew; one tablecloth of diaper for the communion table; two diaper roles and one dowlas role; one brass candlestick; two surplices; one great hanging candlestick with branches of brass.

3

RELIGIOUS CULTURE AND RELIGIOUS CONTEST IN ELIZABETHAN ENGLAND

A VIEW OF POPISH ABUSES YET REMAINING IN THE ENGLISH CHURCH, 1572

Puritan critics of the Church of England appended this 'View of Popish Abuses' to their *Admonition to the Parliament* of 1572. Their aim was to restructure the church by substituting a Presbyterian organization for episcopacy, and to advance the reformation by eliminating all remnants of 'popish' ceremony and belief from the Book of Common Prayer. The contentious and satirical tone of this catalogue of abuses, with its attack on the Elizabethan religious settlement, guaranteed its rejection by political and religious authorities. Local attempts to implement godliness and to eradicate superstition by altering religious ritual repeatedly brought Puritans into conflict with episcopal disciplinarians who demanded strict adherence to the official form of worship. Source: *An Admonition to the Parliament* (Hemel Hempstead? 1572) (*STC* 10847).

Abide patiently the Lord's leisure. Cast thy care upon the Lord, and he will bring it to pass, he will do it. The jeopardous time is at hand, that the wrath of God shall be declared from heaven upon all ungodliness of those seducers that withhold the truth in unrighteousness, and set his commandments at naught, for their own traditions.

Whereas immediately after the last parliament, held at Westminster, begun in 1570, and ended in 1571 the ministers of God's holy word and sacraments were called before her majesty's high commissioners, and enforced to subscribe unto the articles if they would keep their places and livings, and some for refusing to subscribe were unbrotherly and uncharitably entreated and from their offices and places removed: May it please therefore this honourable and high court of parliament, in consideration of the premises, to take a view of such causes, as then did withhold, and now doth the foresaid ministers from subscribing and consenting unto those foresaid articles, by way of purgation to discharge themselves of all disobedience towards the church of God and their sovereign, and by way of most humble entreaty, for the removing away and utter abolishing of all such corruptions and abuses as withheld them, through which this long time brethren have been at unnatural war and strife among themselves, to the hindrance of the gospel, to the joy of the wicked and to the grief and dismay of all those that profess Christ's religion and labour to attain Christian reformation.

The First Article: First, that the book commonly called the book of common prayers for the Church of England, authorized by parliament, and all and every the contents therein be such as are not repugnant to the word of God.

Albeit, right honourable and dearly beloved, we have at all times borne with that which we could not amend in this book, and have used the same in our ministry, so far forth as we might: reverencing those times and those persons in which and by whom it was first authorized, being studious of peace, and of the building up of Christ's church, yet now being compelled by subscription to allow the same, and to confess it, not to be against the words of God in any point but tolerable: We must needs say as followeth, that this book is an unperfect book, culled and picked out of that popish dunghill, the mass book full of all abominations. For some, and many of the contents therein, be such as are against the word of God, as by his grace shall be proved unto you. And by the way, we cannot but much marvel at the crafty wiliness of those men whose parts it had been first to have proved each and every content therein, to be agreeable to the word of God, seeing that they enforce men by subscription to consent unto it, or else send them packing from their callings.

They should first prove, that a reading service by the word of God going before, and with the administration of the sacraments, is according to the word of God, that private communion, private baptism, baptism ministered by women, holy days ascribed to saints, prescript services for them, kneeling at communion, wafer cakes for their bread when they minister it, surplice and cope to do it in, churching of women, coming in veils, abusing the psalm to her, I have lifted up mine eyes unto the hills, etc., and such other foolish things, are agreeable to the written word of the Almighty. But their craft is plain. Wherein they deceive themselves, standing so much upon this word repugnant, as though nothing were repugnant or against the word of God, but that which is expressly forbidden by plain command-ment, they know well enough and would confess, if either they were not blinded, or else their hearts hardened, that in the circumstances each content wherewith we justly find fault, and they too contentiously for the love of their livings maintain, smelling of their old popish priest-hood, is against the word of God. For besides that this prescript form of service as they call it, is full of corruptions, it maintained an unlawful ministry, unable to execute that office.

By the word of God, it is an office of preaching, they make it an office of reading: Christ said go preach, they in mockery give them the Bible, and authority to preach, and yet suffer them not, except that they have new licences. So that they make the chiefest part preaching, but an accessory that is as a thing without which their office may and doth consist. In the scriptures there is attributed unto the minister of God the knowledge of the heavenly mysteries, and therefore as the greatest token of their love, they are enjoined to feed God's lambs, and yet with these, such are admitted and accepted, as only are bare readers that are able to say service and minister a sacrament. And that this is not the feeding that Christ spake of, the scriptures are plain. Reading is not feeding, but it is as evil as playing upon a stage, and worse too. For players yet learn their parts without book, and these, a many of them can scarcely read within book. These are empty feeders, dark eyes, ill workmen to hasten in the Lord's harvest, messengers that cannot call, prophets that cannot declare the will of the Lord, unsavoury salt, blind guides, sleepy watchmen, untrusty dispensers of God's secrets, evil dividers of the word, weak to withstand the adversary, not able to confute, and to conclude, so far from making the man of God perfect to all good works, that rather the quite contrary may be confirmed . . .

In this book, days are ascribed unto saints, and kept holy with fasts on their evens, and prescript service appointed for them, which beside that they are of many superstitiously kept and observed, are also contrary to the commandment of God. Six days shalt thou labour, and therefore we for the superstition that is put in them, dare not subscribe to allow them.

In this book we are enjoined to receive the communion kneeling, which beside that it hath in it a show of papistry doth not so well express the mystery of this holy supper. For as in the Old Testament, eating the paschal lamb standing signified a readiness to pass, even so in receiving it now sitting, according to the example of Christ, we signify rest, that is a full finishing through Christ of all the ceremonial law, and a perfect work of redemption wrought that giveth rest forever. And so we avoid also the danger of idolatry, which was in times past too common, and yet is in the hearts of many, who have not yet forgotten their breaden God, so slenderly have they been instructed? Against which we may set the commandment, Thou shalt not bow down to it, or worship it.

As for the half communion, which is yet appointed like to the commemoration of the mass, we say little of it, saving that we may note, how near the translator bound himself to the mass book, that would not omit it. We speak not of the name of priest wherewith he defaceth the minister of Christ (because the priest that translated it, would perhaps fain have the ministers of Christ to be joined with him) seeing the office of priesthood is ended, Christ being the last priest that ever was. To call us therefore priests as touching our office, is either to call back again the old priesthood of the law, which is to deny Christ to be come, or else to keep a memory of the popish priesthood of abomination still amongst us. As for the first, it is by Christ abolished, and for the second it is of Antichrist, and therefore we have nothing to do with it. Such ought to have no place in our church, neither are they ministers of Christ, sent to preach his gospel, but priests of the pope to sacrifice for the quick and the dead, that is to tread under their feet the blood of Christ. Such ought not to have place amongst us, as the scriptures manifestly teach. Besides that we never read in the New Testament, that this word priest as touching office, is used in the good part . . .

And as for private baptism, that will abide the touchstone. Go ye, saith Christ and teach, baptising them, etc. Now teaching is divorced from communions and sacraments. They may go alone without doctrine. Women that may not speak in a congregation, may yet in time of necessity minister the sacrament of baptism, and that in a private house. And yet this is not to tie necessity of salvation to the sacraments, nor to nuzzle men up in that opinion. This is agreeable with the scriptures, and therefore when they bring the baptized child, they are received with this special commendation. I certify you, that you have done well, and according unto due order, etc. But now we speak in good earnest, when they answer this: Let them tell us, how this gear agreeth with the scriptures, and whether it be not repugnant or against the word of God.

The public baptism, that also is full of childish and superstitious toys. First in their prayer they say that God by the baptism of his son Jesus Christ did sanctify the flood Jordan, and all other waters, to the mystical washing away of sin, attributing that to the sign which is proper to the work of God in the blood of Christ, as though virtue were in water, to wash away sins. Secondly, they require a promise of the godfathers and godmothers (as they term them) which is not in their powers to perform. Thirdly, they profane holy baptism, in toying foolishly, for that they ask questions of an infant, which cannot answer, and speak unto them, as was wont to be spoken unto men, and unto such as being converted, answered for themselves and were baptized. Which is but a mockery of God, and therefore against the Holy Scriptures. Fourthly, they do superstitiously and wickedly institute a new sacrament, which is proper to Christ only, marking the child in the forehead with a cross, in token that hereafter he shall not be ashamed to confess the faith of Christ. We have made mention before of that wicked divorce of the word and sacraments. We say nothing of those that are admitted to be witnesses, what ill choice there is made of them, how convenient it were, seeing the children of the faithful only are to be baptized, that the father should and might, if conveniently, offer and present his child to be baptized, making an open confession of that faith, wherein he would have his child baptized, and how this is used in well-ordered churches.

As for matrimony, that also hath corruptions too many. It was wont to be counted a sacrament, and therefore they use yet a sacramental sign, to which they attribute the virtue of wedlock. I mean the wedding ring, which they foully abuse and dally withal, in taking it up and laying it down. In putting it on, they abuse the name of the Trinity, they make the new married man according to the popish form, to make an idol of his wife, saying: with this ring, I thee wed, with my body I thee worship, etc. And because in popery, no holy action might be done without a mass, they enjoin the married persons to receive the communion (as they do their bishops and priests when they are made, etc.). Other petty things out of the book, we speak not of, as that women contrary to the rule of the apostles, come and are suffered to come bareheaded, with bagpipes and fiddlers before them, to disturb the congregation, and that they must come in at the great door of the church, or else all is marred . . .

They appoint a prescript kind of service to bury the dead. And that which is the duty of every Christian, they tie alone to the minister, whereby prayer for the dead is maintained, and partly gathered out of some of the prayers, where they pray that we with this our brother, and all other departed in the true faith of thy holy name, may have our perfect consummation and bliss, both in body and soul. We say nothing of the threefold peal because that it is rather licensed by injunction than commanded in their book, nor of their strange mourning by changing their garments, which if it be not hypocritical, yet it is superstitious and heathenish, because it is used only of custom, nor of burial sermons, which are put in place of trentals, whereout spring many abuses, and therefore in the best reformed churches are removed. As for the superstitions used both in country and city, for the place of burial, which way they must lie, how they must be fetched to church, the minister meeting them at church stile with surplice, with a company of greedy clerks, that a cross white or black must be set upon the dead corpse, that bread must be given to the poor, and offerings in burial time used, and cakes sent abroad to friends, because these are rather used of custom and superstition, than by the authority of the book. Small commandment will serve for the accomplishing of such things. But great charge will hardly bring the least good thing to pass, and therefore all is let alone, and the people as blind and as ignorant as ever they were. God be merciful unto us.

Churching of women after childbirth smelleth of Jewish purification: their other rites and customs in their lying-in and coming to church, is foolish and superstitious, as it is used. She must lie in with a white sheet upon her bed, and come covered with a veil, as ashamed of some folly. She must offer, but these are matters of custom, and not in the book. But this psalm (as is noted before) is childishly abused, I have lift up mine eyes unto the hills, from whence cometh my help. The sun shall not burn thee by day, nor the moon by night. They pray that all men may be saved, and that they may be delivered from thundering and tempest, when no danger is nigh. That they sing *Benedictus, Nunc Dimittis* and *Magnificat,* we know not to what purpose, except some of them were ready to die, or except they would celebrate the memory of the Virgin, and John Baptist, etc. Thus they profane the Holy scriptures.

In all their order of service there is no edification, according to the rule of the apostle, but confusion, they toss the psalms in most places like tennis balls. The people, some standing, some walking, some talking, some reading, some praying by themselves, attend not to the minister. He again posteth it over, as fast as he can gallop. For either he hath two places to serve, or else there are some games to be played in the afternoon, as lying for the whetstone, heathenish dancing for the ring, a bear or a bull to be baited, or else Jackanapes to ride on horseback, or an interlude to be played, and if no place else can be gotten, it must be done in the church, etc. Now the people sit and now they stand up. When the Old Testament is read, or the lessons, they make no reverence, but when the gospel cometh, then they all stand up. For why, they think that to be of the greatest authority, and are ignorant that the scriptures came from one spirit. When Jesus is named, then off goeth the cap, and down goeth the knees, with such a scraping on the ground, that they cannot hear a good while after, so that the word is hindered, but when any other names of God are mentioned, they make no curtsey at all, as though the names of God were not equal, or as though all reverence ought to be given to the syllables. We speak not of ringing, when matins is done and other abuses incident. Because we shall be answered, that by the book they are not maintained, only we desire to have a book to reform it. As for organs and curious singing, though they be proper to popish dens, I mean to cathedral churches, yet some others also must have them. The queen's chapel, and these churches must be patterns and precedents to the people, of all superstitions . . .

What should we speak of the archbishop's court, since all men know it, and your wisdoms cannot but see what it is. As all other courts are subject to this, by the pope's prerogative, yea, and by the statute of this realm yet unrepealed, so is it the filthy quagmire, and poisoned plash of all the abominations that do infect the whole realm. We speak not of licences granted out of this court to marry in forbidden time, as in Lent, in Advent, in the gang week, when banners and bells with the priest in his surplice, singing gospels, and making crosses, rangeth about in many places, upon the ember days, and to forbidden persons, and in exempt places. We make no mention of licenses, to eat white meat and flesh in Lent, and that with a safe conscience, for rich men that can buy them with money, nor we say nothing how dearly men pay for them. As for dispensations with beneficed boys, tolerations for non-residents, bulls to have two benefices, to have three, to have more, and as many as they list or can get, these are so common, that all godly and good men are compelled with grief of heart to cry out upon such abominations. We omit excommunication for money, absolution for the same, and that by absolving one man for another, which how contrary it is to the scriptures the complaints of many learned men by propositions in open schools proposed, by writings in printed books set out, and by preaching in open pulpits, have been sufficiently witnessed. To conclude, this filthy court hath full power together with the authority of this petty pope, metropolitan and primate of all England, to dispense in all causes, wherein the pope was wont to dispense, under which are contained more cases and causes than we are able to reckon . . .

And as for the commissaries court, that is but a petty little stinking ditch, that floweth out of that former great puddle, robbing Christ's church of lawful pastors, of watchful seniors and elders, and careful deacons. In this court as in the other, one alone doth excommunicate, one alone sitteth in judgement, and when he will, can draw back the judgement which he hath pronounced, having called upon the name of God, and that for money which is called the changing of penance. In this court, for non-payment of two pence, a man shall be excommunicated if he appear not when he is sent for, if he do not as his ordinary would, from whom he had his popish induction and institution, and to whom he hath sworn *canonicam obedientiam,* canonical obedience, if he learn not his catechism like a good boy without book, when it were more meet he should be able to teach others. To conclude: if he be not obedient to all these lord bishop's officers, by and by he must be cut off by excommunication. And, as it is lightly granted and given forth, so if the money be paid and the court discharged, it is as quickly called in again. This court polleth parishes, scourgeth the poor hedge-priests, ladeth churchwardens with manifest perjuries, punisheth whoredoms and adulteries with toyish censures, remitteth without satisfying the congregation, and that in secret places, giveth out dispensations for unlawful marriages, and committeth a thousand such like abominations. God deliver all Christians out of this antichristian tyranny, where the judge's advocates and proctors for the most part are Papists, and as for the scribes and notaries as greedy as cormorants, and if they all should perhaps see this writing, they would be as angry as wasps, and sting like hornets. Three of them would be enough to sting a man to death, for why they are high commissioners.

All this we say springeth out of this pontifical, which we must allow by subscription, setting down our hands, that it is not repugnant or against the word of God, we mean this antichristian hierarchy, and popish ordering of ministers, strange from the word of God, and the use of all well-reformed churches in the world . . .

The Second Article: That the manner and order appointed by public authority about the administration of the sacraments and common prayers, and that the apparel by sufficient authority appointed for the ministers within the Church of England, be not wicked nor against the word of God, but tolerable, and being commanded for order and obedience sake, are to be used.

For the order of administration of sacraments and common prayer, enough is said before, all the service and administration is tied to a surplice, in cathedral churches they must have a cope, they receive the communion kneeling, they use not for the most part common bread according to the word of God, and the statute, but starch bread according to the Injunction. They commonly minister the sacraments without preaching the word. And as for the apparel, though we have been long borne in hand, and yet are, that it is for order and decency commanded, yet we know and have proved that there is neither order, nor comeliness, nor obedience in using it. There is no order in it, but confusion: no comeliness, but deformity: no obedience, but disobedience, both against God and the prince. We marvel that they could espy in their last synod, that a gray amise, which is but a garment of dignity, should be a garment (as they say) defiled with superstition, and yet that copes, caps, surplices, tippets and such like baggage, the preaching signs of popish priesthood, the pope's creatures, kept in the same form to this end, to bring dignity and reverence to the ministers and sacraments, should be retained still, and not abolished. But they are as the garments of the idol, to which we should say, avaunt and get thee hence. They are as the garments of Balamites, of popish priests, enemies to God and all Christians. They serve not to edification, they have the show of evil (seeing the popish priesthood is evil), they work discord, they hinder the preaching of the gospel, they keep the memory of Egypt still amongst us, and put us in mind of that abomination whereunto they in times past have served, they bring the ministry into contempt, they offend the weak, they encourage the obstinate. Therefore can no authority by the word of God, with any pretence of order and obedience command them, nor make them in any wise tolerable, but by circumstances, they are wicked, and against the word of God . . .

The Third Article: That the articles of religion which only concern the true Christian faith, and the doctrine of the sacraments, comprised in a book imprinted: Articles, whereupon it was agreed by both archbishops, etc., and every of them contain true and godly Christian doctrine.

For the articles concerning that substance of doctrine using a godly interpretation in a point or two, which are either too sparely, or else too darkly set down, we were and are ready according to duty, to subscribe unto them. We would to God that as they hold the substance together with us, and we with them: so they would not deny the effect and virtue thereof. Then should not our words and works be divorced, but Christ should be suffered to reign, a true ministry according to the word instituted, discipline exercised, sacraments purely and sincerely ministered. This is that we strive for, and about which we have suffered not as evil-doers, but for resisting popery, and refusing to be strong with the tail of antichristian infection, ready to render a reason of our faith, to be stopping of all our enemies' mouths. We therefore for the church of God's sake, which ought to be most dear unto you, beseech you for our sovereign's sake, upon whom we pray, that all God's blessings may be poured abundantly. We pray you to consider of these abuses to reform God's church according to your duties and callings, that as with one mouth we confess one Christ, so with one consent, this reign of Antichrist may be turned out headlong from amongst us, and Christ Our Lord may reign by his word over us. So your seats shall be established and settled in great assurance, you shall not need to fear your enemies: for God will turn away his threatened plagues from us. Which he in mercy do, for his Christ's sake. Amen.

ARCHBISHOP GRINDAL'S INJUNCTIONS FOR THE LAITY IN THE PROVINCE OF YORK, 1571

As an energetic reforming bishop, Edmund Grindal (1519–83) sought to impose Protestant discipline on the northern province of York. These Injunctions required parish officials to remove and destroy the material apparatus of the Roman Catholic mass, and to provide in its place the books and equipment for English Protestant worship. Grindal also promoted the reformation of manners, the suppression of superstition, control of disorderly customs, and the godly observance of the Sabbath. Grindal's efforts at York earned him the archbishopric of Canterbury in 1575. It may have taken another generation for widespread popish practices to disappear from this part of England.

Source: *Iniunctions Giuen by the most reuerende father in Christ, Edmonde . . . in his Metropoliticall visitation of the Prouince of Yorke* (London, 1571) (*STC* 10375).

[Injunctions 1, 2 and 3 deal with laymen performing clerical offices, provision of pulpits, and the appointment of churchwardens.]

4. That the churchwardens in every parish shall, at the costs and charges of the parish, provide (if the same be not already provided) all things necessary and requisite for common prayer and administration of the holy sacraments . . . especially the Book of Common Prayer, with the new calendar, and a psalter to the same, the English Bible in the largest volume, the two tomes of the Homilies, with the Homilies lately written against rebellion, the table of the Ten Commandments, a convenient pulpit well placed, a comely and decent table, standing on a frame, for the holy communion, with a fair linen cloth to lay upon the same, and some covering of silk, buckram, or other such like for the clean keeping thereof; a fair and comely communion cup of silver, and a cover of silver for the same, which may serve also for the ministration of the communion bread; a decent large surplice with sleeves, a sure coffer with two locks and keys for keeping of the register book, and a strong chest or box for the alms of the poor, with three locks and keys to the same, and all other things necessary in and to the premises; and shall also provide . . . the paraphrases of Erasmus in English upon the gospels, and the same set up in some convenient place within their church or chapel, the charges whereof the parson or proprietary and parishioners shall by equal portions bear, according to the queen's majesty's injunctions; all which books must be whole and not torn or unperfect in any wise. And the churchwardens also shall, from time to time, at the charges of the parish, provide bread and wine for the communion; and for that purpose shall take some order among the parishioners, that every one may pay such a reasonable sum towards the same, as may suffice for the finding of bread and wine for the communion throughout the whole year, so as no communion at any time be disappointed for want of bread and wine.

5. That the churchwardens shall see that in their churches and chapels all altars be utterly taken down, and clear removed even unto the foundation, and the place where they stood paved, and the wall whereunto they joined whited over, and made uniform with the rest, so as no breach or rupture appear. And that the altar stones be broken, defaced and bestowed to some common use. And that the rood lofts be taken down and altered, so that the upper boards and timber thereof, both behind and above where the rood lately did hang, and also the solar or loft be quite taken down unto the cross beam, whereunto the partition between the choir and the body of the church is fastened, and that the said beam have some convenient crest put upon the same. And that all the boards, beams, and other stuff of the rood lofts be sold by the churchwardens to the use of the church, so as no part thereof be kept and observed.

6. That the churchwardens shall, from time to time, see that their churches and chapels and the steeples thereof be diligently and well

repaired with lead, tile, slate, or shingle, limestone, timber, glass and all other necessaries; and that their churches and chapels be kept clean and decently, that they be not loathsome to any, either by dust, sand, gravel, or any filth; and that there be no feasts, dinners, or common drinking kept in the church; and that the churchyard be well fenced, and cleanly kept, and that no folks be suffered to dance in the same.

7. That the churchwardens and minister shall see that antiphoners, mass books, grailes, portesses, processionals, manuals, legendaries, and all other books of late belonging to their church or chapel, which served for the superstitious Latin service, be utterly defaced, rent, and abolished. And that all vestments, albs, tunicles, stoles, fanons, pyxes, paxes, hand-bells, sacring-bells, censers, christmatories, crosses, candlesticks, holy-water stocks, or fat images, and all other relics and monuments of superstition and idolatry, be utterly defaced, broken and destroyed; and if they cannot come by any of the same, they shall present to the ordinary what they cannot come by, and in whose custody the same is, to the intent further order may be taken for the defacing thereof.

8. When any man or woman, dwelling near to the church in any city, borough, or great town, is in passing out of this life, the parish clerk or sexton shall knoll the bell, to move the people to pray for the sick person. And after the time of the departing of any Christian body out of this life, the churchwardens shall see that neither there be any more ringing but one short peal before the burial, and another short peal after the burial, without ringing of any hand-bells, or other superfluous or superstitious ringing, either before or at the time of the burial, or at any time after the same; nor any other form of service said or sung, or other ceremonies used at any burial, than are appointed by the Book of Common Prayer. And also that neither on All Saints' day after evening prayer, nor the day next after, of late called All Souls' day, there be any ringing at all than to common prayer, when the same shall happen to fall upon the Sunday. And that no month-minds or yearly commemorations of the dead, nor any other superstitious ceremonies, be observed or used, which tend either to the maintenance of prayer for the dead, or of the popish purgatory.

[Injunctions 9, 10, 11 and 12 deal with bell-ringing, catechism, communion from the age of fourteen, and commercial activity in churches and churchyards.]

13. That no innkeeper, alehouse-keeper, victualler, or tippler, shall admit or suffer any person or persons in his house or backside to eat, drink, or play at cards, tables, bowls, or other games in time of common prayer, preachings, or reading of homilies, on the Sundays or holy days; and that there be no shops set open on Sundays or holy days, nor any butchers or other suffered to sell meat or other things upon the Sundays or holy days, in like time of common prayer, preaching or reading of the Homilies. And that in any fairs or common markets, falling upon the Sunday, there be

no showing of any wares before all the morning service and the sermon (if there be any) be done. And if any shall offend in this behalf, the church-wardens and sworn-men, after once warning given unto them, shall present them by name unto the ordinary.

[Injunctions 14 and 15 require church attendance.]

16. That no person or persons whatsoever shall wear beads, or pray, either in Latin or in English, upon beads, or knots, or any other like superstitious thing; nor shall pray upon any popish Latin or English Primer, or other like book, nor shall burn any candles in the church superstitiously upon the feast of the Purification of the Virgin Mary, commonly called Candlemas day; nor shall resort to any popish priest for shrift or auricular confession in Lent, or at any other time; nor shall worship any cross or any image or picture upon the same, nor give any reverence thereunto, nor superstitiously shall make upon themselves the sign of the cross when they first enter into any church to pray, nor shall say *De profundis* for the dead, or rest at any cross in carrying any corpse to burying, nor shall leave any little crosses of wood there.

[Injunctions 17 and 18 deal with collections for the poor and yearly peramubulations.]

19. That the minister and churchwardens shall not suffer any lords of misrule, or summer lords or ladies, or any disguised persons or others in Christmas or at May games, or any minstrels, morris dancers, or others, at rushbearings or at any other times, to come unreverently into any church or chapel or churchyard, and there dance or play any unseemly parts with scoffs, jests, wanton gestures, or ribald talk, namely in the time of divine service or of any sermon.

[Injunctions 20, 21, 22, 23, 24 and 25 deal with schoolmasters, parish clerks, and the presentation of offenders.]

ARCHBISHOP GRINDAL'S LETTER TO THE QUEEN, 1576

This document eloquently evokes the tension between the Elizabethan state, headed by a conservative monarch wary of Puritan extremism, and the Elizabethan church, largely run by returned Marian exiles anxious to effect continental-style reforms. In the following uncompromising letter, Edmund Grindal, Archbishop of Canterbury from 1575, remonstrates with the queen regarding her demand that he suppress then-popular public exercises known as 'prophesyings'. These were not, as their name might suggest, devoted to the work of prophecy, but were sessions devoted to the discussion and interpretation of scripture by learned clergy, with both clergy and laity in attendance. Archbishop Grindal's conscientious and impolitic refusal led to his suspension from the jurisdictional and spiritual functions of his office. Although his spiritual duties were eventually restored, Grindal's political disgrace foreshadowed the failure of moderate Puritanism in early modern England.
Source: *The Remains of Archbishop Grindal*, ed. William Nicholson, Parker Society (Cambridge, 1843), pp. 376–90.

With most humble remembrance of my bounden duty to your majesty: It may please the same to be advertised, that the speeches which it hath pleased you to deliver unto me, when I last attended on your Highness, concerning abridging the number of preachers, and the utter suppression of all learned exercises and conferences among the ministers of the church, allowed by their bishops and ordinaries, have exceedingly dismayed and discomforted me. Not so much for that the said speeches sounded very hardly against mine own person, being but one particular man, and not much to be accounted of; but most of all for that the same might both tend to the public harm of God's church, whereof your majesty ought to be *nutricia*,[1] and also to the heavy burdening of your own conscience before God, if they should be put in strict execution. It was not your majesty's pleasure then, the time not serving thereto, to hear me at any length concerning the said two matters then propounded: I thought it therefore my duty by writing to declare some part of my mind unto your highness; beseeching the same with patience to read over this that I now send, written with mine own rude scribbling hand; which seemeth to be of more length than it is indeed: for I say with Ambrose, *Scribo manu mea, quod sola legas.*[2]

Madam, first of all, I must and will, during my life, confess, that there is no earthly creature to whom I am so much bounden as to your majesty; who, notwithstanding mine insufficiency (which commendeth your grace the more) hath bestowed upon me so many and so great benefits as I could never hope for, much less deserve. I do therefore, according to my most bounden duty, with all thanksgiving, bear towards your majesty a most humble, faithful, and thankful heart; and that knoweth he which knoweth all things. Neither do I ever intend to offend your majesty in any thing, unless, in the name of God or of his church, by necessity of office, and burden of conscience, I shall thereto be enforced: and in those cases (which I trust in God shall never be urged upon me) if I should use dissembling or flattering silence, I should very evil requite your majesty's so many and so great benefits; for in so doing, both you might fall into peril towards God, and I myself into endless damnation.

The prophet Ezechiel termeth us, ministers of the church, *speculatores*, and not *adulatores*.[3] If we see the sword coming by reason of any offence towards God, we must of necessity give warning, or else the blood of those that perish will be required at our hands. I beseech your majesty thus to think of me, that I do not conceive any evil opinion of you, although I cannot assent to those two articles then propounded. I do with the rest of all your good subjects acknowledge, that we have received by your government many and most excellent benefits, as, among others, freedom of

94

conscience, suppressing of idolatry, sincere preaching of the gospel, with public peace and tranquillity. I am also persuaded, that even in these matters, which you seem now to urge, your zeal and meaning is to the best. The like hath happened to many of the best princes that ever were: yet have they not refused afterwards to be better informed out of God's word.

King David, so much commended in the scriptures, had no evil meaning, when he commanded the people to be numbered: he thought it good policy in so doing, to understand what forces he had in store to employ against God's enemies, if occasion so required. Yet afterward (saith the scripture) his own heart stroke him; and God, by the prophet Gad, reprehended him for his offence, and gave him for the same choice of three very hard penances, that is to say, famine, war, and pestilence . . .

And so, to come to the present case; I may very well use unto your highness the words of Ambrose above written, *Novi pietatem tuam*, etc.[4] But surely I cannot marvel enough, how this strange opinion should once enter into your mind, that it should be good for the church to have few preachers. Alas Madam! is the scripture more plain in any one thing, than that the gospel of Christ should be plentifully preached; and that plenty of labourers should be sent into the Lord's harvest; which, being great and large, standeth in need, not of a few, but of many workmen? . . .

Public and continual preaching of God's word is the ordinary mean and instrument of the salvation of mankind. St Paul calleth it the ministry of reconciliation of man unto God. By preaching of God's word the glory of God is enlarged, faith is nourished, and charity increased. By it the ignorant is instructed, the negligent exhorted and incited, the stubborn rebuked, the weak conscience comforted, and to all those that sin of malicious wickedness the wrath of God is threatened. By preaching also due obedience to Christian princes and magistrates is planted in the hearts of subjects: for obedience proceedeth of conscience; conscience is grounded upon the word of God; the word of God worketh his effect by preaching. So as generally, where preaching wanteth, obedience faileth.

No prince ever had more lively experience hereof than your majesty hath had in your time, and may have daily. If your majesty come to the city of London never so often, what gratulation, what joy, what concourse of people is there to be seen! Yea, what acclamations and prayers to God for your long life, and other manifest significations of inward and unfeigned love, joined with most humble and hearty obedience, are there to be heard! Whereof cometh this, madam, but of the continual preaching of God's word in that city, whereby that people hath been plentifully instructed in their duty towards God and your majesty? On the contrary, what bred the rebellion in the north? Was it not papistry, and ignorance of

God's word, through want of often preaching? And in the time of that rebellion, were not all men, of all states, that made profession of the gospel, most ready to offer their lives for your defence? Insomuch that one poor parish in Yorkshire, which by continual preaching had been better instructed than the rest (Halifax I mean) was ready to bring three or four thousand able men into the field to serve you against the said rebels. How can your majesty have a more lively trial and experience of the contrary effects of much preaching, and of little or no preaching? The one working most faithful obedience, and the other most unnatural disobedience and rebellion.

But it is thought of some, that many are admitted to preach, and few be able to do it well. That unable preachers be removed is very requisite, if ability and sufficiency may be rightly weighed and judged: and therein I trust as much is, and shall be, done as can be; for both I, for mine own part (let it be spoken without any ostentation) am very careful in allowing such preachers only, as be able and sufficient to be preachers, both for their knowledge in the scriptures, and also for testimony of their good life and conversation. And besides that, I have given very great charge to the rest of my brethren, the bishops of this province, to do the like. We admit no man to the office, that either professeth Papistry or Puritanism. Generally, the graduates of the university are only admitted to be preachers, unless it be some few which have excellent gifts of knowledge in the scriptures, joined with good utterance and godly persuasion. I myself procured above forty learned preachers and graduates, within less than six years, to be placed within the diocese of York, besides those I found there; and there I have left them: the fruits of whose travail in preaching your majesty is like to reap daily, by most assured, dutiful obedience of your subjects in those parts. But, indeed, this age judgeth very hardly, and nothing indifferently of the ability of preachers of our time; judging few or none in their opinion to be able . . .

Now, where it is thought, that the reading of the godly homilies, set forth by public authority, may suffice, I continue of the same mind I was when I attended last upon your majesty. The reading of homilies hath his commodity; but is nothing comparable to the office of preaching. The godly preacher is termed in the gospel *fidelis servus et prudens, qui novit famulitio Domini cibum demensum dare in tempore;*[5] who can apply his speech according to the diversity of times, places, and hearers, which cannot be done in homilies: exhortations, reprehensions, and persuasions, are uttered with more affection, to the moving of the hearers, in sermons than in homilies. Besides, homilies were devised by the godly bishops in your brother's time, only to supply necessity, for want of preachers; and are by the statute

96

not to be preferred, but to give place to sermons, whensoever they may be had; and were never thought in themselves alone to contain sufficient instruction for the Church of England . . .

Now for the second point, which is concerning the learned exercise and conference amongst the ministers of the church: I have consulted with divers of my brethren, the bishops, by letters; who think the same as I do, viz. a thing profitable to the church, and therefore expedient to be continued. And I trust your majesty will think the like, when your highness shall have been informed of the manner and order thereof; what authority it hath of the scriptures; what commodity it bringeth with it; and what incommodities will follow, if it be clean taken away.

The authors of this exercise are the bishops of the diocese where the same is used; who both by the law of God, and by the canons and constitutions of the church now in force, have authority to appoint exercises to their inferior ministers, for increase of learning and knowledge in the scriptures, as to them seemeth most expedient: for that pertaineth *ad disciplinam clericalem*.[6] The times appointed for the assembly is once a month, or once in twelve or fifteen days, at the discretion of the ordinary. The time of the exercise is two hours: the place, the church of the town appointed for the assembly. The matter entreated of is as followeth. Some text of scripture, before appointed to be spoken of, is interpreted in this order: First, the occasion of the place is showed. Secondly, the end. Thirdly, the proper sense of the place. Fourthly, the propriety of the words: and those that be learned in the tongues showing the diversities of interpretations. Fifthly, where the like phrases are used in the scriptures. Sixthly, places in the scriptures, seeming to repugn, are reconciled. Seventhly, the arguments of the text are opened. Eighthly, it is also declared, what virtues and what vices are there touched; and to which of the commandments they pertain. Ninthly, how the text hath been wrested by the adversaries, if occasion so require. Tenthly, and last of all, what doctrine of faith or manners the text doth contain. The conclusion is, with the prayer for your majesty and all estates, as is appointed by the Book of Common Prayer, and a psalm.

These orders following are also observed in the said exercise. First, two or three of the gravest and best learned pastors are appointed of the bishop to moderate in every assembly. No man may speak, unless he first be allowed by the bishop, with this proviso, that no layman be suffered to speak at any time. No controversy of this present time and state shall be moved or dealt withal. If any attempt the contrary, he is put to silence by the moderator. None is suffered to glance openly or covertly at persons public or private; neither yet any one to confute another. If any man utter a wrong sense of the scripture, he is privately admonished thereof, and better instructed by the moderators, and other his fellow-ministers. If any man use immodest speech, or irreverent gesture or behaviour, or otherwise be suspected in life, he is likewise admonished, as before. If any wilfully do break these orders, he is presented to the bishop, to be by him corrected . . .

I trust, when your majesty hath considered and well weighed the premises, you will rest satisfied, and judge that no such inconveniences can grow of these exercises, as you have been informed, but rather the clean contrary. And for my own part, because I am very well assured, both by reasons and arguments taken out of the Holy Scriptures, and by experience (the most certain seal of sure knowledge) that the said exercises, for the interpretation and exposition of the scriptures, and for exhortation and comfort drawn out of the same, are both profitable to increase knowledge among the ministers, and tendeth to the edifying of the hearers, I am forced, with all humility, and yet plainly, to profess, that I cannot with safe conscience, and without the offence of the majesty of God, give my assent to the suppressing of the said exercises: much less can I send out any injunction for the utter and universal subversion of the same. I say with St Paul, 'I have no power to destroy, but to only edify'; and with the same apostle, 'I can do nothing against the truth, but for the truth'.[7]

If it be your majesty's pleasure, for this or for any other cause, to remove me out of this place, I will with all humility yield thereunto, and render again to your majesty that I received of the same. I consider with myself, *Quod horrendum est incidere in manus Dei viventis.*[8] I consider also, *Quod qui facit contra conscientiam (divinis juribus nixam) oedificat ad gehennam.*[9] 'And what should I win, if I gained' (I will not say a bishopric, but) 'the whole world, and lose mine own soul!'[10]

Bear with me, I beseech you, madam, if I choose rather to offend your earthly majesty, than to offend the heavenly majesty of God. And now being sorry, that I have been so long and tedious to your majesty, I will draw to an end, most humbly praying the same well to consider these two short petitions following.

The first is, that you would refer all these ecclesiastical matters which touch religion, or the doctrine and discipline of the church, unto the bishops and divines of your realm; according to the example of all godly Christian emperors and princes of all ages . . . The second petition I have to make to your majesty is this: that, when you deal in matters of faith and religion, or matters that touch the church of Christ, which is his spouse, bought with so dear a price, you would not use to pronounce so resolutely and peremptorily, *quasi ex authoritate,*[11] as ye may do in civil and extern matters; but always remember, that in God's causes the will of God, and not the will of any earthly creature, is to take place. It is the antichristian voice of the pope, *sic volo, sic jubeo; stet pro ratione voluntas.*[12] In God's matters all princes ought to bow their sceptres to the Son of God, and to ask counsel at his mouth, what they ought to do. David exhorteth all kings and rulers to, *serve God with fear and trembling.*

Remember, madam, that you are a mortal creature. 'Look not only (as was said to Theodosius) upon the purple and princely array, wherewith ye are apparelled; but consider withal, what is that that is covered therewith. Is it not flesh and blood? Is it not dust and ashes? Is it not a corruptible body, which must return to his earth again, God knoweth how soon?' Must not you also one day appear *ante tremendum tribunal Crucifixi, ut recipias ibi, prout gesseris in corpore, sive bonum sive malum?*[13]

And although ye are a mighty prince, yet remember that He which dwelleth in heaven is mightier. He is, as the Psalmist sayeth, *terribilis, et is qui aufert spiritum principium, terribilis super omnes reges terrae.*[14]

Wherefore I do beseech you, madam, *in visceribus Christi,*[15] when you deal in these religious causes, set the majesty of God before your eyes, laying all earthly majesty aside: determine with yourself to obey his voice, and with all humility say unto him, *Non mea, sed tua voluntas fiat.*[16] God hath blessed you with great felicity in your reign, now many years; beware you do not impute the same to your own deserts or policy, but give God the glory. And as to instruments and means, impute your said felicity, first, to the goodness of the cause which ye have set forth (I mean Christ's true religion); and, secondly, to the sighs and groanings of the godly in their fervent prayer to God for you; which have hitherto, as it were, tied and bound the hands of God, that he could not pour out his plagues upon you and your people, most justly deserved . . .

Ye have done many things well; but except ye persevere to the end, ye cannot be blessed. For if ye turn from God, then God will turn away his merciful countenance from you. And what remaineth then to be looked for, but only a terrible expectation of God's judgements, and an heaping up of wrath against the day of wrath?

But I trust in God, your majesty will always humble yourself under his mighty hand, and go forth in the zealous setting forth of God's true religion, always yielding due obedience and reverence to the word of God, the only rule of faith and religion.

GEORGE GIFFORD'S *COUNTRY DIVINITY*, 1582

George Gifford's discourse of 'country divinity' drew on his personal experience of the 'village politics' of religion. As incumbent of an Essex parish, he understood the potentially divisive impact of reformation ideals and practices on the face-to-face culture of neighbourliness. Gifford's nonconformity led to his suspension from preaching, but a petition from his parishioners to Lord Burghley secured his reinstatement. His dialogue is remarkable for giving powerfully persuasive arguments to both protagonists: one, an advocate of religious and social transformation; the other, an adherent of older traditions of hospitality and good fellowship. But Gifford, as Zelotes, has the last word.

Source: George Gifford, *A Brief Discourse of Certaine Points of the Religion, Whiche is Among the Common Sort of Christians: Which may be Termed the Country Divinitie: With a Plaine and Manifest Confutation of the Same, After the Order of a Dialogue* (London, 1582) (*STC* 11846), sigs A1–A3.

ZELOTES. Well overtaken my friend.

ATHEOS. I thank you Sir.

ZELOTES. How far do you travel this way?

ATH. Twenty miles . . .

ZELOT. What call ye the town where you dwell?

ATH. G.B.

ZELOT. Have ye a preacher there?

ATH. We have an honest man our curate.

ZELOT. Doth he teach his flock?

ATH. He doth his good will, and more ye cannot require of a man.

ZELOT. Ye did commend him even now, to be an honest man.

ATH. Commend him: yea I may commend him: I am persuaded we have the best priest in the country, we would be loath to forego him for the learnedest of them all.

ZELOT. I pray ye let me hear what his virtues be, for which ye do commend him so highly.

ATH. He is as gentle a person as ever I see: a very good fellow, he will not stick when good fellows and honest men meet together to spend his groat at the alehouse: I cannot tell, they preach and preach, but he doth live as well as the best of them all. I am afraid when he is gone we shall never have the like again.

ZELOT. Be these the great virtues which ye doth commend him for? He may have all these, and yet be more meet for to keep swine, than to be a shepherd over the flocks of Christ, is he able to teach the people, and doth he instruct them in God's word?

ATH. I know not what teaching ye would have, he doth read the service, as well as any of them all, and I think there is as good edifying in those prayers and homilies, as in any that the preacher can make: let us learn those first.

ZELOT. This is not all which is required in a minister, for a boy of ten

100

years old can do all this: doth he not teach them to know the will of God and reprove naughtiness among the people?

ATH. Yes that he doth, for if there be any that do not agree, he will seek for to make them friends: for he will get them to play a game or two at bowls or cards, and to drink together at the alehouse: I think it a godly way, to make charity: he is none of these busy controllers: for if he were, he could not be so well liked of some (and those not of the meanest) as he is.

ZELOT. Do ye call the preachers of God's word busy controllers? Do they go further than God's word doth lead them?

ATH. We may call them busy controllers, I think we shall do nothing shortly, as poor a man as I am, I would not for forty shillings that we had one of them, there be more of my mind.

ZELOT. Some poor men perhaps.

ATH. Nay, the best in the parish, who would not so well like of our curate, if he should meddle that way.

ZELOT. I perceive now what manner of man your curate is, and I see like master like scholar.

ATH. Why so I pray ye?

ZELOT. Why so, I smell how unmeet he is, and also how ignorant you are. Let me question a little while with ye concerning that which ye have uttered.

ATH. I trust I have uttered nothing but that which doth become an honest man.

ZELOT. Nay all your speech doth bewray that you are a carnal man, for you have made a very fine description of a good curate, what mean ye when ye say he is a good fellow, and will not stick to spend his money among good fellows, is it not because he is a pot-companion?

ATH. Do ye mislike good fellowship, is it not lawful for honest men to drink and be merry together?

ZELOT. I do not mislike true friendship, which is in the Lord, knit in true godliness, but I mislike this vice, which overfloweth everywhere, that drunkards meet together and sit quaffing, and the minister which should reprove them, to be one of the chief: when he should be at his study, to be upon the alebench at cards or dice.

ATH. I perceive you are one of those curious and precise fellows, which will allow no recreation, what would ye have men do? We shall do nothing shortly. You would have them sit moping always at their books, I like not that . . .

ATH. If they be so good and godly, how cometh it to pass then, that

101

there is so much debate among them? For I know towns myself, which are even divided one part against another, since they had a preacher, which were not so before. This they gain, that whereas before they loved together, now there is dissention sown among them.

ZELOT.   Now ye discharge your greatest ordinance: I trow ye have now paid it home: It is hard if Satan cannot with this engine overthrow and beat down preaching. But I pray you tell me, can ye put fire and water together but they will rumble? Will ye have light and darkness for to agree as companions together?

ATH.   What is this to the matter?

ZELOT.   Would ye have God and the Devil agree together? Would ye have the godly and the wicked for to be at one? this ye must do, ye look where the fault is to be laid.

ATH.   I think the fault must needs be laid upon the preaching, because they agreed before that came.

ZELOT.   If their agreement together before had been good, then no doubt the preaching that could break it, could not be good: for one good thing cannot destroy another. But the former peace was not in God, but in the flesh: neither was it so great as you would seem for to set it forth, because that the worldlings are always at strife, and one ready for to cut another's throat: but yet their hatred is so exceeding great against the gospel, that in respect of the mind, which they carry towards the professors thereof, they seem among themselves to be at peace, and one to love and make much of another.

ATH.   Where is the fault then for to be laid?

ZELOT.   Upon the wicked which fret and rage against the word, because it layeth open and discloseth their filthiness, and bewrayeth them. For the light (as St Paul saith) doth manifest all things. They pretend other excuses, as though they hated the professors for some evil conditions: but this is very evident, a blind man may almost discern it, that so long as a man is void of religion, and maketh profession of no more then they, so long, although he be full, and swarm with great vices, he is an honest man, but let him follow the word, and be careful for to amend, then there is not a lewder fellow upon earth, divers slanders shall be raised, things shall be reckoned up, which he did seven years agone: and now they hate him like a dog. Light is come into the world, and men love darkness more than light, because their works are evil. Will ye charge Christ and his gospel, because as he sayeth, he came not to send peace, but a sword, to set the father against the son (Matthew 10)? Or will ye lay blame upon those who love the light? Will ye blame St Paul and his preaching because there was stir and hurly-burly almost wheresoever he came? Was he to be blamed, or the wicked infidels, which could not abide to have their sins reproved?

ATH. There be some places where they have grave and learned preachers, and yet there is no such contention in their parishes: I like that well.

ZELOT. You like that well: so doth your master also.

ATH. What mean you by that? Whom do ye call my master?

ZELOT. Even the Devil, for he is content those preachers should ride upon his back, because he is sure they will not spur and gall him: they be very gentle riders. Do ye not think, that if they should set forth God's word as they ought, and spread the light: that all wicked men (of which their parish is full) would storm and fret against them? The Devil himself would fisk about, if they should spur him but a little. But they can tell a smooth tale in the pulpit, garnished with some merry story, for to make the people merry, or else some old rotten allegory: or some far-fetched matter out of some great writers, that the people may be at their wit's end, and admit them. A man would think to see the people come out of the church blowing, that they were fed as full as ticks, when they go home with empty bellies. This I dare warrant, if it be not so, let me lose both mine ears, that go through the parishes of these grave and learned divines, and except such as run to fetch their victuals other where, ye shall not find five among five score which are able to understand the necessary grounds and principles of religion: and yet the people will say they be excellent deep men: But I love not those wells which are so deep that a man can draw no water out of them . . .

ATH. If a man labour all the week truly and honestly, and upon the Sabbath day come to the church and make his prayers, shall we say God regarded not his prayer, because he doth not understand what he prayeth: his intent is good, he doth his good will: he hath a wife and children to provide for, he must follow the world, and let preaching go, or else he shall beg: and so long as he doth hurt no man, but dealeth uprightly: I think God doth not require no more at his hands. Such as have naught else for to do let them seek for knowledge.

ZELOT. Ye are like unto a hedge which is full of briars and pricking thorns, a man cannot lay hold on ye unless ye bring his hedging gloves, and his bill. Ye have many things to shroud yourself under, and to keep the truth from touching of ye, as the Lord in his word hath set forth the whole armour for a Christian soldier: so likewise Satan doth by suggestions teach men to arm themselves against the Lord. But ye must be stripped of your armour, at the least ye must be showed that it is no armour of proof. Ye say that if a man labour truly and honestly all the week, those labour so which do it not alone for necessity, but because God requireth that men should painfully travail: and which have the word of God as a lantern for to guide their steps: for whatsoever a man doth, if it be not in obedience of God in his word, it is sin. To pray upon the Sabbath for fashion sake, is very detestable, because we are in continual danger, and in continual need, and want help continually from the Lord, upon whom our salvation doth daily depend: we are commanded to pray continually, or to have our hearts watching thereunto. To pray without understanding, is not praying but mumming. You speak as though it were a thing which God doth allow, that men should seek more after the world than after God: and so to make the world their God. And because they have wife and children to provide for, therefore they cannot seek to know God. As though we were not commanded to seek first, the kingdom of God, that is to seek that chiefly, and more than the world, and then God hath promised, that all these things shall be cast upon us.

How shall any man be excused when God maketh this promise unto all: as he doth perform it unto as many as do trust him. I have been young (saith the prophet) and now am old, yet did I never see the righteous forsaken, and his seed begging their bread. When ye say he must follow the world, and let preaching go, ye were even as good say, he must follow the Devil, and let God go. And if an ignorant man could come so far, as to deal uprightly, and to hurt no man neither in word nor deed (which notwithstanding they come nothing near) yet this would not serve the turn: for there is a God who will be known and worshipped in that religion which he readieth. Have ye so fleshly eyes that ye can look no higher? Do ye think God requireth no more but an honest and civil conversation towards men? God requireth even of the poor labouring man that he should (if he will be blessed) meditate in his law, or his doctrine day and night (Psalm 1). Likewise when he sayeth that the man is blessed which feareth the Lord, to the end we might know which that man is, he addeth immediately, he hath great delight in

his commandments. But the most part of your honest men nowadays, delight so much in the word of God, and meditate so much in
it, that they care not a button though they never hear it: they love it
and set as much by it as they do an old shoe. And are not so forward
as you do allow, to seek for the knowledge of God, when they have
naught else for to do: for you think ye grant a liberal allowance to
God.

PHILIP STUBBES, THE MANNER OF SANCTIFYING THE SABBATH, 1583

Sabbatarianism, or insistence on strict observance of the Sabbath (Sunday), was a
distinguishing mark of late Elizabethan Puritanism. So too was the polemical dialogue
in which a true believer instructs his less committed junior colleague. In *The Anatomie
of Abuses* the Puritan controversialist Philip Stubbes catalogues the 'wicked and
ungodly pastimes' that drove the English people from God. Stubbes reserved much
of his anger for stage plays and extravagant fashions. In this section he designates
the Sabbath for godly exercises and religious devotion, and attacks those people who
used the Lord's day for work or play. Different views on the discipline of the Sabbath
fuelled the later controversy over the Declaration of Sports.
Source: Philip Stubbes, *The Anatomie of Abuses* (London, 1583) (*STC* 23376), sigs
L2–L4v.

PHILOPONUS. The Sabbath day, of some is well sanctified, namely in hearing
the word of God, preached and interpreted, in private and
public prayers, in singing of godly psalms, in celebrating the
sacraments, and in collecting for the poor and indigent, which
are the true uses and ends whereto the Sabbath was ordained.
But other some spend the Sabbath day (for the most part) in
frequenting of bawdy stage plays and interludes, in maintaining lords of misrule (for so they call a certain kind of play
which they use) May games, church ales, feasts and wakes: in
piping, dancing, dicing, carding, bowling, tennis-playing: in
bear-baiting, cock-fighting, hawking, hunting, and such like.
In keeping of fairs, and markets on the Sabbath. In keeping
courts and leets. In football-playing, and such other devilish
pastimes: reading of lascivious and wanton books, and an
infinite number of such like practices and profane exercises
used upon that day, whereby the Lord God is dishonoured,
his Sabbath violated, his word neglected, his sacraments
contemned and his people marvelously corrupted, and carried away from true virtue and godliness. Lord remove these
exercises from thy Sabbath.

105

SPUDEUS.   You will be deemed too Stoical, if you should restrain men from these exercises upon the Sabbath, for they suppose, that, that day was ordained and consecrate to that end and purpose, only to use what kind of exercises they think good themselves, and was it not so?

PHIL.   After that the Lord Our God had created the world, and all things therein contained, in six days, in the seventh day he rested from all his works (that is, from creating them, not from governing them) and therefore he commanded that the seventh day should be kept holy in all ages to the end of the world: then after that in effect two thousand years, he iterated this commandment, when he gave the law in mount Horeb to Moses, and in him to all the children of Israel, saying, remember (forget it not) that thou keep holy the seventh day etc. If we must keep it holy, then must we not spend it in such vain exercises, as please ourselves, but in such godly exercises as he in his holy word hath commanded. And (in my judgement) the Lord Our God ordained the seventh day to be kept holy, for four causes especially. First, to put us in mind of his wonderful workmanship, and creation of the world and creatures besides. Secondly, that his word (the church assembling together) might be preached, interpreted and expounded, his sacraments ministered sincerely according to the prescript of his word, and that suffrages and prayers both private and public might be offered to his excellent majesty. Thirdly, for that every Christian man might repose himself from corporal labour, to the end they might the better sustain the travails of the week to ensue, and also to the end, that all beasts and cattle, which the Lord hath made for man's use, as helps and adjuments unto him in his daily affairs and business, might rest and refresh themselves, the better to go through in their travails afterward. For, as the heathen Pan knew very well, *sine alterna requie, non est durabile quicquam.* Without some rest or repose, there is not anything durable, or able to continue long. Fourthly, to the end it might be a typical figure, or signitor to point (as it were) with the finger, and to cipher forth and shadow unto us that blessed rest and thrice happy joy which the faithful shall possess after the day of judgement in the kingdom of heaven. Wherefore, seeing the Sabbath was instituted for these causes, it is manifest, that it was not appointed for the maintenance of wicked and ungodly pastimes and vain pleasures of the flesh, which God abhoreth, and all good men from their hearts do loathe and detest.

The man of whom we read in the law, for gathering of a few small sticks upon the Sabbath, was stoned to death, by the commandment of God from the theatre of heaven.

Than if he were stoned for gathering a few sticks upon the Sabbath day, which in cases might be, for necessity's sake, and did it, but once, what shall they be, who all the Sabbath days of their life give themselves to nothing else, but to wallow in all kind of wickedness and sin, to the great contempt both of the Lord, and his Sabbath? And though they have played the lazy lurdens all the week before, yet that day of set purpose, they will toil and labour, in contempt of the Lord and his Sabbath. But let them be sure, as he that gathered sticks upon the Sabbath, was stoned for his contempt of the same so shall they be stoned, yea grinded to pieces for their contempt of the Lord in his Sabbath . . .

But (perchance) you will ask me, whether the true use of the Sabbath consist in outward abstaining from bodily labour and travail? I answer no: the true use of the Sabbath (for Christians are not bound only to the ceremony of the day) consisteth as I have said, in hearing the word of God truly preached, thereby to learn and to do his will, in receiving the sacraments (as seals of his grace towards us) rightly administered, in using public and private prayer, in thanksgiving to God for all his benefits, in singing of godly psalms and other spiritual exercises and meditations, in collecting for the poor, in doing of good works: and briefly in the true obedience of the inward man. And yet notwithstanding, we must abstain from the one, to attend upon the other: that is, we must refrain all bodily labours, to the end that we may the better be resident at these spiritual exercises upon the Sabbath day. This is the true use and end of the Lord his Sabbath, who grant that we may rest in him for ever.

OXFORDSHIRE ARCHDEACONRY COURT, 1584

The ecclesiastical courts not only survived the reformation but expanded their business to regulate the social, moral and religious affairs of both clergy and laity. Periodic visitations by archdeacons, bishops and archbishops always discovered a host of irregularities in need of correction. The church used sanctions of public penance and temporary excommunication to reform popular culture, to improve godly conduct, and to standardize worship with the Book of Common Prayer. Serious offenders were made to dress in a white gown, hold a white candle, and publicly recite before the assembled congregation the details of their crime and their apology. These extracts from an Elizabethan archdeaconry court act book may be compared to the later archiepiscopal returns from the reign of Charles I. They reveal the reactions of ordinary people to the disciplinary activity of the church.

Source: E. R. Brinkworth (ed.), *The Archdeacon's Court: Liber Actorum, 1584,* Oxfordshire Record Society, vol. 23 (Oxford, 1942), pp. 24–52, 124–5.

Richard Cumber of St Ebbe's parish, for brawling in the church and churchyard upon Easter day . . . denied that he did either chide or brawl in the church or churchyard, saving that being urged thereunto by the churchman who called him arrant knave, said that he was not so arrant a knave as the said churchman Matthew Atkins was a lousy knave, and this was all that he said. (Dismissed with warning.)

Margerie Brasehead of Over Hayford, for having a child being not married.

John Hore of the same, for getting of the said Margerie with child. (Made to perform public penance.)

Richard Pym and John Darling, alemen, for molesting the minister in the time of service and the preacher in his sermon . . . said that on Tuesday in the Whitsun week at service time and in the time of sermon there came a stranger into the church with a painted cloth on his back, one William Powell's man of Horton, and otherwise there was no disorder either in the church or churchyard all the holidays. (Dismissed.)

John Stephens and Thomas Cross, the alemen of Blackthorne, for keeping of evil rule in the time of service at their alehouse . . . acknowledged that in time of divine service on Monday in the Whitsun week there was some resort of people to their alehouse, but not at any time other. (Dismissed with warning.)

Gilbert Major of Haley, for working on the holy days . . . denied that he doth usually work either on the Sabbath or festival day, saving on a holiday upon urgent occasion he was constrained to take a few faggots out of the way where they might easily have been lost. (Dismissed.)

Richard East of Suncombe, admitted that he did not communicate this last Easter because his conscience was troubled by the evil speech of Katherine Ginacre, but doth not refuse the Lord's table upon any scruple in religion or otherwise. (Ordered to take communion.)

Thomas Pauling of Stanlake, for not lying with his wife.

Richard Disell of St Nicholas's parish, for working on St John's day last, making of hay.

George Stockton and John Ragnell of Oxford, for bowling in the service time.

Eleanor Stanton of St Ebbe's parish, for scolding in service time . . . said that one William Dawson of the parish of St Magdalen's came divers times unto her and requested her of marriage, and they being promised between themselves with faith and truth the one to the other as man and wife, thereupon she yielded herself unto him and saith that he hath known her carnally and feareth that he hath begotten her with child. (Ordered to perform penance.)

Thomas Hall of Bicester, for shearing of sheep on the Sunday . . . saith he did but help his neighbour who had his sheep in despair. (Dismissed with warning.)

John Hill of Bampton, for incontinency with Mary Child, servant to widow Buckley . . . denied that he had ever attempted her chastity and denied that he frequented the house of the said widow, for that he doth till her land and her other business. (Dismissed.)

Thomas Bradley, curate of Charlbury, for marrying of William Rauckley in Advent.

John Pawling and John Powke, churchwardens of Goring, for dancing and bowling in the churchyard and suffering the same to be digged with swine, and bowling there used . . . acknowledged that some of the town did use to bowl in the churchyard about the procession way, and about half a year ago curate Wright did keep hogs there sometimes. (Dismissed with warning.)

William Horne and Robert Chamberlain, churchwardens of Wootton, for not presenting of evil rule done in the church by the Lord and Lady on Midsummer day . . . said that there was no Lord or Lady this year in Wootton parish, but on Midsummer day last year at evening prayer the youth were somewhat merry together in crowning of lords, and otherwise they know no disorder at all. (Dismissed.)

Richard Huckwell and William Fletcher, churchwardens of Spilsbury, their church hath no scripture written on the walls and the glass windows are broken . . . admitted that their church windows are somewhat in decay. (Ordered to certify repairs.)

James Layon for working on Sundays and holy days . . . acknowledged that upon necessity he hath wrought upon some Sundays in the morning, but notwithstanding he hath orderly kept his divine service. (Dismissed with warning.)

William White of Charlbury, for keeping together with Mary Gillett in one house. Mary Gillett admitted that she doth and hath used the company of William White, who is contracted to her before sufficient witness and meaneth to marry her as soon as he is out of service. (Dismissed.)

John Castell and Robert Mesie, churchwardens of Dunstew, for keeping interludes and plays in the church, and brawling in the church about the same with one old Poulton, and caused Poulton to be cited to Dr Floyd's court, and also for shooting and gaming in the churchyard upon their wake-day at evening prayer . . . acknowledged there was an interlude played in the church of Dunstew upon a Saturday in the evening after service was done about three weeks or a month ago, but by whom they know not, nor whose men they were. And by the consent of Robert Mesie, one of the churchwardens. And they say further that there was no brawling with Poulton at that time. But John Castell saith that he caused Poulton to be cited before Master Doctor Floyd because he burdened him for presenting (Castell's) daughter for disquieting of her neighbours, and also called this same John Castell false forsworn knave. They confess further that upon the Sunday after our first Lady day, being their wake day, there were certain strangers which were at their wake which did shoot at the time of evening prayer.

WILLIAM ALLEN'S *DEFENCE OF ENGLISH CATHOLICS*, 1584

In this treatise the Catholic apologist William Allen (1532–94) set out to answer William Cecil's tract, *The Execution of Justice in England* (1583), which condemned popery as treason deserving of secular punishment. Allen's *Defence*, on one level, is a Roman Catholic narration of persecution and martyrdom analogous to Foxe's *Acts and Monuments*. It is also a painful reminder of England's very recent Catholic past. Allen's protestations of innocence, while undoubtedly true for the majority of loyal Elizabethan Catholics, were not so easily applied to his own actions at this time. He was deeply involved in surreptitious Catholic missionary activity in England, and was party to a plot to depose Queen Elizabeth in favour of the Catholic King Philip of Spain. The founder of the English Jesuit college in Rome, Allen spent most of his adult life in exile, and in 1587 was made a cardinal of the Roman Catholic church.
Source: William Allen, *A True, Sincere, and Modest Defence of English Catholics* (Ingolstadt, 1584) (STC 373), pp. 209–17.

Though in the deep conceiving of this our country's incomparable offence, our hearts be wholly oppressed with fear and heaviness: yet either the force of our peculiar affection towards our flesh and blood, driving us to hope for better then is deserved; or the largeness of God's immeasurable mercies, yielding, contrary to man's demerits, pardon upon repentance; do cause us oftentimes to expect grace and mercy, rather than extreme rigour and judgement.

In which cogitation it cometh often to our minds, that if any thing avert God's ire from our prince and country, it is the abundance of holy blood shed these late years, and ever since the first revolt. Which though by justice, it might cry rather to God for vengeance (and so it doth in respect of the impenitent, and the clamour thereof shall never be void) yet we trust it sueth for mercy, specially in respect of the infinite number of all estates, that never consented to this iniquity. It is the heroical endeavour of a great many zealous priests and worthy gentlemen that continually offer not only their prayers, and other devout and religious offices, but themselves in sacrifice, for the salvation of their best beloved country. It is the ardent and incessant care of his holiness, seeking our reconcilement with charity unspeakable. It is the general conjunction of all Christian minds in the whole world, towards our recovery. No church, no company, monastery or college of name in Christendom, that with earnest devotion and public fasts and prayers, laboureth not to God for mercy towards us. Finally, even those things and persons, that the adversaries account to be the cause of all their troubles and fears, are indeed the only hope of God's mercy, their own pardon, and our country's salvation.

In which case, to deal as freely for a farewell, and as charitably with the Libeller as he would seem to conclude with us: we wish no more for performance of that he proposeth and partly promiseth, but that he were assured of her majesty's and the council's mind therein: or were of such credit with them, that he could bring that to good effect which in covert words he pretendeth, towards us: which is, that he 'doubteth not but her majesty would shed no more the blood of her natural subjects, nor use any more bodily punishments at all, if they would desist from their practices abroad, from their writing of railing books, and from wandering in disguised apparel within the realm; and would employ their travail in the works of light and doctrine, according to the usage of their schools; and content themselves with their profession and devotion'. So the man speaketh howsoever he meaneth.

But (alas) if any mercy, just or tolerable treaty were meant, or ever had been offered to Catholics upon any reasonable conditions whatsoever; our adversaries had never needed to have fallen to such extreme proceedings with their own flesh and blood: nor ever had any such troubles, fears, or dangers been thought upon, whereof now they have so deep apprehension. If any pitiful ear had ever been given by the superiors to the incessant groans, cries, tears, and supplications of their Catholic subjects, desiring but release of their infinitely distressed consciences, tormented by damnable oaths, articles, and exercises of Calvinism, that were forced upon them: if they might have had either by licence or connivance, in never so few places of the realm, never so secretly, never so inoffensively, the exercise of that faith and religion, which all their forefathers since our country was converted, lived and died in; and in which themselves were baptized; and from which by no law of God nor man they can be compelled, to any sect or rite of religion, which they nor their forefathers ever voluntarily accepted of admitted: if of all the noble churches, colleges, and other inestimable provisions of the realm, founded and made only by Catholics and for Catholics, and for no Protestants nor any their sacrilegious ministries at all, some few had been permitted to the true owners, and to that true worship of God, for which they were instituted: if they might have obtained any piece of that liberty, which Catholics enjoy in Germany, Switzerland, or other places among Protestants; or half the freedom that the Huguenots have in France and other countries: yea, or but so much courtesy as the Christians find among the very Turks; or very Jews among Christians; upon any reasonable or unreasonable tribute (which hath been often in most humble and lamentable sort offered and urged): or (to be short) if any respect, care, or compassion in the world had been had, either of Catholic men's souls, bodies, or goods; our adversaries should never have been troubled nor put in jealousy of so many men's malcontentment at home, nor stand in doubt of the departure and absence of so great a number of nobility and principal gentlemen abroad: they should never have had such colleges and seminaries in other princes' dominions, erected and furnished with English youths, the issue whereof is now, and perhaps will be hereafter more and more wonderful to the world: they should not have been controlled in their heresy so zealously and effectually by the priests created at home of old, or lately ordained and sacred abroad: there should have been no cause of writing so many books for defence of our innocency, and the faith of our forefathers; and for our just complaint to the Christian world, of the intolerable rigour or cruelty used against us . . .

Therefore, if such as govern our state under her majesty at this day, cannot be induced to revoke themselves and the whole realm (which were absolutely the best) to the former Catholic state and condition wherein their ancestors left it, and themselves found it, in respect perhaps of some little check or dishonour which they may conceive would ensue by acknowledging their former error; (though in sincere truth it must needs prove finally more dishonourable and dangerous to persevere): yet at the least, let their wisdoms consider, that their principal worldly error was; that in the beginning, or long since, they gave not liberty of conscience to Catholics (being far the greater and more respective part of the realm) as other of their religion and profession have done, to their own great advantage, in Germany and other provinces adjoining; which error (no doubt) might yet in great part or wholly be redressed, if they would but now at length have some pity of their people: the greater part whereof languisheth away in body and soul most lamentably, only upon an obstinate punto[17] and formality (as is thought) of some few particular adversaries, who will not seem to yield in any one iota or circumstance, though never so much commodity might ensue thereof.

Which matter of liberty of conscience we move not perchance, for our own benefit so much, as for our adversary's weal, and worldly security, whereof they will seem to have both mistrust and solicitude. And perhaps the wisdom of God will sound otherwise and say to us, *Nescitis quid petatis*.[18] judging it to be far more to his honour and glory, and the briefer way to salvation of our whole nation, and of more souls in particular, that we should pass through this persecution, and win our own and our brethren's salvation by our blood. And indeed if the German Catholics had been so restrained, persecuted, and put to death, as the English have been these years; and had not gone by halves with the Protestants as in some places they have done: they had had perhaps far more Catholics at this day, and them more zealous; and their whole nation (perchance) reduced ere this: which now, for the Protestants, standeth not so much on their religion or conscience in heresy; as upon their mutual peace, concord, and concurrence with Catholics.

Well, what were best for us in this case God only knoweth. *Nos humanum dicimus propter infirmatem nostram,*[19] as the apostle speaketh. But sure we are, that the first best for our English nation, as well prince as people, were both in respect of God and the world; of themselves, and other men; to restore the state again to the obedience of God's church, and to the happy fellowship of all their forefathers, and other faithful people and princes now living. The next best were in respect of their own security and perpetuity (if the first may not take place) to desist from persecuting their Catholic subjects and brethren, and to grant some liberty for exercise of their consciences, divine offices, and holy devotions; that so they may pray for her majesty and councillors as their patrons, whom now they pray for only as their persecutors.

If to none of these conditions they can be brought, but will have our bodies, goods, life and souls: then let Our Lord God the just arbiter of all things, and judge of princes as well as poor men, and the only comforter of the afflicted, discern our cause. In whose holy name, word and promise, we confidently tell them, and humbly even in Christ's blood pray them, to consider of it; that by no human force or wisdom they shall ever extinguish the Catholic party, overcome the holy church, or prevail against God.

WILLIAM PERKINS, *A GOLDEN CHAIN, OR THE DESCRIPTION OF THEOLOGY*, 1590

William Perkins (1558-1602) was a non-separatist, non-conformist theologian whose influence over Cambridge students was legendary and whose works enjoyed a remarkable authority in the seventeenth century. *A Golden Chaine* was first published in Latin in 1590; it went through fifteen editions, in several languages, over the next twenty years. Perkins combines a meticulous and systematic exposition of Protestant thought with practical and pastoral concerns. Perkins's non-conformity was considered 'Puritan' but his theological style was within the bounds of a 'Calvinist consensus' that characterized the doctrinal politics of the Elizabethan and Jacobean church. Source: William Perkins, *A Golden Chaine, or, the Description of Theologie, containing the order of the causes of salvation and damnation, according to God's word* (Cambridge, 1600 edn) (*STC* 19646), pp. 23, 113–21, 163–7, 176–9.

Of election, and of Jesus Christ the foundation thereof

Predestination hath two parts: election and reprobation (I Thessalonians 5:9). Election is God's decree, whereby on his own free will he hath ordained certain men to salvation, to the praise of the glory of his grace (Ephesians 1:4–6) . . .

Of the degrees of executing God's decree of election

The degrees are in number two: the love of God and the declaration of his love (Ephesians 1:6,9). God's love is that, whereby God doth freely love all such as are chosen in Jesus Christ, though in themselves altogether corrupt (I John 4:19; Romans 5:8, 10).

The declaration of God's love is twofold. The first, towards infants elected to salvation, the second, towards men of riper years. The declaration of God's love towards infants is on this manner: infants already elected, albeit they in the womb of their mother before they were born, or presently after, depart this life, they, I say, being after a secret and unspeakable manner by God's spirit engrafted into Christ, obtain eternal salvation (I Corinthians 12:13; Luke 1:35, 41, 64, 80; Jeremiah 1:5).

I call the manner of infants' salvation secret and unspeakable, because: (1) They want actual faith to receive Christ, for actual faith necessarily presupposeth a knowledge of God's free promise, the which he that believeth, doth apply unto himself; but this, infants cannot any ways possibly perform. And surely if infants should have faith actually, they generally either lose it when they come to men's estate, or at least show no signs thereof, both which they could not do, if before they had received actual faith. Nay we see that in those of riper years, there are not so much as the shadows or sparks of faith to be seen, before they be called by the

114

preaching of the Gospel. (2) Infants are said to be regenerated only in regard of their internal qualities and inclinations, not in regard of any motions, or actions of the mind, will, or affections. And therefore they want those terrors of conscience, which come before repentance as occasions thereof, in such as are of riper years of discretion. Again, they are not troubled with that conflict and combat betwixt the flesh and the spirit, wherewith those faithful ones that are of more years are marvellously exercised.

Concerning the first degree of the declaration of God's love

The declaration of God's love in those of years of discretion hath especially four degrees (Romans 8:30; I Corinthians 1:30). The first decree is an effectual calling, whereby a sinner being severed from the world, is entertained into God's family (Ephesians 2:17, 19). Of this there be two parts. The first is election, which is a separation of a sinner from the cursed estate of all mankind (John 15:19). The second is the reciprocal donation or free gift of God the father, whereby he bestoweth the sinful man to be saved upon Christ, and Christ again actually and most effectually upon that sinful man, so that he may boldly say this thing, namely Christ, both God and man, is mine, and I for my benefit and use enjoy the same. The like we see in wedlock: the husband saith, this woman is my wife, whom her parents have given unto [me],[20] so that, she being fully mine, I may both have her and govern her. Again, the woman may say, this man is mine husband, who hath bestowed himself upon me, and doth cherish me as his wife (Romans 8:32; Isaiah 9:6; John 17:2, 6–7; John 10:29).

Hence cometh that admirable union, or conjunction, which is the engrafting of such as are to be saved into Christ, and their growing up together with him; so that after a peculiar manner, Christ is made the head, and every repentant sinner, a member of his mystical body (John 17:20–1; Ephesians 2:20; John 25:1–2; Ephesians 2:20–2) . . .

A member of Christ is diversely distinguished, and is so either before men or God. Before men they are the members of Christ, who outwardly professing the faith are charitably reputed by the church as true members. But such deceiving at length both themselves and the church, may be reprobates: and therefore in God's presence they are no more true members, than are the noxious humours in a man's body, or a wooden leg or other joint cunningly fastened to another part of the body . . .

Again, members before God, they are such as either are decreed to be so, or actually are so already. Such as are decreed to be so, are they, who, being elect from all eternity, are either as yet not born, or not called (John 10:16).

Actual members of Christ are either living or dying members. An actual living member of Christ is every one elected, which being engrafted by faith and the spirit into Christ, doth feel and shew forth the power of Christ in him.

An actual dying or decaying member is every one truly engrafted into Christ, and yet hath no feeling of the power and efficacy of the quickening spirit in him. He is like unto a benumbed leg without sense, which indeed is part of a man's body, and yet receiveth no nourishment. Such are those faithful ones, who for a time do faint and are overcome under the heavy burden of temptations and their sins; such are also those excommunicate persons, who in regard of their engrafting are true members, howsoever in regard of the external communion with the church and efficacy of the spirit they are not members, till such time as, they being touched with repentance, do begin, as it were, to live again.

God executeth this effectual calling by certain means. The first is the saving hearing of the word God . . . The second is the mollifying of the heart, the which must be bruised in pieces, that it may be fit to receive God's saving grace offered unto it . . . The third is faith, which is a miraculous and supernatural faculty of the heart, apprehending Christ Jesus, being applied by the operation of the Holy Ghost, and receiving him to itself (John 1:12; 6:35; Romans 9:30) . . .

In the work of faith there are four degrees, or motions of the heart, linked and united together, and are worthy the consideration of every Christian.

The first is knowledge of the gospel, by the illumination of God's spirit (Isaiah 53:11; John 7:3) . . . The second is hope of pardon, whereby a sinner, albeit he yet feeleth not that his sins are certainly pardoned, yet he believeth that they are pardonable (Luke 15:18). The third is an hungering and thirsting after that grace which is offered to him in Christ Jesus, as a man hungereth and thirsteth after meat and drink (John 6:35; 7:37; Revelation 21:6; Matthew 5:6). The fourth is the approaching to the throne of grace, that there flying from the terror of the law, he may take hold of Christ and find favour with God (Hebrews 4:16) . . . The fifth, arising of the former, is an especial persuasion imprinted in the heart by the Holy Ghost, whereby every faithful man doth particularly apply unto himself those promises which are made in the gospel (Matthew 9:2; 15:28; Galatians 2:20). This persuasion is, and ought to be, in every one, even before he have any experience of God's mercies (Matthew 15:22–7; John 20:29; Hebrews 11:1).

In philosophy, we first see a thing true by experience, and afterward give our assent unto it. As in natural philosophy: I am persuaded that such a water is hot, because when I put mine hand into it, I perceive by experience an hot quality. But in the practice of faith it is quite contrary. For first, we must consent to the word of God, resisting all doubt and diffidence, and afterward will an experience and feeling of comfort follow (II Chronicles 20:20) . . .

Concerning the decree of reprobation

The decree of reprobation is that part of predestination whereby God, according to the most free and just purpose of his will, hath determined to reject certain men unto eternal destruction and misery, and that to the praise of his justice (Romans 9:21; I Peter 2:8; Jude 5:4; I Thessalonians 5:9). In the scriptures, Cain and Abel, Ishmael and Isaac, Esau and Jacob, are propounded unto us as types of mankind partly elected and partly rejected.

Neither do we here set down any absolute decree of damnation, as though we should think that any were condemned by the mere and alone will of God, without any causes inherent in such as are to be condemned . . . Again, the decree of God is secret: (1) Because it ariseth only from the good pleasure of God, unsearchable and adored of the very angels themselves. (2) Because it is not known but by that which is after it, namely by the effects thereof.

Concerning the execution of the decree of reprobation

Reprobates are either infants or men of riper age. In reprobate infants, the execution of God's decree is this: as soon as they are born, for the guilt of original and natural sin being left in God's secret judgement unto themselves, they dying are rejected of God for ever (Romans 5:14; 9:11). Reprobates of riper age are of two sorts: they that are called (namely by an uneffectual calling) and they that are not called. In the reprobates which are called the execution of the decree of reprobation hath three decrees, to wit, an acknowledgement of God's calling, a falling away again, and condemnation.

The acknowledgement of God's calling is whereby the reprobates for a time do subject themselves to the calling of God, which calling is wrought by the preaching of the word (Matthew 22:14). And of this calling there are five other degrees.

The first is an enlightening of their minds, whereby they are instructed of the Holy Ghost to the understanding and knowledge of the word (Hebrews 6:4; 2 Peter 2:20).

117

The second is a certain penitency, whereby the reprobate: (1) doth acknowledge his sin; (2) is pricked with the feeling of God's wrath for sin; (3) is grieved for the punishment of sin; (4) doth confess his sin; (5) acknowledgeth God to be just in punishing sin; (6) desireth to be saved; (7) promiseth repentence in his misery or affliction, in these words, 'I will sin no more' (Matthew 27:3; Hebrews 12:17; I Kings 21:27; Numbers 23:10; Psalms 78:32–5).

The third degree is a temporary faith, whereby the reprobate doth confusedly believe the promises of God made in Christ. I say *confusedly*, because he believeth that some shall be saved, but he believeth not that he himself particularly shall be saved, because he being content with a general faith, doth never apply the promises of God to himself, neither doth he so much as conceive any purpose, desire, or endeavor to apply the same, or any wrestling or striving against security or carelessness and distrust (James 2:19; Matthew 13:20–1; John 2:23–4).

The fourth is a tasting of heavenly gifts: as of justification and of sanctification, and of the virtues of the world to come. This tasting is merely[21] a sense in the hearts of the reprobates, whereby they do perceive and feel the excellency of God's benefits, notwithstanding they do not enjoy the same. For it is one thing to taste of dainties at a banquet, and another thing to feed and to be nourished thereby (Hebrews 6:4).

The fifth degree is the outward holiness of life for a time, under which is comprehended a zeal in the profession of religion, a reverence and fear towards God's ministers, and amendment of life in many things (Mark 6:20; Acts 18:13; Hosea 6:4).

The second degree of the execution of God's counsel of reprobation in men of ripe age which are called, is a falling away again, which for the most part is effected and wrought after this manner. First, the reprobate is deceived by some sin. Secondly, his heart is hardened by the same sin. Thirdly, his heart being hardened, it becommeth wicked and perverse. Fourthly, then followeth his incredulity and unbelief, whereby he consenteth not to God's word, when he hath heard and known it. Fifthly, an apostacy, or falling away from faith in Christ, doth immediately follow this unbelief (Hebrews 3:12–13; I Timothy 1:9) . . . After apostacy followeth pollution, which is the very fullness of all iniquity, altogether contrary to sanctification (Genesis 15:16).

The third degree is damnation, whereby the reprobates are delivered up to eternal punishment. The execution of damnation beginneth in death, and is finished in the last judgement (Luke 16:22) . . .

Of the application of predestination

The judgement and discerning of a man's own predestination is to be performed by means of these rules which follow.

I. The elect alone, and all they that are elect, not only may be, but also in God's good time are, sure of election in Christ to eternal life (I Corinthians 2:12; II Corinthians 13:5).

II. They have not this knowledge from the first causes of election, but rather from the last effects thereof; and they are especially two: the testimony of God's spirit, and the works of sanctification (II Peter 1:10; Romans 8:16).

III. If any doubt of this testimony it will appear unto them, whether it come from the spirit of God, or of their own carnal presumption . . .

IV. If the testimony of God's spirit be not so powerful in the elect, then may they judge of their election by that other effect of the Holy Ghost, namely, sanctification. Like as we use to judge by heat that there is fire when we cannot see the flame itself.

V. And of all the effects of sanctification, these are most notable: (1) To feel our wants, and in the bitterness of heart to bewail the offense of God in every sin. (2) To strive against the flesh; that is, to resist and to hate the ungodly motions thereof, and with grief to think them burdenous and troublesome. (3) To desire earnestly and vehemently the grace of God and merit of Christ to obtain eternal life. (4) When it is obtained, to account it a most precious jewel (Philippians 3:8). (5) To love the minister of God's word in that he is a minister, and a Christian in that he is a Christian; and for that cause, if need require, to be ready to spend our blood with them (Matthew 10:41; I John 3:16). (6) To call upon God earnestly, and with tears. (7) To desire and love Christ's coming and the day of judgement, that an end may be made of the days of sin. (8) To fly all occasions of sin, and seriously to endeavour to come to newness of life. (9) To persevere in these things to the last gasp of life. Luther hath a good sentence for this purpose: 'He that will serve God, must', saith he, 'believe that which cannot be seen, hope for that which is deferred, and love God, when he showeth himself an enemy, and thus remain to the end'.

VI. Now, if so be all the effects of the spirit are very feeble in the godly, they must know this, that God trieth them, yet so, as they must not therewith be dismayed, because it is most sure, that if they have faith but as much as a grain of mustard seed, and be as weak as a young infant is, it is sufficient to engraft them into Christ; and therefore they must not doubt of their election because they see their faith feeble and the effects of the Holy Ghost faint within them.

VII. Neither must he, that as yet hath not felt in his heart any of these effects, presently conclude that he is a reprobate, but let him rather use the word of God and the sacraments, that he may have an inward sense of the power of Christ drawing him unto him, and an assurance of his redemption by Christ's death and passion.

VIII. No man may peremptorily set down that himself or any other is a reprobate. For God doth oftentime prefer those which did seem to be most of all estranged from his favour, to be in his kingdom above those who in man's judgement were the children of the kingdom. Hence is it that Christ saith: 'The publicans and harlots go before you', and 'many a one is called at the eleventh hour', as appeareth by that notable example of the thief upon the cross.

The uses which may be made of this doctrine of predestination are very many. First, for our instruction, we are taught these things:

I. That there is neither any justification by works, nor any works of ours that are meritorious. For election is by the free grace of God and therefore in like sort is justification. For, as I said before, the cause of the cause is the cause of the thing caused. And for this reason, in the work of salvation grace doth wholly challenge all to itself (Romans 11:5; 2 Timothy 1:9; Philippians 1:29; Romans 3:24; Titus 3:5; Ezekiel 36:27; Romans 6:23).

II. That astrology, teaching by the casting of nativities what men will be, is ridiculous and impious, because it determineth that such shall be very like in life and conversation, whom God in his predestination hath made unlike . . .

III. That God is most wise, omnipotent, just and merciful (Ephesians 1:5).

Secondly, being the servants of God we are admonished:

I. To fight against all doubting and diffidence of our salvation, because it neither dependeth upon works, nor faith, but upon God's decree which is immutable (Matthew 24:24; Luke 10:20; Romans 8:33; 2 Timothy 2:19). This teacheth that the anchor of hope must be fixed in the truth and stability of the immutable good pleasure of God, so that, albeit our faith be so tossed as that it is in danger of shipwreck, nevertheless it must never sink to the bottom, but even in the midst of danger take hold upon repentance, as on a board, and so recover itself.

II. To humble our souls under the mighty hand of God, for we are as clay in the hand of the potter (Romans 9:21).

III. To give all glory to God (Thessalonians 2:13).

IV. To bear crosses patiently (Romans 8:29; Philippians 3:10).

V. To do good works (Ephesians 2:10).

SAMUEL WARD'S DIARY, 1595

The diary of Samuel Ward (1572–1643), written while a student at Cambridge, records the profound religious self-consciousness of this budding Calvinist academic. For him, and for like-minded Puritans, God was the constant judge and companion of his life. His diary was a register of the tribulations of conscience as well as a record of providences.

SAMUEL WARD

Ward later served as a royal chaplain, professor of divinity, and master of Sidney
Sussex College.
Source: M. M. Knappen (ed.), *Two Elizabethan Puritan Diaries* (London, 1933), pp.
104–8.

25 May Think how blockish men are that never think of God and their
salvation. Remember God's mercy toward thee, in giving thee grace at the
end of thy prayer to pray heartily unto thee, whereas in the beginning thou
wast blockish. Thy unwillingness to pray and thy backwardness to any good
exercise of Christianity. Think of the good motion which God put in thy
mind, that is of the frowardness and backwardness to serve God. How that
it is a very preposterous thing that, seeing God hath set us in this world,
especially to serve him and glorify, and how that nothing conduceth more
to the true service and glory of God than often to hear his word, to call
upon him, and other such Christian exercises, yet for a man to be weary of
this service, yea to think much to call twice a day upon God, or to serve
him one day in a week. A man must therefore labour above all things for
alacrity in God's service. And I must learn to desire more after the Sundays
than the Mondays.

26 May How God gave this morning, being Sunday, before thou rise,
some good meditation against wearisomeness in God's service. Thy
dullness this day in hearing God's word. Thy carelessness and impotency
in exhorting thy Christian brethren. Thy unwillingness to pray. The little
affection I had in praying in S. J.'s study. Remember thy promise now, when
thou art not well, how if God restore thee to health thou wilt be careful to
perform all Christian duties. Remember this.

27 May Thy overmuch delight in these transitory pleasures of this world.

28 May How it pleased God to detain the sense of my sins from me in
my prayer, howsoever I called often for the sight thereof, but I must
attribute it to mine own wants in prayer. How it pleased God to give
thee some insight into the state of salvation at thy evening prayers. Thy
conceit of God, not as he is omnipotent, omnipresent, most just, most
good, most merciful.

29 May How it pleased God to give you grace to pray in the morning.
How that upon Mr Nowell's death we took occasion, M. W., S. S. and I, to

121

talk much upon the vanity of this life. My negligence in calling to mind Mr Sheaf his sermon.

30 May   My negligence in my studies. My ignorance in a special point of divinity, of our sanctification. How that I can hardly be brought to make profession of God externally. How it pleased God to give me grace to call upon him at night.

31 May   My not feeling of the reverence which I ought to have in the sight of God. My want of preparation for the Sabbath ensuing.

1 June   My late rising in the morning to sanctify the Sabbath. My negligence all that day, and idleness in performing the duties of the Sabbath. My want in not meditating sufficiently on the creatures, as also in prayer. My by talk in the bed, of other matters than are not meet to be talked of on the Sabbath. My ill dream . . .

14 June   My negligence in not calling upon God before I went to the chapel, and the little desire I had there to call on God, and my drowsiness in God's service. My sins even through the whole day, being Sunday: (1) My negligence aforesaid. (2) My hearing of the sermon without that sense which I should have had. (3) In not praying to God to bless it to me afterward. (4) In not talking of good things at dinner, being the *posteriorums* day.[22] (5) In the immoderate use of God's creatures. (6) In sleeping immediately after dinner. (7) In not preparing me to sermon till it tolled. (8) In sluggish hearing of God's words, and that for my great dinner. (9) In hearing another sermon sluggishly. (10) In returning home and omitting our repetition of sermons, by reason my countryman Eubanks was with me. (11) In not exhorting him to any good thing. (12) In not going to evening prayers. (13) In supping liberally, never remembering our poor brethren. (14) In not taking order to give the poor women somewhat at seven o'clock. (15) My dullness in stirring of my brother to Christian meditations. (16) My want of affections in hearing the sermons repeated. (17) My sluggishness in prayer, and thus sin I daily against thee, O Lord.

4

THE JACOBEAN CHURCH

BISHOP MATTHEW'S REPORT ON THE HAMPTON COURT CONFERENCE, 1604

James I convened the Hampton Court Conference to enquire into the complaints and concerns of English Puritans, whose pleas for a more reformed church were revived when the Scottish king ascended to the English throne. Representatives from both the Puritan and conformist clergy assembled to debate issues of clerical education and maintenance, ecclesiastical discipline and church ceremonies. Tobie Matthew (1546–1628) attended as Bishop of Durham. In his report to the Archbishop of York, Matthew presents the conference as a model of decorum, moderation and 'princely clemency' towards the Puritans, whose hopes for further reformation were disappointed. Only one Puritan petition at the conference bore successful fruit, though it is not mentioned in Matthew's account. This was the plan for a new translation of the Bible, completed in 1611 under King James's patronage as the 'Authorized Version'. Source: Edward Cardwell, *A History of Conferences and Other Proceedings Connected with the Revision of the Book of Common Prayer from the Year 1558 to the Year 1690* (Oxford, 1840), pp. 161–6.

May it please your grace: Upon Thursday the 12th of January, my lord's grace of Canterbury, with the Bishops of London, Durham, Winchester, Worcester, St David's, Chichester, Carlisle, Peterborough, and myself, out of the privy chamber, were sent for by his majesty into an inner withdrawing chamber; where in a very private manner, and in as few words, but with most gracious countenance, he imparted to us, first, the cause wherefore we were called up; which was, for the reformation of some things amiss in ecclesiastical matters, supposed, and by some complained of. Next, how desirous he was, and we ought to be, that the kingdom of Ireland might be reduced to the true knowledge of God, and true obedience. To which latter, without the former, he could never hope to find among them. Lastly, his majesty gave us to understand, that the day was somewhat mistaken, being meant by him to be the Saturday after: at which time his majesty willed us to repair to the court again.

Which, when we did accordingly, his highness, about eleven of the clock, in his privy chamber, in the presence of the privy council only, sitting on his right hand, and all the bishops on his left, made an excellent oration of an hour long, declaring, that religion was the soul of a kingdom, and unity the life of religion. That as both among the Jews and the heathen, so among the Christian emperors, their chiefest care was first to establish God's worship. And that in this realm of England, as sundry of the kings had been religious in their kind, of ancient time, so in this latter age there had been made divers alterations; as, by King Henry the Eighth in some points; by King Edward in many more; by Queen Mary, who crossed them both; and lastly, by Queen Elizabeth, who reformed her sister's superstitions, and established the church of God here, in the doctrine of Christ, and discipline agreeable to the same. Whereunto, because some preachers in sundry parts of the realm did not so submit themselves, but that some contradiction and discontentment did arise long since, and increase of late, little less than to a schism (a point most perilous as well to the common weal as to the church) therefore he had convened us, the reverend fathers, to consult with us: first, apart from our opposites, for avoiding contention towards us and them, and for his own resolutions in some particulars, which the contrary faction imputed partly to the Book of Common Prayer, and partly to the form of church government here. Which said particulars were: (1) The form of absolution after the public confession of sins. (2) The manner of confirmation of children. (3) The toleration of private baptism to be done by laymen or women. (4) Many great errors and abuses, crept in under the title of excommunication, and by the corrupt dealing of chancellors, officials, etc. Against all which his majesty did argue and dispute at large.

And after answer severally made by my lords grace of Canterbury, and the bishops of London and Winchester chiefly, his highness so scholastically and effectually replied, that what with rejoining and surrejoining, four long hours were spent in that day's conference, to our exceeding great admiration of his majesty's not only rhetorical and logical, but theological and juridical discourses. As also, in the end, to his good satisfaction in all such objections as he propounded; giving present order, that for the present clearing of some doubts and misconstructions here and there, some few words, not in the body of the sense, but in the rubrics, or titles, of some of the aforesaid particulars, should, in the next edition of the common prayer book, be inserted, by way rather of some explanation, than of any alteration at all.

Upon Monday his majesty appointed certain of the best learned of the preciser sort to be before him in the privy chamber, to hear what they could object; viz. Dr Reynolds, Dr Sparke, Mr Chatterton, and Mr Knewstubbs: to whom his highness used more short and round speech: and admitted only two bishops to be present, to be named by my lords grace of Canterbury; who sent thither the bishops of London and Winchester, while we the rest were with him, setting down the form of the former points. The doctors named divers abuses, but insisted chiefly upon the confirmation, the cross in baptism, the surplice, private baptism, kneeling at the communion, reading of the *Apocrypha*, subscriptions to the Book of Common Prayer and articles; one only translation of the Bible to be authentical, and read in the church; the censure of excommunication for so small causes; the corruptions in the bishops' and archdeacons' courts, committed by their chancellors, commissaries, officials, registers, and such like officers; together with their immoderate exactions and fees, to be reformed. Of all which, as also concerning the oath (upon many and sundry catching articles unto the preachers) *ex officio,* to entangle them: which one of them compared to the Spanish inquisition.

After that his majesty had, in most excellent and extraordinary manner, disputed and debated with them, and confuted their objections; being therein assisted now and then, for variety sake rather than for necessity, by the two bishops before-named, from eleven of the clock until after four; with some sharp words among, he favourably dismissed them for that time; requiring them to give their attendance here again on the Wednesday after, before himself and his council, and all the bishops, to receive such order and directions as he should be pleased to give therein.

According to which appointment, we and they altogether presented our selves. And after that his majesty had summarily repeated unto us what had passed between him and them on the Monday, and began to set down the courses he would have to be observed in some of the foresaid points in controversy, Mr Chatterton and Mr Knewstubbs moved his highness, with all submission, to have the cross in baptism utterly forborne, and kneeling at the communion. Which being utterly for divers causes denied them, yet by their importunity on behalf of certain preachers in Lancashire, who had taken great pains against the Papists, and done much good among the people, his highness was contented, out of his princely clemency, so far to condescend unto them that a letter should be written to the Bishop of Chester, to bear with their weakness for some time, and not proceed over hastily and roughly against any of them, until, by conference between the bishop and them, they might be persuaded to conform themselves to us, and the rest of their brethren; advising Mr Chatterton and Mr Knewstubbs, by their letters or otherwise, to deal with those preachers to submit themselves to the judgement of the church, and to avoid all singularity, the mother of schisms and disorder.

Which done, his majesty assigned his council and all the bishops forth-with to go and consult together in the council chamber, as well upon the premises that needed any amends, as also how religion might be planted upon the borders of England and Scotland, and likewise in Wales, but especially in his kingdom of Ireland; wherein he made demonstration of his exceedingly princely care and godly zeal, with most vehement and deep impression in all our ears and hearts, for the salvation of the souls of that forlorn people, and for the discharge of his own and all our Christian duties. Naming withal some whom he thought fittest to be employed, to take care for the expedition of that principal design.

Immediately whereupon, all the most honourable privy council and we going together, agreed to set down several courses for the better perfor-mance of all and every the matters aforementioned: some of them and us to employ our selves, some in one thing and some in another. The copy of which general project I will send your grace so soon as I can procure it of my lord Cecil: to whom his highness did deliver it to be recorded in the council book: adding thereunto an earnest exhortation and charge unto both the chancellors of the universities there present, and to the bishops, to be much more careful hereafter than heretofore, not to suffer any person in any college, that shall be given to defend any heresy, or disposed to maintain any schismatical tricks, (as he termed them) what other good gifts or eloquence soever they have. For the more learning, saith he, without humility and obedience, the more pernicious to the church and commonweal. Lastly, to look better to the education of noblemen and gentlemen's sons, many of which he was informed to have been by popish tutors and teachers dangerously corrupted.

And requiring the bishops to be so much the more vigilant in their calling, as the adversaries are no less diligent than the Devil himself in perverting the people, we were most benignly and graciously dismissed for that time.

Thus much I thought it my duty in gross to advertise your grace, as I promised, presuming that some other, as Sir John Bennet, hath already or will shortly certify all in more particular: wishing that you had been here at the conference, which in my opinion would have wrought in you as great comfort and joy as ever happened to you in this mortal life; to see and hear so worthy a king and priest in one person, with so sacred a majesty, to propose, discuss, and determine so many, so necessary, and so important matters, so readily, so soundly, as I never look to see or hear the like again. God, even the God of our fathers, prosper and protect his highness and all his posterity, as he hath rejoiced the hearts of all us, his humble and obedient clergy; hoping also, that it will work, if not perfect contentment, yet much more quietness in all those that were before otherwise affected.

CONSTITUTIONS AND CANONS ECCLESIASTICAL, 1604

The Canons of 1604, an explication and codification of English ecclesiastical law, launched the Elizabethan church into the seventeenth century. Drawn up by the bishops in Convocation and endorsed by royal assent, they reiterated the ideals of uniformity and discipline set forth in episcopal visitation articles and the Book of Common Prayer. Ministers who refused to acknowledge by subscription that the prayer book 'containeth in it nothing contrary to the word of God' (Canon 36) were subject to suspension. Canon 30, the longest of all, attempted to assure moderate Puritans that the sign of the cross in baptism was not a popish remnant. Other canons specified standards of religious behaviour for both laity and clergy, with injunctions against indecency, irreverence, immorality and disorder.
Source: *Constitutions and Canons Ecclesiastical* (1604) (*STC* 10069).

5 Impugners of the articles of religion, established in the Church of England, censured

Whosoever shall hereafter affirm, that any of the nine and thirty articles agreed upon by the archbishops and bishops of both provinces, and the whole clergy, in the convocation holden at London, in the year of Our Lord God one thousand five hundred sixty-two, for the avoiding of diversities of opinions, and for the establishing of consent touching true religion, are in any part superstitious or erroneous, or such as he may not with a good conscience subscribe unto, let him be excommunicated *ipso facto*, and not restored, but only by the archbishop, after his repentence, and public revocation of such his wicked errors.

6 Impugners of the rites and ceremonies, established in the Church of England, censured

Whosoever shall hereafter affirm, that the rites and ceremonies of the Church of England by law established are wicked, antichristian, or superstitious, or such as, being commanded by lawful authority, men, who are zealously and godly affected, may not with any good conscience approve them, use them, or, as occasion requireth, subscribe unto them, let him be excommunicated *ipso facto*, and not restored until he repent, and publicly revoke such his wicked errors.

7 *Impugners of the government of the Church of England by archbishops, bishops, etc., censured*

Whosoever shall hereafter affirm, that the government of the Church of England under his majesty by archbishops, bishops, deans, archdeacons, and the rest that bear office in the same, is antichristian, or repugnant to the word of God, let him be excommunicated *ipso facto*, and so continue until he repent, and publicly revoke such his wicked errors.

18 *A reverence and attention to be used within the church in time of divine service*

In the time of divine service, and of every part thereof, all due reverence is to be used; for it is according to the apostle's rule, let all things be done decently and according to order; answerable to which decency and order, we judge these our directions following: No man shall cover his head in the church or chapel in the time of divine service, except he have some infirmity; in which case let him wear a nightcap or coif. All manner of persons then present shall reverently kneel upon their knees, when the general confession, litany, and other prayers are read; and shall stand up at the saying of the belief, according to the rules in that behalf prescribed in the Book of Common Prayer: and likewise when in time of divine service the Lord Jesus shall be mentioned, due and lowly reverence shall be done by all persons present, as it hath been accustomed; testifying by these outward ceremonies and gestures, their inward humility, Christian resolution, and due acknowledgment that the Lord Jesus Christ, the true and eternal Son of God, is the only saviour of the world, in whom alone all the mercies, graces, and promises of God to mankind, for this life, and the life to come, are fully and wholly comprised. None, either man, woman, or child, of what calling soever, shall be otherwise at such times busied in the church, than in quiet attendance to hear, mark, and understand that which is read, preached, or ministered; saying in their due places audibly with the minister, the confession, the Lord's Prayer, and the Creed; and making such other answers to the public prayers, as are appointed in the Book of Common Prayer; neither shall they disturb the service or sermon, by walking or talking, or any other way; nor depart out of the church during the time of service and sermon, without some urgent or reasonable cause.

30 *The lawful use of the cross in baptism explained*

We are sorry that his majesty's most princely care and pains taken in the conference at Hampton Court, amongst many other points, touching this one of the cross in baptism, hath taken no better effect with many, but that still the use of it in baptism is so greatly stuck at and impugned. For the further declaration therefore of the true use of this ceremony, and for the removing of all such scruple as might any ways trouble the consciences of them who are indeed rightly religious, following the royal steps of our most worthy king, because he therein followeth the rules of the scriptures, and the practice of the primitive church; we do commend to all the true members of the Church of England these our directions and observations ensuing . . .

It must be confessed, that in process of time the sign of the cross was greatly abused in the Church of Rome, especially after that corruption of popery had once possessed it. But the abuse of a thing doth not take away the lawful use of it. Nay, so far was it from the purpose of the Church of England to forsake and reject the churches of Italy, France, Spain, or any such like churches, in all things which they held and practised, that, as the *Apology of the Church of England* confesseth, it doth with reverence retain those ceremonies, which doth neither endamage the church of God, nor offend the minds of sober men; and only departed from them in those particular points, wherein they were fallen both from themselves in their ancient integrity, and from the apostolical churches, which were their first founders. In which respect, amongst some other very ancient ceremonies, the sign of the cross in baptism hath been retained in this church, both by the judgement and practice of those reverend fathers and great divines in the days of King Edward the Sixth, of whom some constantly suffered for the profession of the truth; and others being exiled in the time of Queen Mary, did after their return, in the beginning of the reign of our late dread sovereign, continually defend and use the same. This resolution and practice of our church hath been allowed and approved by the censure upon the communion book in King Edward the Sixth his days, and by the harmony of confessions of later years: because indeed the use of this sign in baptism was ever accompanied here with such sufficient cautions and exceptions against all popish superstition and error, as in the like cases are either fit or convenient.

First, the Church of England, since the abolishing of popery, hath ever held and taught, and so doth hold and teach still, that the sign of the cross used in baptism is no part of the substance of that sacrament: for when the minister, dipping the infant in water, or laying water upon the face of it (as the manner also is) hath pronounced these words, 'I baptize thee in the name of the Father, and of the Son, and of the Holy Ghost', the infant is fully and perfectly baptized. So as the sign of the cross being afterwards used, doth neither add any thing to the virtue and perfection

129

of baptism, nor being omitted doth detract any thing from the effect and substance of it.

Secondly, it is apparent in the communion book, that the infant baptized is, by virtue of baptism, before it be signed with the sign of the cross, received into the congregation of Christ's flock, as a perfect member thereof, and not by any power ascribed unto the sign of the cross. So that for the very remembrance of the cross, which is very precious to all them that rightly believe in Jesus Christ, and in the other respects mentioned, the Church of England hath retained still the sign of it in baptism; following therein the primitive and apostolical churches, and accounting it a lawful outward ceremony and honourable badge, whereby the infant is dedicated to the service of him that died upon the cross, as by the words used in the Book of Common Prayer it may appear.

Lastly, the use of the sign of the cross in baptism, being thus purged from all popish superstition and error, and reduced in the Church of England to the primary institution of it, upon those true rules of doctrine concerning things indifferent, which are consonant to the word of God, and the judgement of all the ancient fathers, we hold it the part of every private man, both minister and other, reverently to retain the true use of it prescribed by public authority; considering that things of themselves indifferent do in some sort alter their natures, when they are either commanded or forbidden by a lawful magistrate; and may not be omitted at every man's pleasure, contrary to the law, when they be commanded, nor used when they be prohibited.

74 Decency in apparel enjoined to ministers

The true, ancient, and flourishing churches of Christ, being ever desirous that their prelacy and clergy might be had as well in outward reverence, as otherwise regarded for the worthiness of their ministry, did think it fit, by a prescript form of decent and comely apparel, to have them known to the people, and thereby to receive the honour and estimation due to the special messengers and ministers of Almighty God: we, therefore, following their grave judgement, and the ancient custom of the Church of England, and hoping that in time newfangleness of apparel in some factious persons will die of itself, do constitute and appoint, that the archbishops and bishops shall not intermit to use the accustomed apparel of their degrees. Likewise all deans, masters of colleges, archdeacons, and prebendaries, in cathedral and collegiate churches (being priests or deacons) doctors in divinity, law, and physic, bachelors in divinity, masters of arts, and bachelors of law, having any ecclesiastical living, shall usually wear gowns with standing

130

collars and sleeves straight at the hands, or wide sleeves, as is used in the universities, with hoods and tippets of silk or sarcenet, and square caps. And that all other ministers admitted or to be admitted into that function shall also usually wear the like apparel as is aforesaid, except tippets only. We do further in like manner ordain, That all the said ecclesiastical persons above mentioned shall usually wear in their journeys cloaks with sleeves commonly called priests' cloaks, without guards, welts, long buttons, or cuts. And no ecclesiastical person shall wear any coif or wrought nightcap, but only plain nightcaps of black silk, satin, or velvet. In all which particulars concerning the apparel here prescribed, our meaning is not to attribute any holiness or special worthiness to the said garments, but for decency, gravity, and order, as is before specified. In private houses, and in their studies, the said persons ecclesiastical may use any comely and scholar-like apparel, provided that it be not cut or pinked; and that in public they go not in their doublet and hose, without coats or cassocks; and that they wear not any light-coloured stockings. Likewise poor beneficed men and curates (not being able to provide themselves long gowns) may go in short gowns of the fashion aforesaid.

75 Sober conversation required in ministers

No ecclesiastical person shall at any time, other than for their honest necessities, resort to any taverns or ale-houses, neither shall they board or lodge in any such places. Furthermore, they shall not give themselves to any base or servile labour, or to drinking or riot, spending their time idly by day or by night, playing at dice, cards, or tables, or any other unlawful games: but at all times convenient they shall hear or read somewhat of the holy scriptures, or shall occupy themselves with some other honest study or exercise, always doing the things which shall appertain to honesty, and endeavouring to profit the church of God; having always in mind, that they ought to excel all others in purity of life, and should be examples to the people to live well and christianly, under pain of ecclesiastical censures, to be inflicted with severity, according to the qualities of their offences.

82 A decent communion table in every church

Whereas we have no doubt, but that in all churches within the realm of England, convenient and decent tables are provided and placed for the celebration of the holy communion, we appoint, that the same tables shall from time to time be kept and repaired in sufficient and seemly manner, and covered, in time of divine service, with a carpet of silk or other decent stuff, thought meet by the ordinary of the place, if any question be made of it, and with a fair linen cloth at the time of the ministration, as becometh that table, and so stand, saving when the said holy communion is to be administered: at which time the same shall be placed in so good sort within the church or chancel, as thereby the minister may be more conveniently heard of the communicants in his prayer and ministration, and the communicants also more conveniently, and in more number, may communicate with the said minister; and that the Ten Commandments be set upon the east end of every church and chapel, where the people may best see and read the same, and other chosen sentences written upon the walls of the said churches and chapels, in places convenient; and likewise that a convenient seat be made for the minister to read service in. All these to be done at the charge of the parish.

88 Churches not to be profaned

The churchwardens or questmen and their assistants shall suffer no plays, feasts, banquets, suppers, church ales, drinkings, temporal courts, or leets, lay-juries, musters, or any other profane usage, to be kept in the church, chapel, or churchyard, neither the bells to be rung superstitiously upon holy days or eves abrogated by the Book of Common Prayer, nor at any other times, without good cause to be allowed by the minister of the place, and by themselves.

109 Notorious crimes and scandals to be certified into ecclesiastical courts by presentment

If any offend their brethren, either by adultery, whoredom, incest, or drunkenness, or by swearing, ribaldry, usury, and any other uncleanness, and wickedness of life, the churchwardens, or questmen, and sidemen, in their next presentments to their ordinaries, shall faithfully present all and every of the said offenders, to the intent that they, and every of them, may be punished by the severity of the laws, according to their deserts: and such notorious offenders shall not be admitted to the holy communion, till they be reformed.

ARCHBISHOP BANCROFT'S LETTER REGARDING CATHOLIC RECUSANTS, 1605

In this letter, Richard Bancroft (1544–1610), the newly appointed Archbishop of Canterbury, instructs his bishops on the detection, treatment and punishment of

English Catholics who refused to attend the services of the Church of England. Written before the Gunpowder Plot (and therefore less prone to propagandistic exaggeration of the extent of covert Catholicism), Bancroft's letter provides evidence that, despite half a century of Protestant evangelism, the persistence of Catholicism was still a significant problem to early seventeenth century administrators.

Source: E. Cardwell, *Documentary Annals of the Church of England* (Oxford, 1844), pp. 96–101.

Salutatem in Christo.[1] I have written to your lordship before concerning your proceeding with your factious ministers, and that you should not desist by depriving one, two, or three at once, until you have purged your diocese of them; now I am to signify unto you, that his most excellent majesty hath, with the admiration of all that heard him, most fully, rarely, and resolutely declared himself (as often heretofore) touching such courses, as he wisheth should be held with popish recusants, being most desirous to rid his kingdom as well of these pestiferous adversaries, as of the former; to which purpose he hath dealt very thoroughly and privily both with the lords of his right honourable privy council, and with his judges; expecting likewise that we, who are bishops, should not be negligent in discharging of our duties, so far as lieth in us, for the furthering and effecting of so royal and so religious a designment.

As therefore my place requireth, and not without due and careful deliberation, I do commend to your good lordship (as I also have done to the rest of our brethren) these particular points following to be thoroughly by you observed: first, your lordship is not to depend altogether upon the 114th Canon, expecting still the minister's diligence in presenting of recusants, but to use your own best endeavour, by the labour and means of all your officers and friends, to inform yourself as well of the number, as of the qualities of them; and the same to certify unto me with all convenient speed.

Secondly, because order and discretion in all proceedings are principally to be observed (whereof without my advice, your lordship will be sufficiently mindful) and for that there being differences in the dispositions of the said popish recusants, and cannot all of them be reformed together, your lordship is to take notice by all the means before expressed, first, of all the recusants in your diocese, who they be, that are the most busy in seeking to seduce others either abroad, or at home in their own families, by bringing up their children in popery, and refusing to entertain any to serve them, especially in places of trust, that are not recusants; secondly, of all such persons of any note, who are become recusants, since his majesty's coming into England, and of them that are the most insolent, as the manner of those usually is, who are newly seduced.

133

Thirdly, these three observations thus promised, your lordship is to procure, as much as in you lieth, that for the faithful accomplishment of the 66th Canon, no pains may be spared in conferring with the said recusants, especially with the two sorts before mentioned, who are the heads and leaders of the rest, that thereby (if it be possible) they may be reduced from their errors, and no sweet or kind means omitted for the recovering of them to the truth.

Fourthly, in this conference you are to do your best for the reclaiming of those, that are already excommunicated in their private parishes, with whom if such travail shall nothing prevail, because it is either obstinately rejected, or wilfully contemned, then let them be publicly denounced in your cathedral church for excommunicate persons, without any forbearance or partiality, according to the 65th Canon, if happily such a notorious punishment may be a means to bring them to repentance.

Fifthly, if you have in your diocese sundry of the first sort, of the said busy and seducing recusants, not yet excommunicated (with whom conference will prevail no more, than with the former beforementioned) then call two or three of the chiefest of them (for dignity, place, and perverseness, such as are heads and leaders of the rest) forthwith by your ordinary authority; and if either they will not appear, after sufficient admonition to be carefully executed, so as they may not plead any probable ignorance, or appearing, shall obstinately refuse to go to church (as our phrase is) let them be *in scriptis*[2] excommunicated, and after forty days certified unto the chancery. This direction, touching the said first sort, will serve for the second, such as are of latter years revolted.

Sixthly, of those that before stood excommunicated, and so have been publicly denounced according to the said canon, if there be amongst them any of the said two sorts, then let two or three of the principallest of them, as is aforesaid, that have stood excommunicated forty days, be presently certified unto the said court. And for your better encouragement herein, if you shall advertise me of any such certificate, I will use my uttermost endeavour to procure the writ *De excommunicato capiendo*,[3] and take such order as that the same shall be faithfully and speedily served; that so they, who have not learned how to use their former liberty, may be better instructed by chastisement in prison.

Your lordship knoweth, that the people are commonly carried away by gentlemen recusants, landlords, and other ringleaders of that sort, so as the winning or punishing of one or two of them is a reclaiming, or kind of bridling of many, that do depend upon them; which hath induced me to prescribe to your lordship by the directions precedent such a moderation and course, as I think fit to be generally pursued; hoping that when they, who have been seduced under pretence of toleration, or I know not what vain imagined thing, shall hereby find that such disobedient persons are no longer to be borne with, but that the laws, made in that behalf, are carefully to be executed, they will be better advised, and reform themselves; and that the rest of us such simple people will be more heedful hereafter, that they be not misled and carried away by lewd persuasions of any person whatsoever.

Lastly, we that are bishops, being all of us (as is supposed) justices of the peace, it is much marvelled, that so many priests and Jesuits range about in our dioceses, without any impeachment or regard almost had of them; we ourselves seldom or never seeking after them; it is said, that our remissness therein doth discourage the rest of the justices of the peace from taking such pains in that behalf, as heretofore they have been accustomed, and that they would be as ready as they were to join with us in that service, if they might see our willingness thereunto, either by effecting something ourselves, or by our intelligence (having all the ministers of our diocese at our commandment) would give them our best directions, where those imposters might be met with, and apprehended. These things, I fear, may justly be objected against some of us; and I am driven now and then into some straits, how to excuse such our security. I do therefore very heartily pray your lordship, to think thereof, not that I have any cause to suspect you to be one of the number (if I shall speak properly), but rather to inform you what is expected at our hands, that with better discouragement we may therein discharge our duties.

WILLIAM BRADSHAW'S *ENGLISH PURITANISM*, 1605

As a phenomenon most often described by its opponents, 'Puritanism' is one of the most elusive categories of religious description in post-reformation England. In this treatise, the controversial lecturer William Bradshaw (1571–1618) outlines what he claims are the 'main opinions of the rigidest sort that are called Puritans in the realm of England.' It is characteristic of the period that Bradshaw identifies issues of ecclesiastical polity and practice, not doctrine, as areas differentiating Puritans from their conformist Protestant brethren. Jacobean Puritanism was, for the most part, a movement assimilated within the Church of England, although this was later to change.
Source: William Bradshaw: *English Puritanisme: Containeing the Maine Opinions of the Rigidest Sort of those that are Called Puritanes in the Realme of England* (Amsterdam? 1605) (*STC* 3516), sigs A2–A4v, preface.

It cannot be unknown unto them that know anything, that those Christians in this realm which are called by the odious and vile name of Puritans, are accused by the prelates to the king's majesty and the state to maintain many absurd, erroneous, schismatical, and heretical opinions, concerning religion, church government and the civil magistracy. Which hath moved me to collect (as near as I could) the chiefest of them, and to send them naked to the view of all men that they may see what is the worst that the worst of them hold. It is not my part to prove and justify them. Those that accuse and condemn them must in all reason and equity prove their accusations or else bear the name of unchristian slanderers. I am not ignorant that they lay other opinions (yea some clean contradictory to these) to the charge of these men, the falsehood whereof we shall (it is to be doubted) have more and more occasion to detect. In the meantime all enemies of divine truth shall find, that to obscure the same with calumnations and untruths is but to hide a fire with laying dry straw or tow upon it. But thou mayest herein observe, what a terrible popedom and primacy these rigid Presbyterians desire. And with what painted bugbears and scarecrows the prelates go about to fright the states of this kingdom withal. Who will no doubt one day see, how their wisdoms are abused.

Concerning religion or the worship of God in general

Imprimis, they hold and maintain that the word of God contained in the writings of the prophets and apostles, is of absolute perfection, given by Christ the head of the church, to be unto the same, the sole canon and rule of all matters of religion, and the worship and service of God whatsoever. And that whatsoever done in the same service and worship cannot be justified by the said word, is unlawful. And therefore that it is a sin, to force any Christian to do any act of religion or divine service, that cannot evidently be warranted by the same.

2. They hold that all ecclesiastical actions invented and devised by man, are utterly to be excluded out of the exercises of religion; especially such actions as are famous and notorious mysteries of an idolatrous religion, and in doing whereof, the true religion is conformed (whether in whole or in part) to idolatry and superstition.

3. They hold that all outward means instituted and set apart to express and set forth the inward worship of God, are parts of divine worship and that not only all moral actions but all typical rites and figures ordained to shadow forth in the solemn worship and service of God, any spiritual or religious act or habit in the mind of man, are special parts of the same; and therefore that every such act ought evidently to be prescribed by the word of God, or else not to be done; it being a sin to perform any other worship to God, whether external or internal, moral or ceremonial, in whole or in part, then that which God himself requires in his word.

4. They hold it to be gross superstition, for any mortal man to institute and ordain as parts of divine worship, any mystical rite and ceremony of

religion whatsoever, and to mingle the same with the divine rites and mysteries of God's ordinance. But they hold it to be high presumption to institute and bring into divine worship such rites and ceremonies of religion, as are acknowledged to be no parts of divine worship at all, but only of civil worship and honour: For they that shall require to have performed unto themselves a ceremonial obedience service and worship, consisting in rites of religion to be done at that very instant that God is solemnly served and worshipped, and even in the same worship make both themselves and God also an idol. So that they judge it a far more fearful sin to add unto, and to use in the worship and service of God or any part there of such mystical rites and ceremonies as they esteem to be no parts or parcels of God's worship at all, than such as in a vain and ignorant superstition, they imagine and conceive to be parts thereof.

5. They hold that every act or action appropriated and set apart to divine service and worship, whether moral or ceremonial, real or typical, ought to bring special honour unto God and therefore that every such act ought to be apparently commanded in the word of God, either expressly, or by necessary consequent.

6. They hold that all actions whether moral or ceremonial appropriated to religious or spiritual persons, functions, or actions, either are or ought to be religious and spiritual. And therefore either are or ought to be instituted immediately by God, who alone is the author and institutor of all religious and spiritual actions, and things: whether internal or external, moral or ceremonial.

ARCHBISHOP ABBOT'S LETTER REGARDING PREACHING, 1622

In the final years of his reign, exasperated by increasing public criticism of his foreign policy (which was popularly considered to be too lenient towards international Catholicism), James I issued 'Directions to Preachers', which forbade any preacher to discuss matters of state, and allowed only preachers above the rank of dean to discuss 'the deep points of predestination, election [or] rebrobation'. The association of Calvinist teaching with political opposition serves as a harbinger of the declining fortunes of orthodox Calvinism in the reign of Charles I. In this letter George Abbot (1562–1633), Archbishop of Canterbury since 1611, explains the king's purpose in suppressing preaching that was theologically or politically sensitive. Abbot refers to the consternation produced by the 'Directions' and alludes to an increase of civil disturbance in the kingdom at this time.
Source: *Records of the Old Archdeaconry of St Albans: A Calendar of Papers AD 1575 to AD 1637*, H. R. Wilton Hall (ed.) (St Albans, 1908), pp. 150–2.

I doubt not but before this time you have received from me the directions of his most excellent majesty concerning preaching and preachers, which are so graciously set down that no godly or discreet man can otherwise than acknowledge that they do tend much to edification if he do not take them up upon report, but do punctually consider the tenor of the words as they lie and do not give an ill construction to that which may receive a fair interpretation. Notwithstanding because some few churchmen, and many of the people have sinisterly conceived as we here find, that those instructions do tend to the restraint of the exercise of preaching, and do in some sort abate the number of sermons and so consequently by degrees do make a breach to ignorance and superstition, his majesty of his princely wisdom hath thought fit that I should advertise your lordship of the grave and weighty reasons which induced his highness to prescribe that which is done.

You are therefore to know, that his majesty being much troubled and grieved at the heart to hear every day of so many defections from our religion both to Popery and Anabaptism or other points of separation in some part of this kingdom, and considering with much admiration what might be the cause thereof, especially in the reign of such a king who doth so constantly profess himself an open adversary to the superstition of the one and madness of the other, his princely wisdom could fall upon no one greater probability than the lightness, affectedness and unprofitableness of the kind of preaching which hath of late years been too much taken up in court, university, city and country.

The usual scope of very many preachers is noted to be a serving up in points of divinity too deep for the capacity of the people, for a mustering up of much reading, or a display of their own wit, or an ignorant meddling with civil matters as well in the private or several parishes and corporations as in the public of the kingdom, or a venting of their own distastes, or a smoothing up of those idle fancies which in this blessed time of so long a peace do boil in the brains of unadvised people, or lastly a rude and undecent railing not against the doctrines (which when the text shall occasion the same is not only approved but much recommended by his royal majesty) but against the persons of Papists and Puritans. Now the people bred up with this kind of teaching and never instructed in the catechism and fundamental grounds of religion are for all this airy nourishment, no better than *abrasae tabulae,* new table books ready to be filled up either with the manuals and catechisms of the popish priests or the papers and pamphlets of Anabaptists, Brownists and Puritans.

His majesty calling to mind the saying of Tertullian, *Id verum quod primum,*[4] and remembering with what doctrine the Church of England in her first most happy reformation did drive out the one and keep the other from poisoning and infecting the people of this kingdom doth find that the scope of this doctrine is contained in the articles of religion, the two books of Homilies, the lesser and the greater catechism which his majesty doth therefore recommend again in these directions as the themes and proper subjects of all sound and edifying preaching. And so far are those directions from abating it his majesty doth expect at our hands that it should increase the number of sermons by renewing upon every Sunday in the afternoon in all parish churches throughout the kingdom the primitive and most profitable exposition of the catechism wherewith the people, yea very children, may be timely seasoned and instructed in all the heads of Christian religion. The which kind of teaching (to our amendment be it spoken) is more diligently observed in all the reformed churches of Europe than of late it hath been here in England. I find his majesty much moved with this neglect and resolved (if we that are his bishops do not see a reformation thereof which I trust we shall) to recommend it to the care of the civil magistrate so far is his highness from giving the least discouragement to solid preaching or discreet or religious preachers. To all these I am to add that it is his majesty's princely pleasure that both the former directions and these reasons of the same be fairly written in every register's office to the end that every preacher of what denomination soever, may if he be so pleased take out copies of either of them with his own hand *gratis*, paying nothing in the name of fee or expedition. But if he do use the pains of the register or his clerks then to pay some moderate fee to be pronounced in open court by the chancellors and commissaries of the place, taking the directions and approbation of my lords the bishops.

SAMUEL GARDINER, *THE FOUNDATION OF THE FAITHFUL*, 1611

The reign of James I is often described as a golden age of English pulpit oratory. In this sermon extract, and those that follow, we glimpse the diversity of theological, ecclesiastical, and rhetoric styles characteristic of the period. Gardiner's sermon is a good example of Calvinist orthodox preaching. Its meticulously detailed explanation of the 'comfortable doctrine' of predestination owes much to William Perkins's *A Golden Chain*, Article 17 of the Thirty-Nine Articles, and classical logic.
Source: Samuel Gardiner, *The Foundation of the Faythful: in a Sermon delivered at Paul's Cross* (London, 1611) (*STC* 11577), sigs. A6–A8.

The foundation of the Lord remaineth sure, and hath his seal. The Lord knoweth who are his: And let every one that calleth upon the name of the Lord, depart from iniquity (2 Timothy 2:19).

First, *a posteriori*,[5] God's purpose to save the elect in this world, is absolutely constant. Therefore he calleth, justifieth, regenerateth them, so qualifieth them with the induments[6] and ornaments of his spirit, so governeth them, and giveth them the gift of perseverance, as he never repenteth himself of these collated benefits, inasmuch as repentance cannot fall upon him, as scripture before taught us. God followeth his chosen with an indivisible, unwearisome, and eternal love; so saith God in Jeremiah: I have loved thee with an everlasting love.[7] So sayeth Christ in John: Forasmuch as he loved his own which were in the world, unto the end he loved him.[8] But he willeth and worketh nothing now, which was not willed and determined by him from all eternity: wherefore this foundation is of absolute stability.

A priori,[9] we plead thus; election is only in God, and not in man, inasmuch as election was before the creation, and so before man: We were chosen (saith the apostle) before the world's foundation.[10] Again, if election be a part of divine providence, and providence is God's: the sequence is natural, that election must be in God, and no part thereof may cleave to man's thumbs. And hence also the deduction is as needful, that it is eternal and immutable, as consisting in God only, in whom all things are according to his nature, without variableness or shadow of change. Stood the foundation of our election upon no surer ground than man, it would soon be turned up, for Euripus[11] changeth not oftener than man. And what may man do simply by himself towards his own salvation? He that is a reprobate can lay to himself a sure foundation whereupon he may build his own damnation; inasmuch as not being sufficiently supported by the hand of God (God not being bound unto him thereunto) he simply can bring forth nothing but fruits unto death, with willfulness enough; and so undo himself. But election cannot so be made sure of the part of the elect, as by nature mutable, and as so continually and grievously sinful: So, as so far as it layeth in them, they quite strip themselves of the graces of God, and if doom should be denounced according to their deeds, there were no foundation made for them in heaven.

The effects of election are in the persons themselves that are elected, as their vocation passive, and so their justification and regeneration in this sense; also faith, and the works of faith, and at last their glorification in like manner. Wherefore these effects in us that are of the elect, admit an alteration in respect of ourselves. Whereupon by nature, faith and regeneration may be lost of us; and of righteous we may become unrighteous, and so fall from grace and perish. But in regard of predestination, and divine decree which is in God, and so immutable: it cannot be, that these gifts of God and these effects of predestination should be quite without effect; and therefore having dependence on God, our salvation is most safe.

JOHN BUCKERIDGE, *A SERMON TOUCHING PROSTRATION AND KNEELING*, 1618

In this sermon John Buckeridge (1562–1631), who became Bishop of Rochester in 1611, underscores the patriarchal basis of kingly authority, and connects this political theory to a startling endorsement of ceremonies as essential parts of divine worship rather than adiaphora.

Source: John Buckeridge, *A Sermon Preached Before His Majesty at Whitehall . . . Touching Prostration and Kneeling* (London, 1618) (STC 4005), pp. 7–8.

Venite adoremus; O come, let us worship, let us fall down, and kneel (or weep) before the Lord our Maker (Psalm 95:6).

Now there is a threefold *venite*; the first, *singulare*, particular or singular in every particular man; for man is a little world, or city, or kingdom in himself. The spirit is to rule, and all the powers of soul and body must obey. Memory must record all God's blessings, and our own duties; reason must apprehend and believe them; will must choose, and love them; and affection must desire them. The senses must be shut up, that they wander not, but ascend and behold; the eyes must see God's beauties, not gad after vanities, and send tears as ambassadors; the ears must attend the truth, not leasings; the tongue must sound forth the sacrifice of prayer and praise; the hands must be lifted up as an evening sacrifice, to entreat pardon, and bestow alms; and the knees must be bowed, that God who resisteth the proud, may behold the humble afar off; and the whole man must be offered up as a living sacrifice to God, *ut totus hic sit, et totus in Coelo offeratur*, that the whole man being in the temple may at the same instant be presented to God in heaven.

The second is, *privatum*, the private call of the master of the family; which is another little kingdom, and hath all the societies of man and wife, father and son, master and servant in it: as the kingdom is the great family, consisting of many families, and the power of the king is no other but *Patria Potesta*, that fatherly power that was placed by God immediately in Adam over all the families that issued from him. In which, as David said, no deceitful person shall dwell in my house:[12] so every master must say, No recusant in God's worship shall rest within my doors. If he will not go to God's house, and adore his maker, and receive the blessed body and blood, *Non habitabit in domo mea*, He shall not hide his head in my house, if he be ashamed to show his face in God's houses. Our most religious David, that sits upon the throne of this kingdom, and suffers none to serve him, a king on earth; unless he will also with him serve the king of heaven, may be a singular light, a pattern to all masters in this kind. And surely he can never be a true servant to a man in earth, that is not a devout and religious servant to God in heaven; if he be false to God, he will never be true to him that is but the image, and represents the person of God on earth.

The third is, *publicum*, the public call, when he calls all, who hath the authority to call all; that is the king's call: to which every one that is a part or member of the great family, and receives protection and direction from him must be obedient; and not only one family, or one kingdom, but as many families or kingdoms as are subject to his dominion. All his kingdoms must be obedient to his *venite*, and join together, not only in *unitate*, in the unity and substance of religion, and worship of God, but also *in uniformitate*, in uniformity of outward order and ceremony of God's service, if possibly it may be; especially in all the parts of my text, of adoration, and prostration and kneeling, which are not ceremonies, but parts of divine worship; and for disobedience must be subject to his coercion, who bears not the sword in vain.

LANCELOT ANDREWES, 'A SERMON BEFORE THE KING', 1621

Like his fellow bishop John Buckeridge, Lancelot Andrewes (1555–1626) was an anti-Calvinist ceremonialist whose sermons, collected and published in 1629 were to inspire Laudian divines in the reign of Charles I. In the passage below, Andrewes's rhetoric connects the political concepts of monarchical dignity, authority and prerogative to a brisk criticism of prevailing religious thought. Calvinist theology, identified here with the Five Articles ratified by the international Synod of Dort (1618–19), is clearly indicted as politically and spiritually presumptuous.

Source: Lancelot Andrewes, 'A sermon preached before the king's majesty at White-hall on the first of April 1621, being Easter day', in *XVCI Sermons by the Right Honorable and Reverend Father in God, Lancelot Andrewes, late Lord Bishop of Winchester* (London, 1629) (*STC* 606), pp. 548–9.

Dicit ei Jesus, Noli me Tangere (John 20:17).[13]

The truth is, in the natural body the eye is a most excellent part, but withal so tender, so delicate, it may not endure to be touched, no, though it ail nothing, be not sore at all. In the civil body the like is: there are in it both persons and matters, whose excellency is such they are not familiarly to be dealt with by hand, tongue, or pen, or any other way. The persons, they are as the apple of God's own eye, *christi Domini*.[14] They have a peculiar *nolite tangere*, by themselves. Wrong is offered them, when after this, or in familiar or homely manner, any touch them. The matters likewise, princes' affairs, secrets of state, David calleth them *magna et mirabilia super se*,[15] and so *super nos*[16] points too high, too wonderful for us to deal with. To these also, belongs this 'touch not'.

And if of king's secrets this may truly be said, may it not as truly of God, of his secret decrees? May not they, for their height and depth, claim to this *noli* too? Yes sure; and I pray God, he be well-pleased with this licentious touching, nay tossing his decrees of late; this sounding the depth of his judgements with our line and lead, too much presumed upon by some in these days of ours. *Judicia eius abyssus multa* (saith the psalmist): His judgements are the great deep.[17] St Paul, looking down into it, ran back, and cried, O the depth! the profound depth! not to be searched, past our fathoming or finding out.[18] Yet are there in the world that make but a shallow of this great deep, they have sounded it to the bottom. God's secret decrees they have them at their fingers' ends, can tell you the number and order of them just, with 1. 2. 3. 4. 5. Men that (sure) must have been in God's cabinet, above the third heaven[19] where St Paul never came. Mary Magdalen's touch was nothing to these.

RICHARD SHELDON, *A SERMON LAYING OPEN THE BEAST AND HIS MARKS*, 1622

Sheldon's sermon on Revelation 14:9–11, preached at Paul's Cross, London, in 1622, is a good example of severe political criticism disguised as a protestation on behalf of the king. Sheldon's concerns about popery can be interpreted as a warning to James I concerning his relations with Catholic Spain. His tactics were unsuccessful, for this sermon earned him a censure and its publication was postponed.
Source: Richard Sheldon, *A Sermon Preached at Paul's Cross: Laying Open the Beast, and his Marks*, (London, 1625) (*STC* 22398), pp. 48–50.

Cast your eyes round about this present world, reflect your memories into generations, all generations past; and show me (if you can) any state or kingdom, which having once fully (fully I say) shaken off the papal yoke, by a perfect reformation, did ever settledly receive the same again? . . . Such a change was royally impossible: for how possible, that our religious David, should not be *semper idem*, always the same? How possible but he, who hath gone in and out before us in this holy war? . . . How possible (I say) that he, who hath so happily begun in the spirit, should end in the flesh? Shall any of us, dare to be so irreverent against majesty (so Christian a majesty) as once to think, that he will do aught against the knowledge of his own conscience (a sin against the Holy Ghost)? Or that he will suffer, that truth to be imprisoned, impugned, which his royal pen hath so learnedly and christianly defended and maintained? Far be all surmises from the hearts and tongues of all dutiful subjects, who also ever will (as they ought) interpret *Arcana Regni*, secrets of state, in the best sense. But, if we will not persuade ourselves, that such a change is royally impossible; in regard we have a religious, learned and resolved prince, in all points of Christianity; yet let us be persuaded, that such an alteration is royally impossible, in respect we have an intelligent, and a politic wise prince: for who cannot but know, that with such a change he must put on *Iugum Exactoris*, the very yoke of the exactor, and that he and his successors, must of absolute monarchs, and sovereign commanders, become blind devouts to papal briefs, and hedge servants also to the sovereign lord (of all lords) the pope.

CEREMONIALISM AND ITS DISCONTENTS

THE KING'S DECLARATION OF SPORTS, 1633

The king's *Declaration to His Subjects Concerning Lawfull Sports* gave royal authority to the pursuit of 'honest mirth or recreation' on Sundays and holy days, and thereby sabotaged the sabbatarian campaign for the reformation of manners. This so-called 'Book of Sports' made little stir when James I issued it in Lancashire in 1618, but when Charles I reissued the *Declaration* in 1633, to be read from pulpits throughout the land, it led to a wave of protest by Puritan divines. At stake were competing views of harmony and order and different notions of religious obligation. While the king encouraged the robust pleasures of the laity, including social dancing and springtime festivities, more austere reformers thought these activities incompatible with serious godly devotion. The *Declaration* may have sharpened the cultural and religious polarization that some scholars perceive as a factor in the English civil wars.
Source: *The Kings Maiesties Declaration to His Subiects, Concerning Lawfull Sports to be vsed* (London, 1633) (*STC* 9257).

Our dear father of blessed memory, in his return from Scotland, coming through Lancashire, found that his subjects were debarred from lawful recreations upon Sundays after evening prayers ended, and upon holy days; and he prudently considered that, if these times were taken from them, the meaner sort that labour hard all the week should have no recreations at all to refresh their spirits. And after his return, he further saw that his loyal subjects in all other parts of his kingdom did suffer in the same kind, though perhaps not in the same degree; and did therefore in his princely wisdom publish a declaration to all his loving subjects concerning lawful sports to be used at such times, which was printed and published by his royal commandment in the year 1618, in the tenor which hereafter followeth.

By the king. Whereas upon our return the last year out of Scotland, we did publish our pleasure touching the recreations of our people in those parts under our hand; for some causes us thereunto moving, we have thought good to command these our directions then given in Lancashire,

145

with a few words thereunto added, and most appliable to these parts of our realms, to be published to all our subjects.

Whereas we did justly in our progress through Lancashire rebuke some Puritans and precise people, and took order that the like unlawful carriage should not be used by any of them hereafter, in the prohibiting and unlawful punishing of our good people for using their lawful recreations and honest exercises upon Sundays, and other holy days, after the afternoon sermon or service, we now find that two sorts of people wherewith that country is much affected, we mean Papists and Puritans, have maliciously traduced and calumniated those our just and honourable proceedings. And therefore, lest our reputation might upon the one side (though innocently) have some aspersion laid upon it, and that upon the other part our good people in that country be misled by the mistaking and misinterpretation of our meaning, we have therefore thought good hereby to clear and make our pleasure to be manifested to all our good people in those parts.

It is true that at our first entry to this crown and kingdom we were informed, and that too truly, that our county of Lancashire abounded more in popish recusants than any county of England, and thus hath still continued since, to our great regret, with little amendment, save that, now of late, in our last riding through our said county, we find both by the report of the judges, and of the bishop of that diocese, that there is some amendment now daily beginning, which is no small contentment to us.

The report of this growing amendment amongst them made us the more sorry, when with our own ears we heard the general complaint of our people, that they were barred from all lawful recreation and exercise upon the Sunday's afternoon, after the ending of all divine service, which cannot but produce two evils: the one the hindering of the conversion of many, whom their priests will take occasion hereby to vex, persuading them that no honest mirth or recreation is lawful or tolerable in our religion, which cannot but breed a great discontentment in our people's hearts, especially of such as are peradventure upon the point of turning. The other inconvenience is, that this prohibition barreth the common and meaner sort of people from using such exercises as may make their bodies more able for war, when we or our successors shall have occasion to use them; and in place thereof sets up filthy tipplings and drunkenness, and breeds a number of idle and discontented speeches in their alehouses. For when shall the common people have leave to exercise, if not upon the Sundays and holy days, seeing they must apply their labour and win their living in all working days?

Our express pleasure therefore is, that the laws of our kingdom and canons of the church be as well observed in that county, as in all other places of this our kingdom: and on the other part, that no lawful recreation shall be barred to our good people, which shall not tend to the breach of our aforesaid laws and canons of our church: which to express more particularly, our pleasure is, that the bishop, and all other inferior church-men and churchwardens, shall for their parts be careful and diligent, both to instruct the ignorant, and convince and reform them that are misled in religion, presenting them that will not conform themselves, but obstinately stand out, to our judges and justices: whom we likewise command to put the law in due execution against them.

Our pleasure likewise is, that the bishop of that diocese take the like straight order with all the Puritans and precisians within the same, either constraining them to conform themselves or to leave the county, according to the laws of our kingdom and canons of our church, and so to strike equally on both hands against the contemners of our authority and adversaries of our church. And as for our good people's lawful recreation, our pleasure likewise is, that after the end of divine service our good people be not disturbed, letted or discouraged from any lawful recreation, such as dancing, either men or women, archery for men, leaping, vaulting, or any other such harmless recreation, nor from having of May games, Whitsun ales, and morris dances, and the setting up of maypoles and other sports therewith used: so as the same be had in due and convenient time, without impediment or neglect of divine service; and that women shall have leave to carry rushes to the church for the decorating of it, according to their old custom. But withal we do here account still as prohibited all unlawful games to be used upon Sundays only, as bear- and bull-baitings, interludes, and at all times in the meaner sort of people by law prohibited, bowling.

And likewise we bar from this benefit and liberty all such known recusants, either men or women, as will abstain from coming to church or divine service, being therefore unworthy of any lawful recreation after the said service, that will not first come to the church and serve God: prohibiting in like sort the said recreations to any that, though conform in religion, are not present in the church at the service of God, before their going to the said recreations. Our pleasure likewise is, that they to whom it belongeth in office, shall present and sharply punish all such, as in abuse of this our liberty, will use these exercises before the end of all divine services for that day. And we likewise straightly command that every person shall resort to his own parish church to hear divine service, and each parish by itself to use the said recreation after divine service: prohibiting likewise any offensive weapons to be carried or used in the said times of recreation: and our pleasure is, that this our declaration shall be published by order from the bishop of the diocese, through all the parish churches, and that both our judges of our circuit and our justices of the peace be informed there-of . . .

Now out of a like pious care for the service of God, and for suppressing of any humours that oppose truth, and for the ease, comfort, and recreation of our well-deserving people, his majesty doth ratify and publish this our blessed father's declaration: the rather, because of late in some counties of our kingdom, we find that under pretence of taking away abuses, there hath been a general forbidding, not only of ordinary meetings, but of the feasts of the declaration of the churches, commonly called wakes. Now our express will and pleasure is, that these feasts, with others, shall be observed, and that our justices of the peace, in their several divisions, shall look to it, both that all disorders there may be prevented or punished, and that all neighbourhood and freedom, with manlike and lawful exercises be used. And we further command all justices of assize in their several circuits to see that no man do trouble or molest any of our loyal and dutiful people, in or for their lawful recreations, having first done their duty to God and continuing in obedience to us and our laws: and for this we command all our judges, justices of the peace, as well within liberties as without, mayors, bailiffs, constables, and other officers, to take notice of, and to see observed, as they tender our displeasure. And we further will that publication of this our command be made by order from the bishops, through all the parish churches of their several dioceses respectively.

Given at our palace of Westminster, the eighteenth day of October, in the ninth year of our reign.

BISHOP PIERS'S REPORT ON SOMERSET PARISH FEASTS, 1633

Many parishes traditionally augmented their funds by sponsoring feasts or 'ales' (drinking parties) on the anniversaries of their patron saints. While some of these customary festivities declined with the advance of the reformation, others flourished with official encouragement in the reign of Charles I. In this report from Somerset, closely contemporary with the *Declaration . . . Concerning Lawfull Sports*, William Piers, the new Bishop of Bath and Wells, assures William Laud, the new Archbishop of Canterbury, of the decency, orderliness, value and antiquity of parish feasts. Source: Public Record Office, London, SP 16/250/20.

I find by the several answers of three score and twelve ministers, beneficed men in whose parishes these feasts are kept, as followeth. First, that they have been kept not only this last year, but also for many years before, as long as they have lived in their several parishes, without any disorders. Secondly, that upon the feast days, which are for the most part everywhere upon Sundays, the service of the church hath been more solemnly performed, and the church hath been better frequented both in the forenoons and in the afternoons, than upon any other Sunday in the year. Thirdly, that they have not known nor heard any disorders in the neighbouring towns, where the like feasts are kept. Fourthly, that the people do very much desire the continuance of these feasts. Lastly, that all these ministers are of opinion, that it is fit and convenient these feast days should be continued, for a memorial of the dedications of their several churches, for the civilizing of people, for their lawful recreations, for the composing of differences by occasion of the meeting of friends, for the increase of love and amity, as being feasts of charity, for the relief of the poor, the richer sort keeping then in a manner open house, and for many other reasons.

This is the sum of their several free and voluntary answers, which I have in writing under their own hands, and will be ready to show if they be required, which course I took because it might not be given out hereafter by those who condemn these feasts, that I did mistake either their words or their meaning. And I do verily believe that if I had sent for an hundred more of the clergy within my diocese, I should have received the same answer from them all . . .

I find that throughout Somersetshire there are not only feasts of dedication, but also in many places church ales, clerk ales, and bid ales. The feasts of dedication are more general, and generally they are called feast days, but in diverse places they are called revel days. They are not known among the ignorant by the name of feasts of dedication, but all scholars acknowledge them to be in the memory of their several dedications, and some ministers of late have taught them so. Divers churches are dedicated here to the Holy Trinity, and they are kept upon Trinity Sunday; but almost all those feasts which are kept in memory of the dedication of churches unto saints, are kept upon some Sundays, either before or after the saints' days; because, as I conceive, on the week days the people have not had leisure to celebrate these feasts. And I find that almost all the feasts of dedication are kept in the summer time, between Our Lady day and Michaelmas, because that time of the year is most convenient for the meeting of friends from all places. In some places they have solemn sermons preached by divines of good note, and also communion upon their feast days; and in one place in this county the parish holds land by their feast. And one minister, who hath been a great traveller, hath inserted in his answer, that in some reformed churches, namely in Switzerland, these feasts of dedication are observed.

149

I find also that the people generally would by no means have these feasts taken away; for when the constables of some parishes came from the assizes about two years ago, and told their neighbours that the judges would put down these feasts, they answered that it was very hard if they could not entertain their kindred and friends once in a year, to praise God for his blessings, and to pray for the king's majesty, under whose happy government they enjoyed peace and quietness; and they said they would endure this judge's penalties rather than they would leave off their feast days . . .

Moreover, I find that the chiefest cause of the dislike of these feasts among the preciser sort is because they are kept upon Sundays, which they never call but Sabbath days, upon which they would have no manner of recreation, nay, neither roast nor sod. And some of the ministers who were with me have ingeniously confessed, that if the people should not have their honest and lawful recreations upon Sundays after evening prayer, they would go either into tippling houses, and there upon their ale-benches talk of matters of the church or state, or else into conventicles.

Concerning church ales, I find that in some places the people have been persuaded to leave them off, in other places they have been put down by the judges and justices, so that now there are very few of them left. But yet I find, that by church ales heretofore, many poor parishes have cast their bells, repaired their towers, beautified their churches, and raised stocks for the poor; and not by the sins of the people, as some humourists have said, but by the benevolence of people at their honest and harmless sports and pastimes; at which there hath not been observed so much disorder, as is commonly at fairs and markets.

Touching clerk ales, which are lesser church ales for the better maintenance of parish clerks, they have been used, until of late, in divers places; and there was good reason for them; for in poor country parishes, where the wages of the clerk is very small, the people thinking it meet that the clerk should duly attend at church, and [not] lose by his office, were wont to send him in provision, and then feast with him, and give him more liberally than their quarterly payments would amount unto in many years. And since these have been put down some ministers have complained unto me, that they are afraid they shall have no parish clerks for want of maintenance for them.

There is another kind of public meeting called a bid ale, when an honest man decayed in his estate is set up again by the liberal benevolence and contribution of friends at a feast; but this is laid aside almost in every place.

150

HENRY BURTON, *A DIVINE TRAGEDY LATELY ACTED*, 1636

The London Puritan minister Henry Burton (1578–1648) blamed the king's Book of Sports for the Sabbath-breaking and libertinism of the mid-1630s. In his view the 'arch patrons' of the book, the king and Archbishop Laud, were responsible for angering God. God, however, did not sit idly watching the profanation of his holy days, but actively intervened to make chilling examples of selected offenders. In this catalogue of 'judgements', illicitly printed in 1636, Burton found satisfaction in local manifestations of divine wrath. An implacable enemy of Archbishop Laud, Burton was punished in 1636 by deprivation of his ministry and cropping of his ears.
Source: *A Divine Tragedie Lately Acted, Or A collection of sundry memorable examples of God's judgements upon Sabbath-breakers* (1636) (*STC* 4140.7).

A collection of sundry memorable examples of God's judgements upon Sabbath-breakers

These examples of God's judgements hereunder set down, have fallen out within the space of less than two years last past, even since the Declaration for Sports (tolerated on the Lord's day) was published, and read by many ministers in their congregations. For hereupon ill-disposed people (being as dry fuel, to which fire being put quickly flameth forth; or as waters pent up and restrained being let loose, break forth more furiously) were so encouraged, if not enraged, as taking liberty dispensed, thereby so provoked God, that his wrath in sundry places hath broken out to the destruction of many, would to God to the instruction of any. And the judgements are so much the more remarkable, that so many in number, as here are observed (besides many more, no doubt, which have not come to our ears) should fall within so narrow a compass of time so thick, and that in so many places . . . So many there are of them as it were too heathenish to impute them to chance, and too much stupidity, and envy of God's glory, not to acknowledge the special hand of God in them, upon such transgressors of his own sacred day.

Example 1   A woman about Northampton, the same day that she heard the book for sports read, went immediately, and having three pence in her purse, hired a fellow to go to the next town to fetch a minstrel, who coming, she with others fell a-dancing, which continued within night; at which time she was got with child, which at the birth she murdering, was detected and apprehended, and being convented before the justice, she confessed it, and withal told the occasion of it, saying it was her falling to sport on the Sabbath, upon reading of the book, so as for this treble sinful act, her presumptuous profaning of the Sabbath, which brought her adultery and that murder. She was according to the law, both of God and man, put to death; much sin and misery followeth upon Sabbath-breaking.

Example 2   Also at Northampton, in the last Easter assizes, there was a young man who formerly by seeing the example of good people in the due sanctification of the Lord's day or Sabbath, had begun to reform his former loose kind of life, and to frame his conversation according to God's word, and that in the well-keeping of the Sabbath, abstaining therein from sports and pastimes, and spending the whole day in the public and private duties of it. But when once he heard of the publishing of the book for sports and pastimes, he fell back again to his former wallowing, and being taken as he was picking a pocket, when the judges were in the church, upon examination confessed what he had formerly been, and how he had been reformed, and that upon the publishing of the said book, he was encouraged to run riot afresh by which means he fell into this impiety and iniquity, for the which he suffered death.

Example 10   At Thornton near Westchester, the people there upon the first publishing of the book, prepared for a solemn summer ale. The bringing in of their Lady Flora should have been guarded with a martial troop; the lustiest wench and stoutest young man in the town were chosen to be the purveyors for cakes, and for ribbons for favours. The solemnity was to be on the Monday, but the preparation on the Lord's day. This lusty tall maid, on the Saturday before, went to the mill to fetch home the meal for cakes on her head, she being strong and able for the purpose. But in the way, passing by a hedge, she was suddenly struck by a divine stroke, and fell into the ditch, where she was found dead. She was suffered to lie abroad in that pickle all the Lord's day, till Monday morning, when the coroner being sent for, she was thence carried to her grave immediately, where all her solemnity was buried with her, and all her vain thoughts in that very day, wherein the great solemnity should have been. And see what a good effect this wrought in the whole town. First, all their mirth was turned into mourning, no summer ale kept, and besides that, they being moved by the dreadful stroke of God, took their maypole down, which they had before set up, and never after would presume to set it up again, or to have any more summer ales, or May games. God grant they continue in their sober minds, and that all others would learn to be wise by their example.

Example 16 At Dartmouth, 1634, upon the coming forth and publishing of the book for sports, a company of younkers[1] on May day morning before day went into the country to fetch home a maypole with drum and trumpet; whereat the neighbouring inhabitants were affrighted, supposing some enemies had landed to sack them. The pole being thus brought home, and set up, they began to drink healths about it, and to it, till they could not stand so steady as the pole did, whereupon the mayor and justice bound the ringleaders over to the sessions; whereupon these complaining to the archbishop's vicar-general, then in his visitation, he prohibited the justices to proceed against them in regard of the king's book. But the justices acquainted him they did it for their disorder, in transgressing the bounds of the book, hereupon these libertines scoffing at authority, one of them fell suddenly into a consumption, whereof he shortly after died. Now although this revelling was not on the Lord's day, yet being upon any other day, and especially May day, the maypole set up thereon, giving occasion to the profanation of the Lord's day, the whole year after, it was sufficient to provoke God to send plagues and judgements among them.

Example 23 In the edge of Essex near Brinkley, two fellows working in a chalk pit, the one was boasting to his fellow how he had angered his mistress with staying so late at their sports the last Sunday night, but he said he would anger her worse the next Sunday. He had no sooner said this, but suddenly the earth fell down upon him, and slew him outright, with the fall whereof his fellow's limb was broken, who had been also partner with him in his jollity on the Lord's day, escaping with his life, that he might tell the truth, that God might be glorified, and that by this warning he might repent of his sin, and reform such his profaneness, and remain as a pillar of salt, to season others with fear by his example.

Example 27 At Ovingdean in Sussex about nine or ten miles from Alfriston, one John Arcold, of the age of one or two and twenty years, eldest son to John Arcold, a blacksmith dwelling in Alfriston, with other younkers would needs fall a-ringing of the bells on a Sabbath day, presuming the book for sports gave them full liberty so to do. One of the churchwardens, Robert Kenward, hindered them from their jangling; whereupon the said Arcold and his companions fell in some contestation with him, telling him that though he hindered them now, yet they would ring the next Sunday, whether he would or no. But the said John Arcold, the ringleader, before the next Sunday came, was struck with a sickness in which he continued a fortnight or three weeks till he died, in which time

Robert Kenward the churchwarden, repairing to him, and putting him in mind of his bold affronting of him, he seemed to be sorry for it, and promised if God would be pleased to restore him again to his health, he would never do the like. God make his surviving companions, and all others, wise by his example.

Example 33   At Ivy Hinckley, a mile from Oxford (about the time when maypoles are set up) on the Lord's day after evening prayer, when most of the town were at the maypole, one John Cooper, servant to master Tinmore of the said town, going along the street, a maid out of a window in John Nicols's house not far from the maypole, called to him to come in thither; where also was another maid and a young man named Christopher Young, servant to master Willis of the said town. John Cooper at first refused to come to them, but the maid earnestly entreating him, he yielded to her, and being come in sat down by the other two, where having sat awhile the aforesaid Christopher Young spied a gun over the chimney, which he supposing not to be charged, fondly took down, and fell a-tampering with it, and first levelled at the maids, and after held it up against John Cooper as he sat, and unwittingly lifting up the cock, it struck fire and the piece discharged, and shot the said John Cooper through the shoulder, so that he died presently, being heard only to say, O Lord.

Example 43   At Glastonbury in Somersetshire, at the setting up of a maypole, it miscarrying fell upon a child, and slew it, and it is reported that it was the churchwarden's child, who was the chief stickler in the business. Also when the maypole in the same town was again the second time a-setting up, a fire took in the town, so as all the people about the maypole were forced to leave it and to run to the quenching of the fire.

Example 55   Upon May eve, Thomas Tree of Gloucester, carpenter in the parish of St Michael, some coming unto him and asking him whether he would go with them to fetch the maypole, he swore by the Lord's wounds that he would, though he never went more. Now whilst he was working on the maypole on May day morning, before he had finished his work, the Lord smote him with such a lameness and swelling in all his limbs that he could neither go nor lift his hands to his mouth to feed himself, but kept his bed for half a year together, and still goes lame to this day.

These examples of divine justice, so notorious, so remarkable both for number and variety, having fallen out in so narrow a compass of time, and

154

so dispersed over the whole land as every particular place and country might take special notice thereof; if they will not take and make impression in our stony hearts to move us to speedy repentance (as for many other enormities and crying sins, so in special) for this our ringleading sin of the heathenish profanation of the Sabbath or Lord's day, what plea can we make for ourselves why the Lord of the Sabbath should not send some universal, epidemical, sweeping calamity upon the land, sparing neither small nor great? And now that the plague and pestilence begins to break forth, and spreads itself much amongst us, the Lord shooting these his terrible venomous arrows, from which not even princes' nor prelates' palaces can secure themselves from becoming his butts and marks, what can we more impute it unto, as the cause thereof, than to this grand sin of the profanation of the Sabbath or Lord's day, occasioned so much the more by the publishing of the late book for sports, and that by the ministers themselves?

ARCHBISHOP LAUD'S VISITATION OF LEICESTERSHIRE, 1634

William Laud (1573–1645) was the architect and lightning-rod of Charles I's religious policies. Like his predecessors as Archbishop of Canterbury, Laud conducted visitations in order to promote religious conformity, to detect irregularities, and to punish offenders. These extracts from Laud's 1634 visitation of Leicestershire, within the diocese of Lincoln, show his concern for reverent behaviour, liturgical decorum, and ceremonial discipline. The placement of the communion table and the gestures and positions of the celebrants were recurrent points of friction between Caroline conformists and Puritans. Brought down by his enemies during the English revolution, Laud was executed in 1645.

Source: Percival Moore (ed.), 'The Metropolitical Visitation of Archdeacon [sic] Laud' *Associated Architectural Societies Reports and Papers*, vol. 29 (1907), pp. 477–534.

Evington: the communion table in the church of Evington shall be placed at the upper end of the chancel, close unto the wall, and be set that the ends thereof may stand north and south.

St Mary in Arden: Mary, the wife of Thomas Pope, for refusing to be churched according to the order of the church, and for standing excommunicate.

Pickwell: John Ball, for working on the Sabbath day. Ball answered, that he did dress a lamb that was eaten with maggots upon a Sunday, which lamb was ready to perish, but that he did not otherwise work upon the Sabbath. (Dismissed with a warning.)

Wislow cum Newton: Mr Thomas Coltman presented for that he refuseth to receive the communion at the hands of our minister, because he will not give it him standing but kneeling. (Excommunicated after fruitless citations.)

Bowden Magna: William Johnson senior, for standing up and not kneeling down when the Lord's Prayer and other prayers are read in church.

Easton Magna: Mr Black of Thorpe Langton, for reading divine service . . . in his cloak and without a surplice, being first desired by Bringhurst Wignail, one of the churchwardens, to wear the said surplice.

Shilton: Thomas Charlton and Judith his wife, for clandestine marriage, being married out of the archdeaconry.

Appleby: Hugh Foster, for a popish recusant, and for not bringing his child to public baptism.

Shenton: Mr Joshua Man, the minister, doth not catechize on Sundays in the afternoon, nor doth read service on Wednesdays. (Ordered to bring certificate of compliance.)

Thornton: Mr James Errycke, vicar, for not reading prayers on Wednesdays and Fridays. (Ordered to bring certificate of compliance.)

Bitteswell: William Feakes presented for comparing the pulpit cloth, which was commanded by the ordinary to be bought, to a saddle cloth, after a disgraceful and contemptuous manner, before the churchwardens and others in the church porch.

Desford: Will Owen, for a common drunkard, and for defaming in a scandalous manner the women of our town, giving forth that there were not above one or two honest women in all the town.

Kirby in Glenfield: there is wanting a decent carpet of silk[2] or some other decent stuff, and a table for the degrees of marriage, and a decent surplice.

Kirby: consecrated ground in Kirby is profaned and polluted by the swine of Thomas Summerfield, and other nasty beasts, which do also break down and spoil the young trees lately set to grow forth [to] ornament and fence off the church.

Shearsby: William Throne, presented for going to plough on St Martin's day last and being absent from prayer.

Bitteswell: Robert Lord the younger, for playing at nine men's morris in the churchyard on Sunday. (Admonished and dismissed.)

Somerby: Thomas Hill, for being churchwarden and yet a very frequent sleeper in the church.

Bottesford: Elizabeth Lamb for standing excommunicate, and not proving her husband's will nor taking administration of his goods.

Garthorpe: Michael Robinson, late churchwarden, for neglecting his office and suffering dogs to come into the church, which have defiled the church and disturbed the minister.

Leicester: Mr William Kinnes, clerk, for reading prayers in St Martin's church without a surplice. (Inhibited.)

Shepshed: the churchwardens, when they go to search alehouses and other places for idle company on Sundays in service time, they have found Papists and others in idle sort, and stayed and drunk with them.

Leicester: whereas it was complained that Mr Browne, parson of Loughborough, doth use to cause the communion table to be removed out of the chancel into the body of the church at the time of administration of the communion, the visitor [representing Archbishop Laud] did enjoin Mr Browne henceforth to administer the communion in the chancel and not elsewhere.

Anstey: John Middleton, for his great and gross abusing our painful, orderly and peaceable minister in uncivil, unbeseeming and scandalous speeches, to the disparagement of his ministry.

Worthington: Mr Matthews, minister there, for delivering the communion to some certain persons sitting. (Dismissed after submission.)

Mountsorrel: the chapel of St Nicholas for being ruinated and decayed . . . and the font that was a horse-trough is now made a font again.

Quorndon: the communion table, the cloth and the cover of the font are insufficient and indecent.

Loughborough: Mr Brown, parson, for wishing his workmen that were taking down the loft commanded to be taken down by Dr Aylett, visitor to the Lord Grace of Canterbury, not to take it down, and wishing them to work but slowly.

All Saints, Leicester: Mr Ward, vicar there, for not catechizing on Sundays in the afternoon, and for reading prayer and churching a woman in St Martin's church on Wednesday, 1 October, 1634, without gown and surplice, being only in a cloak.

St Mary's, Leicester: the communion table shall be placed at the upper end of the south aisle upon the highest ascent there, the ends thereof standing north and south and close unto the wall under the great window, and the minister shall administer communion there and not remove the table from there unto any other part of the church.

Bitteswell: Edward and John Dillingham are notorious Puritans. Gone into New England.

RICHARD MONTAGUE'S ARTICLES OF ENQUIRY FOR THE DIOCESE OF NORWICH, 1638

Periodic visitations allowed ecclesiastical officials to investigate the quality and conduct of the clergy, the moral and religious condition of the laity, and physical arrangements in the church. The 1638 visitation of the diocese of Norwich, covering most of the counties of Norfolk and Suffolk, was typically wide ranging. Richard Montague (1577–1641), however, was a notorious anti-Calvinist, an arch ceremonialist and a strict disciplinarian. His concern for the beauty of holiness, the dignity of priesthood, reverence for the altar and fastidiousness in worship, put him well beyond the mainstream of early seventeenth-century religious opinion. Episcopal insistence on veils at churching, kneeling in worship, and rails for the communion table, fed the frustration that fuelled the Civil War.

Source: *Articles of Enquiry and Direction for the Diocese of Norwich, In the first Visitation of the Reverend Father in God, Richard Mountaigu* (London, 1638) (*STC* 10299).

Concerning the church and chancel

Is it time for you, O ye, to dwell in ceiled houses, and the house of the Lord to lie waste? (Haggai 1:4.)

1. Have you any church for divine service, or hath it been or is it demolished, the parishioners forced to repair unto their neighbours for sacrament and sacramentals, if so, by whose default, usurpation, or impiety is it done?

2. Is your church, though remaining, yet ruined or decayed in any part of the frame, fabric, structure, walls, roof or otherwise, within or without, if so, wherein, how much, by whose fault is it?

3. Is your church leaded, tiled, slated, shingled, thatched with straw or reed all through or in part?

4. Have you a steeple of stone, brick or timber adjoining to your church in good state and reparations, wherein have you any bells hanging, and how many; or do they hang in some low shed, under a roof of boards and timber, or have they been taken down and sold away, when and by whom?

5. Is your church floor decently paved with brick and paving tile, or is it only floored with earth; when the ground is broken up for burials, which was not wont to be, is it again renewed, levelled, paved; if not, by whose default is it; and the money taken by the churchwardens for such burials, how is it accounted for, and expended?

6. Is your church sweetly and cleanly kept, dust, cobwebs and the like nuisances being weekly carried forth, the walls whited and kept fair, are the seat and pews built of an uniformity, or do they hinder and encumber their neighbours in hearing God's word and service?

7. Do men and women sit together in those seats, indifferently and promiscuously, or as the fashion was of old, do men sit together, upon one side of the church and women upon the other?

8. Is your chancel divided from the nave, or body of your church with a partition of stone, boards, wainscot, grates, or otherwise, wherein is there a decent strong door to open and shut, as occasion serveth, with lock and

158

key to keep out boys, girls, irreverent men and women, dogs, cats from coming to besoil or to profane the Lord's table?

9. Is your chancel well paved with brick, paving tile, or so; doth it altogether lie upon a flat or hath it ascents up into the altar?

10. Is your church scaffolded in part, or throughout, do those so made annoy any man's seat or hinder the lights of any windows in the church; is your chancel surrounded with seats, wherein your parishioners commonly use to sit, which take up the room too much and encroach upon the propriety of the minister?

11. Are the light and windows of your church and chancel clear, not dammed up, well mullioned, well glazed and kept clean?

12. Be the doors of your church strong and decently made with good locks and keys, and be they kept shut, except at time of divine service, or other necessary cause of ingress, to keep out passengers, carriers of burdens, children playing, or the like?

13. Doth any man teach children to read or write in your church or chancel?

14. Be furniture for soldiers, ladders or any timber or implements brought into the church, and there disposed of, as in a storehouse? Are any meeting for rates, taxations, levies or the like made in the church, especially at the communion table, by parishioners?

Concerning the churchyard and other consecrated appendages to that holy place

Put off thy shoes from thy feet, for the place whereon thou standeth is holy ground. (Joshua 5:15.)

1. Have you any appropriated churchyard or doth your church stand in open field, without any surrounding or enclosure?

2. Are dead bodies buried in such open and unfenced places, if any such be?

3. If you have a several churchyard, is it well enclosed and fenced with mounds, ditches, hedges, walls, pales or the like; if otherwise, by whose default is it?

4. The graves there, be they conveniently covered, made seven foot deep, kept from scraping of dogs, rooting up of hogs, fouling and polluting otherwise, as the resting places of Christians dead?

5. Though the surface of the soil and the grass there growing, if any such be, are the minister's, yet it being consecrated ground, is not to be profaned by feeding and dunging of cattle.

6. Is it therefore all or in part at any time, let or hired out to be employed for pinfolds of sheep, stalls for oxen or horses, booths or standings for chapmen, at any time of any fair or market, nor to dry

clothes there, tanned leather or the like? For, of the base-court of the temple, said Our Saviour, have these things hence.

7. Much less is it to be unhallowed with dancings, morrises, meetings at Easter, drinkings, Whitsun ales, midsummer merriments or the like, nor by stool ball, football, wrestlings, wasters or boys' sports; if such abuse hath been committed, say by whom, whose procurement, countenance or abetting.

8. Is your churchyard or any part thereof, made a laystall or dunghill, or be any such impious nuisances laid near unto the pale or mounds thereof? Let the offenders be named upon enquiry and presented.

9. Hath any neighbouring *quidam* or great man, encroached upon any part of the churchyard, enclosing it to his garden, hop-yard, stable-yard or so? Present him or them so transgressing.

10. Be there any houses fronting or abutting your churchyard, the dwellers wherein do annoy, soil and profane the churchyard by washing of bucks, emptying of sinks, chamber-pots or the like, by easing of nature either way within that place, or under and against the church walls?

11. If timber trees have been felled which grew in the churchyard, by the minister, churchwardens, parishioners or others, and sold, let the delinquents be presented.

12. Is there a mansion house and glebe belonging to your parsonage and vicarage; if none house, by whom and how long since was it ruined; if there be an house, is it kept in good reparations, water-tight and wind-tight, by the incumbent, whereof the archdeacon properly and principally should take notice?

13. If there be a glebe belonging to the incumbent, hath any part thereof been leased out by the patron incumbent and diocesan, of what quantity is it; hath there been upon survey a terrier thereof made; as also of pensions or portions of tithes in other parishes due to yours, and is this returned into the bishop's registry?

14. Have any monuments or tombs of the dead, in your church or churchyard been cast down, defaced, ruined; any arms or pictures in glass windows been taken down, especially of Our Saviour hanging on the cross, in the great east window, and white glass or other set up in place thereof; have any leaden or brazen inscriptions upon grave stones been defaced, purloined, sold, by whom?

Of sacred utensils, church ornaments, ministers' vestments

How shall I come before the Lord, or appear before my God? Answer: as becometh Saints.

1. Is there in your church a font for the sacrament of baptism, fixed unto the lord's freehold, and not moveable, of what materials is it made,

where is it placed, whether near unto the church door to signify our entrance into God's church by baptism; is it covered, well and cleanly kept; at time of baptism is it filled with water clean and clear, or is some basin, bowl or bucket filled with water set therein?

2. Have you a comely and convenient pew of wainscot for your minister to read divine service in; doth it stand in the face of the congregation, as much as conveniently may be, so that they may behold and hear and understand the minister in what he readeth or prayeth; have you a cloth and cushion for it to be laid upon the desk?

3. Have you a Bible of the largest volume and biggest letter, a service book in folio, with the reading psalms; the order of consecrating bishops; of ordaining priests and deacons; be they well and fairly bound and embossed, and at end of divine service are they clasped, to keep out dust, soil and prevent tearing of the leaves?

4. Have you two fair large surplices for your minister to officiate divine service in, that the one may be for change when the other is at washing; and also serve for him that at communion assisteth the chief minister, that no part of divine service may be done but with and in ministerial vestments?

5. Of what assize be the surplices, large or scantling, of what cloth, coarse or fine, what are they worth if they were to be sold; for not cheapness but decentness is to be respected in the things of God?

6. Have you a register book for the christenings, marriages, burials, of parchment well bound and kept in a chest for church utensils; are the names and surnames, the day, month and year duly and truly registered, to remain upon record, for clearing of many doubts about inheritances, etc.; and is a transcript thereof brought into the bishop's register yearly, within a month after the Annunciation or 25th of March?

7. Is your communion table or altar of stone, wainscot, joiner's work, strong, fair and decent; what is it worth in your opinion, were it to be sold?

8. Have you a covering or carpet of silk, satin, damask or some more than ordinary stuff to cover the table with at all times, and a fair clean linen covering at time of administering the sacrament?

9. Have you a chalice or communion cup with a cover of silver, flagon of pewter or tin, if not, rather of silver, to put the wine in which is to be consecrated and not to be brought and set on the table in wicker bottles or tavern wine-pots, which being of vulgar, common and profane employments ought not to be presented at the Lord's table?

10. Have you a dish or patten of the same materials for the bread, as also a corporas cloth or napkin of fine linen, to cover the bread consecrated, which cannot all at once be contained in the patten, and to fold up what is not used at communion? Are all these sacred utensils clean kept, washed, scoured, rubbed as often as need or convenience requireth?

11. Is your communion table enclosed and ranged about with a rail of joiner's and turner's work, close enough to keep out little dogs or cats from going in and profaning that holy place, from pissing against it, or worse; and is there a door of the same work to open and shut; do any persons presume to enter thereinto, except such as be in holy orders?

12. Is the communion table fixedly set, in such convenient sort and place within the chancel, as hath been appointed by authority, according to the practice of the ancient church, that is, at the east end of the chancel, close unto the wall, upon an ascent or higher ground, that the officiating priest may be best seen and heard of the communicants, in that sacred action?

13. Whether is the communion table removed down at any time, either for or without communion, into the lower part of the chancel or body of the church, by whom, at whose instance, direction or command is it done?

14. Is the wine for communion white or reddish, which should resemble blood, and doth more effectually represent the Lord's passion upon the cross, whereof the blessed sacrament is a commemorative representation?

15. If the consecrated wine fail or sufficeth not, doth your minister, before he give it to the communicants, consecrate that also which is newly supplied as the former, or doth he give it as it cometh from the tavern? For there is no sacrament until the word of institution be pronounced upon it: This is my blood, etc.

16. Doth he instead of wine, give water unto any person that is abstentious and naturally cannot endure wine, such person ought rather to abstain altogether, than to receive a popish half-communion, against Our Saviour's institution? For only institution makes a sacrament, and if God dispense, he doth excuse from ordinary course and tie.

Of divine service, sacraments, and sacramentals

When thou goest into the house of God, look unto thy feet, and be more ready to hear than to offer the sacrifice of fools, for they consider not that they do evil. (Eccles. 5:1)

1. Is divine service orderly performed in your church upon appointed times, as the Book of Common Prayer prescribeth?

2. Do your parishioners come late to church, and not at the beginning of divine service, to make their humble confession unto Almighty God, and by coming late, deprive themselves of the benefit of absolution, and so become unprofitable hearers and petitioners in that holy action; do any depart before service is done, and the blessing pronounced by the priest?

3. Doth any parishioner or foreigner come into the church with an hawk on his fist, and a hawking pole in his hand, with spaniels coupled, to

the disturbance of the auditory, profanation of the church, contempt of God and his service; a course never practised amongst pagans?

4. Do any of your parish sixteen years old or upward absent themselves commonly from church, or do they use any gaming or exercise in church time, do they go into taverns, inns or alehouses, to bowl or tipple upon Sundays and holy days, in time of divine service?

5. Do any keep open shops, sell wares ordinarily on Sundays or holy days?

6. Be there any recusants in your parish, do they keep any priest or schoolmaster in their houses, who refuse to come to church and receive the communion; doth he or they labour to seduce or draw others from the church and profession established, not contenting themselves with their own opinions?

7. Have any in your parish retained, sold, or dispersed books unlawful and scandalous, written by Papists or Puritan sectaries?

8. Do any of your parish leave their own church, minister and service, and repair to other churches ordinarily, where a more sanctified (in their opinion) minister preacheth powerfully to their edification?

9. Is there any in your parish who refuse to come to church, have their children baptized, receive the communion of the minister, because he is no preacher?

10. Is any of your parish a common blasphemer of God's holy name, a common swearer, drunkard, usurer, foul-mouthed speaker, etc.? Have any such not been presented, have they been admitted to the sacraments?

11. Be there any in your parish who deny, or persuade others to deny, the king's authority over all persons, in all causes within his realm?

12. Do any write or publicly speak against anything in the Book of Common Prayer, the confession of the church made in 1562, or against any of the rites and ceremonies used and authorized in the church for divine service, or against the hierarchical government thereof, by archbishops, bishops, archdeacons, etc., affirming it unlawful, antichristian, against God's word, and that the government by pastors, doctors, lay-elders is the sceptre of Jesus Christ?

13. Do your parishioners at their entrance within the church doors use that comely and decent deportment, which is fitting for God's house, where God, whom heaven and earth cannot contain, is fain to dwell, and doth manifest his goodness and mercy to man out of his word; do they uncover their heads, sit bare all service time, kneel down in their seats, bow towards the chancel and communion table, and use those several postures which fit the several acts and parts of divine service?

14. That is, do they reverently kneel at confession, absolution, the Lord's Prayer, the church prayers and petitions or collects, as becometh suitors unto God; do they stand at the creed, as avowing their belief in the face of heaven and earth, men and angels, at the doxology, or Glory to the

163

Father, against the oppugners of the Trinity, which in the primitive church was repeated at the end of every psalm, standing also at the reading of the gospel, and bending or bowing at the glorious, sacred and sweet name of Jesus, pronounced out of the gospel read?

15. Do your parishioners accompany the minister in his perambulation in Rogation week, not only to set out and continue the known bounds of the parish, but especially upon view and sight, to consider the fruits of the earth then in prime, then upon the viewing or impairing, to give God thanks for his goodness on them, to procure by prayer the continuance of them, to deprecate his anger, and entreat his future blessing upon them; for what the eye seeth the heart rueth, and more effectually representeth?

16. Doth your minister officiate divine service in due place, upon set times, in the robes, habit and apparel of his order, with a surplice, a hood, a gown, a tippet, not in a cloak, or sleeveless jacket, an horseman's coat, and peradventure a sword hanging by his side, for such I have known?

17. Doth he use the absolution to be pronounced on penitents, not as it is a declaration of forgiveness, but as a prayer thus, Thou pardonest and absolvest all those, who unfeignedly believe thy gospel?

18. Doth he read the psalms, first and second lesson, the psalms properly appointed for set days, according to the Book of Common Prayer, not as it happeneth upon opening of the book as he fancieth, or make choice of; doth he plainly and diligently only read the chapters, or doth he appoint, or comment upon them, and draweth uses from to his auditory?

19. Doth he instead of collects and prayers of the church, substitute prayers of his own devising, motion, or effusion?

20. Doth he upon Wednesdays and Fridays ordinarily, and at other extraordinary times appointed by the ordinary, read and pray the litany, and doth he especially on Sundays, read the second or latter service, at the communion table, as the ancient tradition of the church was used to do . . . and not in his pew or reading seat, though there be no communion?

21. Doth he catechize at least half an hour before divine service, his parishioners in the afternoon, as he is enjoined, but not enjoined to preach a popular sermon?

22. Doth he commonly, or of set purpose in his popular sermons, fall upon those much disputed and little understood doctrines of God's eternal predestination, of election, antecedaneons, of reprobation, irrespective, without sin foreseen; of free will; of perseverance and not falling from grace, points obscure, unsolvable, unfordable, untraceable, at which that great apostle stood at gaze with: *Oh the height and depth of the riches, both of the wisdom and knowledge of God! how unsearchable are his judgements and his ways past finding out* (Rom. 11:33)?

23. Are his sermons long, beyond the compass of an hour, be his prayers before and after sermon drawn out at length, to equal if not exceed

his sermon, or doth he as he should, conform himself unto the prayer, which is recommended as a form, Canon 55, consisting of prayer, praise, thanksgiving, for the living and the dead, by way of commemoration, that the righteous may be had in everlasting remembrance, God be glorified in and for them, and the living incited to follow them?

Of the sacraments and sacramentals, remembered in the service book

Acoedad verbum ad Elementum, et fie Sacramentum.[3]

Baptism

1. First, for baptism, public and private, doth your minister teach, or do any of your parish hold, that the sacrament of baptism is not of absolute and indispensable necessity unto salvation, in God's ordinary course and dispensation with man, but either eternal election sufficeth or original sin, which infants only have, condemneth none, and therefore regard not, but only for fashion sake to require it?

2. Doth therefore your minister teach the necessity of it, and admonish his parishioners not to defer it, which is a common fault to put it off, till provision can be made for inviting and entertaining of gossips, and of friends or neighbours, or other put-offs, of no necessity?

3. Doth your minister baptize the child at the font, or at his pew, in a basin of water, thither brought and set upon some moveable frame, or perhaps in a bucket, or a bowl-dish, doth he use rose-water or other liquor than pure, mere water from the well, etc.?

4. Doth he refuse to baptize the child unless the father will make public profession he taketh it to be his own, and not begotten in adultery, which of my knowledge, hath been practiced by some indiscreet zealots of the preciser cut?

5. Doth he refuse to baptize any child born in bastardy or out of wedlock, any stranger casually born in his parish?

6. Doth he admit or procure the father to be godfather to his own child, or young children under age, who cannot render an account of their faith, or never were confirmed, being not capable to understand what they do or undertake?

7. In the ancient church the child to be baptized was thrice dipped in the font, in the name of the Father, of the Son, and of the Holy Ghost, semblably is he to be thrice aspersed with water on his face, the priest using those sacramental words, after which act, doth he receive the child into his arms, unto Christ's flock, and then set the badge of Christianity upon him, signing him with the sign of the cross?

8. Doth he according to his own direction to the godfathers, and appointment of the communion book, when the child by him catechized,

can render an account of his faith, transmit him to the bishop, to receive farther confirmation of the graces of God's spirit upon him?

9. That this religious and ancient course may the better be observed, and facilitated the more, doth the minister diligently, at times appointed, catechize the children and youth of the parish, in the church catechism, and none other publicly? Do any refuse to send their children or servants to be catechized; do any sent, refuse to come, or answer, of what condition are they, upon what cause is their refusal?

10. In administration of private baptism, in cases of absolute exigency, doth your minister, being requested and sent for, refuse to go, and baptize the child in danger of death?

Of marriage

11. Concerning marriage, are the banns asked three several times openly in the church, upon three several Sundays or holy days?

12. Or is a licence or dispensation for asking the banns brought from the bishop's court, and presented to the minister before marriage?

13. Is marriage solemnized with licence, or after banns asked, in the church and not clandestinely in a private house, before or after the hours of eight and twelve in the forenoon, in Lent or other prohibited times?

14. Are any married without a ring, joining of hands, or the fees laid down upon the book?

15. Hath your minister married any under twenty-one years without the consent of parents or guardians first signified?

Churching of women after childbirth

26. Doth your minister refuse to church any woman after childbirth, doth he administer it at home, without great cause, to such as will not come to church out of willful scrupulosity?

27. Doth he administer it in his pew or reading seat, using the words of the service in general, as if he intended it to all in the church, or doth he descend unto her feet in the church, and there perform it, or doth he go up into the chancel, the women also repairing thither, kneeling as near the communion table as may be, and if there be a communion, doth she receive?

28. Doth she come to church in her ordinary habit, and wearing apparel or with a fair veil dependent from her head to her shoulders and back, that she may be distinguished from her accompanying neighbours, and that such as take notice of it be thereby put in mind for her, and with her, to give God thanks for her deliverance?

Concerning the sacrament of the Lord's Supper

Do this, as often as you do it, in remembrance of me.

In the primitive church, this sacrament was frequented and celebrated daily, especially in times of persecution, that being suddenly seized on, they might not depart without their *Viaticum.*[4] Afterward it fell down to every Sunday, which was one cause amongst others of that phrase, *Dominicum celebrare.*[5] In process, they became *Mensurna,* monthly, and in latter times, devotion slacking, men were confined to at least thrice in one year, especially at Easter, which is the limitation in our church.

1. Is this blessed sacrament therefore administered in your church every month upon the first Sunday in the month, at least thrice in the year, whereof Easter is one time?

2. Is any public notorious, scandalous offender admitted thereto without satisfaction made unto the church, reconcilement with enemies, confession of his faults, and promise made of amendment?

3. To which end and intent, doth the minister admonish his parishioners, to conform themselves, that they receive not their own damnation, as not discerning the Lord's body?

4. Doth he especially exhort them to make confession their sins, to himself or some other learned, grave and discreet confessor, especially in Lent, against that holy time of Easter, that they may receive comfort and absolution, so to become worthy receivers of such sacred mysteries?

5. He is not to admit boys or girls thereto under sixteen years of age, nor any young person who hath not rendered an account of his faith, and is not confirmed by the bishop, is this observed or not? For better performing whereof, is there yearly a particular note taken of every household in the parish, how many heads in each household are there, which be capable of receiving the communion?

6. Are the names of such as intend to receive, taken by the minister overnight or the day before, they repairing unto him, that he may examine or instruct them, they pay their offerings and not disquiet that sacred action in the chancel, by collecting of them, then or there, and that he may proportion the multitude of receivers, according to the capacity of his chancel, and not be pestered or crowded with multitudes, who thereby may be occasioned to sit in their pews in the church, and not draw near, unto the altar or holy table?

7. Before the communicants ascend up into the chancel, out of their seats in the church, that exhortation is to be said, which in the communion book beginneth, We be come together at this time, etc., and then this exhortation, Dearly beloved we are come together, etc. When after this exhortation, the communicants are come up into the chancel, before they dispose themselves to kneel in their several places, this is to be said, You

that do truly and earnestly repent you of your sins, etc. Is this order of the communion book observed, if not, let it be amended hereafter?

8. Doth he first receive himself, in both kinds (for I have known where the minister hath received last) upon his knees, at the altar, having consecrated the bread and wine, by the solemn and powerful words of Our Saviour, and none other?

9. Doth he next to himself give it to clergymen, if any be present, that they may assist him in giving the cup, and afterwards to every communicant, not standing, going up and down, but humbly expecting till it be brought and presented unto him, receive from the minister, meekly kneeling upon his knees, which is the fitting posture for communicants?

10. Doth he deliver bread and cup severally to each communicant, and not in gross to all, or some part, using the words, The body of Our Lord Jesus Christ, which was given for thee; the blood of Our Lord Jesus Christ shed for thee; at pronunciation of which words directed unto them, each several communicant was wont in the primitive church to say Amen, as professing his consent unto, and approbation of the truth thereof; which words cannot be used, being spoken not severally, but in gross, to many at one time.

11. Is the bread and wine of the best sort, fine, clean, sweet, not musty or unsavoury; which, beside the profanation, of my knowledge hath been occasion to some of turning Papists, who could not swallow it in disrelishment, and abhorred such negligence and contempt of Christ's institution in their minister?

12. And whereas it offendeth many that we sometimes call the Lord's table an altar, and dispose of it altar-wise, that we use the phrase of Sacrament of the Altar; in oppugning whereof, it hath been charged with popery, and constantly but ignorantly affirmed that in the primitive church, it was not named an altar for three hundred years after Christ. To give satisfaction herein and hereabout, both to priests and people, I avow, upon certain knowledge, out of my poor reading, that for all the time articulate, the word table is not above thrice used, but ever altar; and of ecclesiastical writers within that time, only Dionysus Areopagita hath it, and that but once and occasionally; which assertion, I am sure, cannot be refelled; and therefore, if we will, as we profess to do, follow the course and practice of the ancient, primitive, apostolical church, we ought not to traduce or be offended at the name, thing, or use of altar, whereat manifold sacrifice is offered to God.

CHRISTOPHER DOW'S NARRATIVE OF THE RISE AND PROGRESS OF THE 'DISCIPLINARIANS', 1637

Countering charges that the ceremonialists were guilty of innovation, or backsliding towards Rome, the Laudian Christopher Dow constructed a partisan chronology of

religious conflict that is analogous to Rose Hickman's or Robert Parkyn's. Dow sees Jacobean moderate Puritanism as the source of religious conflict in the reign of Charles I. In his view, the Puritan clergy were over-represented as preachers in the previous reign, and their increased access to the pulpit allowed them to instil a corrosive heterodoxy that stemmed from their disdain for ceremonial discipline.
Source: Christopher Dow, *Innovations Unjustly Charged upon the Present Church and State* (London, 1637) (*STC* 7090), pp. 191–8.

It was one of the greatest evils that ever happened to this church, that in the infancy of the reformation (which was happily begun in the reign of King Edward of happy memory) many for conscience sake and to avoid the storm of persecution which fell in the days of Queen Mary, betaking themselves to the reformed churches abroad, and especially to Geneva, were drawn into such a liking of the form of discipline then newly erected by Master Calvin there, that returning home, they became quite out of love with that which they found here established by authority: insomuch, that set on by the persuasions and examples of John Knox and other fiery-spirited zealots in Scotland, they attempted and by all means endeavoured to advance their strongly-fancied platform of Genevan discipline.

For the bringing about whereof, the course they then took for the drawing of the people to a liking of their intentions, was, to pick quarrels against the names, and titles given to the fathers and governors of our church, apparel of ministers, and some ceremonies in the Book of Common Prayer retained and prescribed, which they taxed of superstition, and remnants of popery. And afterward when T. C.[6] and others (who had also been at Geneva) had drunk in the opinion of Master Beza, who by that time, had promoted the discipline there invented by his master, and made it one of the especial notes of the true church, as if it had till then been maimed and imperfect: what books were then written, what seeming humble motions made, what pamphlets, pasquils, libels, flew abroad; yea, what violent attempts, plots, conspiracies and traitorous practices were then set on foot, by the men of that faction, are at large set forth in divers books of that argument, and are yet fresh in the memories of many alive at this day.

What the care and courageous zeal of the governors of this church and state then was, for the preventing and overthrowing of these men's desperate designs, the flourishing and peaceful estate which this church hath since by their means enjoyed, doth abundantly speak. For the authors of these innovations, troubles and disorders, receiving just and public censure, according to their several demerits; they which remained well-willers and abettors of that cause, were glad to lie close, and carry themselves more warily than before, and to wait some better opportunity for the effecting of their purpose. Which they apprehending to be offered

169

at the coming of King James to this crown, began again to move, but so, as beginning as it were at their old ABC their complaint was principally against the use of ceremonies, subscription, and sundry things formerly questioned by their predecessors in the Book of Common Prayer. And when that learned and judicious king had out of his wise and gracious disposition, vouchsafed to take their complaint into his serious consideration, and to grant them a solemn and deliberate hearing in the conference held at Hampton Court; the success of that conference (to use the words of his royal proclamation) was such as happeneth to many other things which moving great expectation before they be entered into, in their issue produce final effects. For (to give the sum of that which there followed) mighty and vehement informations were found to be supported with so weak and slender proofs; that the wise king and his council, seeing no cause to change anything, either in the Book of Common Prayer, doctrine or rites established; having caused some few things to be explained, he by his royal proclamation commanded a general conformity of all sorts, requiring the archbishops and bishops to see that conformity put in practice.

Being thus frustrate of their hopes of bringing in their darling platform, some of the principal among them, remaining stiff in their opinion, and opposition to authority, received a just censure, and suffered deprivation; others (grown wiser by the example of their fellows suffering) that they might save their reputation, and yet continue in their places, invented a new course, and yielded a kind of conformity, not that they thought any whit better of the things, but for that they held them (though in themselves unlawful) not to be such, as for which a man ought to hazard not his living (that might favour of covetousness), but his ministry, and the good which God's people might, by that means, receive. This project prevailed with many, to make them come off to a subscription, and yet gave them liberty, in private, and where they might, freely, and with safety, to express themselves, to show their disaffection to the things to which they had subscribed, resolving not to practice what they had professed, nor to use the ceremonies enjoined, further than they should be compelled. And, for this cause, they did wisely avoid all occasions that might draw them to the public profession of conformity by using the ceremonies, and betook themselves to the work of preaching, placing themselves (as much as might be) in lectures and (where any of them were beneficed) getting conformable curates under them to bear the burden of the ceremonies.

Thus saving themselves, and maintaining their reputation with the people, they gained the opportunity to instill into them their principles, not only of dislike of the church government and rites, but also of the doctrine established: and though (through the vigilancy and care of those that have sat at the stern in this church) they have been hitherto hindered from erecting their altars of Damascus publicly in our temples, yet have they (using this art now a long time) in an underhand way brought up the use of their own crochets, and erected a new church both for doctrine and discipline far differing from the true and ancient English church: and made, though not a local (as some more zealous among them have, by removing to Amsterdam and New England) yet a real separation, accounting themselves the wheat among the tares, and monopolizing the names of *Christians, God's children, professors*, and the like: styling their doctrine, *the gospel, the word*, and their preachers, *the ministers, the good ministers, powerful preachers*, and by such other distinctive names. As for all other men they account them no better than *pagans, or heathens*, baptized with *outward baptism*, which, as one of them once expressed it in a sermon (though I tremble to relate it) did no more to the making of them Christians, than the washing of a dog's leg. Their usual names by which they use to note out those that are not of their tribe, are, *the wicked, carnal, men of no religion, unconverted, wretched beasts.* And, when they are most charitable, *civil honest men* (which yet is no commendation, because with them, civil honesty is no better than a smooth Devil), men that have *good natural parts, some common gifts of grace*, which a reprobate may have; or (if their charity haply do enlarge itself more than ordinary) men that have *some good things in them*, or *some small beginnings of grace*.

But for preachers that suit not their humour, that is, all that are thoroughly conformable (who subscribe and practise, not groan, murmur and complain) their best terms of them are, *formalists, time-servers, men pleasers, enemies of grace and sincerity*, etc. As for the bishops, let Master Burton[7] tell you under what names they use to cloak their conceit of their persons and places . . .

As their faith is new, so are many acts of God's worship new too; I'll begin with the principal of them all, their prayers: which are far different from the prayers of the Church of England: for first, our church appointeth public prayers, after a set and solemn form; prayers received from the ancient church of Christ, and venerable for their antiquity; prayers, wherein the meanest in the congregation, by reason of the continual use, may join in, and help to set upon God with an army of prayers: prayers composed with that gravity, with such pious, and soul-ravishing strains, with those full, and powerful expressions of heavenly affection, that I suppose the world, setting them aside, hath not the like volume of holy orisons. But these are by them slighted and vilified, in whose mouths the short and pithy prayers of the church are but shreds and pieces, and not worthy the name of prayers, and the litany accounted conjuring. And instead of these regular devotions, they have brought in a long prayer, freshly conceived, and brought forth by the minister, and that (God knows) many times in bald and homely language, such as wise men would be ashamed to tell a tale in, even to their equals, with many gasping, and unseemly pauses, and multitudes of irksome tautologies, and (which is none of the least defects of it) in which none of the congregation is able to join with him or to follow him, as not knowing, no, nor the speaker himself sometimes, what he is about to say.

Again, the Church of England hath consecrated certain places to be houses of public prayer, which places so consecrated and appropriated to that holy service, they judge fit that public prayer be there made, as in the places where God is in a more special manner present: but these places are by them contemned, and every place, a parlour, barn, or playhouse, accounted as holy and fit as they, for public prayer or any other act of God's worship . . .

If we pass from prayer to the sacraments, which, as our church teaches, are moral instruments to convey those graces unto the receivers, which the outward signs visibly represent; and so, that in baptism infants receive remission of their sins, and are truly regenerate: these men will allow the sacraments no such virtue, accounting them as bare signs and seals of that grace which they have already received, if they be elect; if otherwise, they hold them to be but as seals set to a blank, being to no purpose, and of no value; acknowledging no such tie between the act of God and the priest, that what the priest shall do visibly, God should be thought, at the same time, and by that means, to effect inwardly by his grace and holy spirit. And therefore when (according to our form of ministration of baptism) they are to say that the child baptized is regenerate, some of them are fain to interlace 'we hope' and think it true, only in the judgement of charity, or in case they be elected; in which case some think (though others strongly contradict) they may be said truly to be regenerate in baptism. Of the same strain is their doctrine of the blessed eucharist; wherein they acknowledge no power of consecration in the priest; no other presence of Christ than by way of representation; no other exhibition than by way of signation or obsignation; nor other grace conveyed, but in seeming or (at best) the only the assuring of what they had before; which (if they have not) they must want, for all that the sacrament can do. Thus have they made these saving ordinances of God, of none effect through their traditions.

ROBERT SKINNER, A SERMON PREACHED BEFORE THE KING AT WHITEHALL, 1634

This sermon provides a good example of the concepts underpinning the Laudian emphasis on the holiness of God's house in the ordering and appointing of church furnishings, altar policies and communion practices. In relating the idea of the 'beauty of holiness' to the eucharist, Robert Skinner, a court chaplain to Charles I, produces an argument that re-emphasizes the presence of Christ in the communion elements. Old-style Calvinists like Grindal or Abbot would have considered this superstitious, while Puritan critics were alarmed and dismayed at these 'innovations' in theology and liturgy.

Source: Robert Skinner, *A Sermon Preached Before the King at White-Hall* (London, 1634) (*STC* 22628), pp. 20–3.

O worship the Lord in the beauty of holiness (Psalm 96:9).

In his holy courts, or in his holy sanctuary; for who can doubt but the beauty of holiness must needs be holy? And that apparently in a double regard: first, because the place of God's worship was hallowed ever, and set apart to holy uses, for so were altars afore the law, and after them the tabernacle, and after that the temple. And by the same right churches, and chapels at this day . . . And it stands with all good reason and religion, that houses of God be sequestered now by solemn consecration, as well as heretofore . . .

And can any Christian doubt, whether [the Lord] be present in our Christian congregations? Where holy prayers are poured forth, his holy gospel preached, his holy sacraments administered, his most holy body and blood communicated? Is it not deep infidelity and heresy, to think Christ to be absent from his body and blood? Most certainly present he is, though not by his glorious, yet in a singular way, by his gracious presence. Ye may as well (saith St Chrysostom) shut God out of heaven as exclude him hence . . . Holy then we see, because the Lord is there by his holy presence.

And now it begins to be open day with us, we may clearly perceive, why the prophet would have us worship rather in the place of holiness than elsewhere: because the Lord is sure to be found there. And we are to seek the Lord, as well where, as while he may be found. Where will ye enquire of the master, but at his house? . . . Where shall ye hope to find the king, so soon as in his court? So the king of heaven will be found . . . in his holy court, above any other place.

6

RELIGIOUS REVOLUTION

THE ROOTS AND BRANCHES PETITION, 1640

This London petition has come to be known by its most famous phrase, which demands that episcopacy, 'with all its dependencies, roots and branches, be abolished'. It represents an urban Puritan reaction to Laudian policy, which enforced stringent uniformity to a sacramentalism apparently akin to Roman Catholic practice. It also challenges Laudian doctrinal positions, which promoted a less Calvinist interpretation of the Thirty-Nine Articles. The petitioners associated government by bishops with a variety of abuses both social and religious, including the abandonment of reformed orthodoxy, an increase in overt and insolent popery, and (in a complaint reminiscent of Gifford's *Country Divinity*) the decline of neighbourliness brought about by contention between clergy and laity.
Source: S. R. Gardiner (ed.), *Constitutional Documents of the Puritan Revolution, 1625–1660* (2nd edn, Oxford, 1899), pp. 137–44.

To the Right Honourable the Commons House of Parliament. The humble petition of many of his majesty's subjects in and about the City of London and several counties of the Kingdom

Whereas the government of archbishops and lord bishops, deans and archdeacons, etc., with their courts and ministrations in them, have proved prejudicial and very dangerous both to the church and commonwealth, they themselves having formerly held that they have their jurisdiction or authority of human authority, till of these later times, being further pressed about the unlawfulness, that they have claimed their calling immediately from the Lord Jesus Christ, which is against the laws of this kingdom, and derogatory to his majesty and his state royal. And whereas the said government is found by woeful experience to be a main cause and occasion of many foul evils, pressures and grievances of a very high nature unto his majesty's subjects in their own consciences, liberties and estates, as in a schedule of particulars hereunto annexed may in part appear.

We therefore most humbly pray, and beseech this honourable assembly, the premises considered, that the said government, with all its dependencies, roots and branches, may be abolished, and all laws in their behalf

174

made void, and the government according to God's word may be rightly placed amongst us: and we your humble suppliants, as in duty we are bound, will daily pray for his majesty's long and happy reign over us, and for the prosperous success of this high and honorable court of parliament.

A particular of the manifold evils, pressures and grievances caused, practised and occasioned by the prelates and their dependents:

1. The subjecting and enthralling all ministers under them and their authority, and so by degrees exempting them from the temporal power; whence follows,

2. The faint-heartedness of ministers to preach the truth of God, lest they should displease the prelates; as namely, the doctrine of predestination, of free grace, of perseverance, of original sin remaining after baptism, of the Sabbath, the doctrine against universal grace, election for faith foreseen, free will against Antichrist, non-residents, human inventions in God's worship; all which are generally withheld from the people's knowledge, because not relishing to the bishops.

3. The encouragement of ministers to despise the temporal magistracy, the nobles and gentry of the land; to abuse the subjects, and live contentiously with their neighbours, knowing that they, being the bishops' creatures, shall be supported.

4. The restraint of many godly and able men from the ministry, and thrusting out of many congregations their faithful, diligent and powerful ministers, who lived peaceably with them, and did them good, only because they cannot in conscience submit unto and maintain the bishops' needless devices; nay, sometimes for no other cause but for their zeal in preaching, or great auditories.

5. The suppressing of that godly design set on foot by certain saints, and sugared with many great gifts by sundry well-affected persons for the buying of impropriations, and placing of able ministers in them, maintaining of lectures, and founding of free schools, which the prelates could not endure, lest it should darken their glories, and draw the ministers from their dependence upon them.

6. The great increase of idle, lewd and dissolute, ignorant and erroneous men in the ministry, which swarm like the locusts of Egypt over the whole kingdom; and will they but wear a canonical coat, a surplice, a hood, bow at the name of Jesus, and be zealous of superstitious ceremonies, they may live as they list, confront whom they please, preach and vent what errors they will, and neglect preaching at their pleasures without control.

7. This discouragement of many from bringing up their children in learning; the many schisms, errors, and strange opinions which are in the

church; great corruptions which are in the universities; the gross and lamentable ignorance almost everywhere among the people; the want of preaching ministers in very many places both of England and Wales; the loathing of the ministry; and the general defection to all manner of profaneness.

8. The swarming of lascivious, idle, and unprofitable books and pamphlets, play-books and ballads; as namely, Ovid's *Fits of Love, The Parliament of Women*, which came out at the dissolving of the last parliament; Barns's *Poems*, Parker's *Ballads*, in disgrace of religion, to the increase of all vice, and withdrawing of people from reading, studying, and hearing the word of God, and other good books.

9. The hindering of godly books to be printed, the blotting out or perverting those which they suffer, all or most of that which strikes either at popery or Arminianism; the adding of what or where pleaseth them, and the restraint of reprinting books formerly licensed, without relicensing.

10. The publishing and venting of popish, Arminian, and other dangerous books and tenets; as namely, 'That the Church of Rome is a true church, and in the worst times never erred in fundamentals'; 'that the subjects have no propriety in their estates, but that the king may take from them what he pleaseth'; 'that all is the king's, and that he is bound by no law', and many other, from the former whereof hath sprung,

11. The growth of popery and increase of Papists, priests and Jesuits in sundry places, but especially about London since the Reformation; the frequent venting of crucifixes and popish pictures both engraven and printed, and the placing of such in bibles.

12. The multitude of monopolies and patents, drawing with them innumerable perjuries; the large increase of customs and impositions upon commodities, the ship money, and many other great burdens upon the commonwealth, under which all groan.

13. Moreover, the offices and jurisdictions of archbishops, lord bishops, deans, archdeacons, being the same way of church government, which is in the Romish church, and which was in England in the time of popery, little change thereof being made (except only the head from whence it was derived), the same arguments supporting the pope which do uphold the prelates, and overthrowing the prelates, which do pull down the pope; and other reformed churches, having upon their rejection of the pope cast the prelates out also as members of the beast. Hence it is that the prelates here in England, by themselves or their disciples, plead and maintain that the pope is not Antichrist, and that the Church of Rome is a true church, hath not erred in fundamental points, and that salvation is attainable in that religion, and therefore have restrained to pray for the conversion of our sovereign lady the queen. Hence also hath come:

14. The great conformity and likeness both continued and increased of our church to the Church of Rome, in vestures, postures, ceremonies

and administrations, namely as the bishops' rochets and the lawn-sleeves, the four-cornered cap, the cope and surplice, the tippet, the hood, and the canonical coat; the pulpits clothed, especially now of late, with the Jesuits' badge upon them every way.

15. The standing up at *Gloria Patri* and at the reading of the gospel, praying towards the east, the bowing at the name of Jesus, the bowing to the altar towards the east, cross in baptism, the kneeling at the communion.

16. The turning of the communion table altar-wise, setting images, crucifixes, and conceits over them, and tapers and books upon them, and bowing or adoring to or before them; the reading of the second service at the altar, and forcing people to come up thither to receive, or else denying the sacrament to them; terming the altar to be the mercy-seat, or the place of God Almighty in the church, which is a plain device to usher in the mass.

17. The christening and consecrating of churches and chapels, the consecrating of fonts, tables, pulpits, chalices, churchyards, and many other things, and putting holiness in them; yea, reconsecrating upon pretended pollution, as though everything were unclean without their consecrating; and for want of this sundry churches have been interdicted, and kept from use as polluted.

18. The liturgy for the most part is framed out of the Romish breviary, rituals, mass-book, also the book of ordination for archbishops and ministers framed out of the Roman pontifical.

19. The multitude of canons formerly made, wherein among other things excommunication, *ipso facto*, is denounced for speaking of a word against the devices abovesaid, or subscription thereunto, though no law enjoined a restraint from the ministry without subscription, and appeal is denied to any that should refuse subscription or unlawful conformity, though he be never so much wronged by the inferior judges. Also the canons made in the late sacred synod, as they call it, wherein are many strange and dangerous devices to undermine the gospel and the subjects' liberties, to propagate popery, to spoil God's people, ensnare ministers, and other students, and so to draw all into an absolute subjection and thraldom to them and their government, spoiling both the king and the parliament of their power.

20. The countenancing plurality of benefices, prohibiting of marriages without their licence, at certain times almost half the year, and licensing of marriages without banns asking.

21. Profanation of the Lord's day, pleading for it, and enjoining ministers to read a declaration set forth (as it is thought) by their procurement of tolerating of sports upon that day, suspending and depriving many godly ministers for not reading the same only out of

177

conscience, because it was against the law of God so to do, and no law of the land to enjoin it.

22. The pressing of the strict observation of the saints' days, whereby great sums of money are drawn out of men's purses for working on them; a very high burden on most people, who getting their living on their daily employments, must either omit them, and be idle, or part with their money, whereby many poor families are undone, or brought behindhand; yet many churchwardens are sued, or threatened to be sued by their troublesome ministers, as perjured persons, for not presenting their parishioners who failed in observing holy days.

23. The great increase and frequency of whoredoms and adulteries, occasioned by the prelates' corrupt administration of justice in such cases, who taking upon them the punishment of it, do turn all into monies for the filling of their purses; and lest their officers should defraud them of their gain, they have in their late canon, instead of remedying these vices, decreed that the commutation of penance shall not be without the bishops' privity.

24. The general abuse of that great ordinance of excommunication, which God hath left in his church as the last and greatest punishment which the church can inflict upon obstinate and great offenders; and the prelates and their officers, who of right have nothing to do with it, do daily excommunicate men, either for doing that which is lawful, or for vain, idle and trivial matters, as working, or opening a shop on a holy day, for not appearing at every beck upon their summons, not paying a fee, or the like; yea, they have made it, as they do all other things, a hook or instrument wherewith to empty men's purses, and to advance their own greatness; and so that sacred ordinance of God, by their perverting of it, becomes contemptible to all men, and is seldom or never used against notorious offenders, who for the most part are their favorites.

25. Yea further, the pride and ambition of the prelates being boundless, unwilling to be subject either to man or laws, they claim their office and jurisdiction to be *Jure Divino*, exercise ecclesiastical authority in their own names and rights, and under their own seals, and take upon them temporal dignities, places and offices in the commonwealth, that they may sway both swords.

26. Whence follows the taking commissions in their own courts and consistories, and where else they sit in matters determinable of right at common law, the putting of ministers upon parishes, without the patron's and people's consent.

27. The imposing of oaths of various and trivial articles yearly upon churchwardens and sidesmen, which they cannot take without perjury, unless they fall at jars continually with their ministers and neighbours, and wholly neglect their own calling.

28. The exercising of the oath *ex officio*, and other proceedings by way

of inquisition, reaching even to men's thoughts, the apprehending and detaining of men by pursuivants, the frequent suspending and depriving of ministers, fining and imprisoning of all sorts of people, breaking up of men's houses and studies, taking away men's books, letters, and other writings, seizing upon their estates, removing them from their callings, separating between them and their wives against both their wills, the rejecting of prohibitions with threatenings, and the doing of many other outrages, to the utter infringing the laws of the realm and the subjects' liberties, and ruining of them and their families; and of later time the judges of the land are so awed with the power and greatness of the prelates, and other ways promoted, that neither prohibition, *Habeas Corpus*, nor any other lawful remedy can be had, or take place, for the distressed subjects in most cases; only Papists, Jesuits, priests, and such others as propagate Popery or Arminianism, are countenanced, spared, and have much liberty; and from hence followed amongst others these dangerous consequences.

1. The general hope and expectation of the Romish party, that their superstitious religion will ere long be fully planted in this kingdom again, and so they are encouraged to persist therein, and to practise the same openly in divers places, to the high dishonour of God, and contrary to the laws of the realm.

2. The discouragement and destruction of all good subjects, of whom are multitudes, both clothiers, merchants and others, who being deprived of their ministers, and over-burdened with these pressures, have departed the kingdom to Holland, and other parts, and have drawn with them a great manufacture of cloth and trading out of the land into other places where they reside, whereby wool, the great staple of the kingdom, is become of small value, and vends not; trading is decayed, many poor people want work, seamen lose employment, and the whole land is much impoverished, to the great dishonour of this kingdom and blemishment to the government thereof.

3. The present wars and commotions happened between his majesty and his subjects of Scotland, wherein his majesty and all his kingdoms are endangered, and suffer greatly, and are like to become a prey to the common enemy in case the wars go on, which we exceedingly fear will not only go on, but also increase to an utter ruin of all, unless the prelates with their dependences be removed out of England, and also they and their practices, who, as we under your honour's favours, do verily believe and conceive have occasioned the quarrel.

All which we humbly refer to the consideration of this honourable assembly, desiring the Lord of heaven to direct you in the right way to redress all these evils.

THE PROTESTATION OATH, 1641

Reacting to wild invasion scares, rumours of plots and fears that the Protestant reformation was about to be undone, members of parliament, both commons and lords, subscribed to the Protestation Oath in May 1641. The oath was soon adopted by activists outside of parliament, and in January 1642 it was extended to adult males throughout England. More people subscribed to this document than were ever invited to vote in parliamentary elections; approximately two-thirds wrote marks instead of signatures, providing a very rough gauge of literacy levels. Ostensibly the Protestation supported the established order against the alleged popish innovations of prelacy and Arminianism, but some subscribers also construed it to defend the church against sectarian attacks on the Thirty-Nine Articles. The promise to defend 'the true reformed Protestant religion, expressed in the doctrine of the Church of England', commanded wide support, but left open the divisive issues of religious ceremonies and discipline.

Source: *Fifth Report of the Royal Commission on Historical Manuscripts* (London, 1876), Part I, Appendix 3.

I, *A. B.*, do in the presence of Almighty God, promise, vow and protest to maintain and defend, as far as lawfully I may, with my life, power and estate, the true reformed Protestant religion, expressed in the doctrine of the Church of England, against all popery and popish innovations within this realm, contrary to the same doctrine, and according to the duty of my allegiance, his majesty's royal person, honour and estate, as also the power and privileges of parliaments, the lawful rights and liberties of the subjects, and every person that maketh this protestation, in whatsoever he shall do in the lawful pursuance of the same; and to my power, and as far as lawfully I may, I will oppose and by all good ways and means endeavour to bring to condign punishment all such as shall, either by force, practice, counsels, plots, conspiracies, or otherwise, do anything to the contrary of anything in this present protestation contained; and further, that I shall in all just and honourable ways, endeavour to preserve the union and peace betwixt the three kingdoms of England, Scotland and Ireland: and neither for hope, fear, nor any other respect, shall relinquish this promise, vow and protestation.

THE SOLEMN LEAGUE AND COVENANT, 1643

Adoption of the Solemn League and Covenant secured Scottish support for the parliamentary enemies of Charles I at a critical stage in the first Civil War. Like the Protestation, it was intended to be subscribed throughout the land. If fully implemented it would have replaced the episcopacy of the Church of England with a Presbyterian organization, and the ceremonies of the prayer book with worship of the kind set forth in the Directory for Public Worship. But Presbyterians never attained dominance among the proliferating religious options of the 1640s and 1650s. Copies of the Solemn League and Covenant were ceremonially burned at the Restoration in 1660.

Source: S. R. Gardiner (ed.), *Constitutional Documents of the Puritan Revolution, 1625–1660* (2nd. edn, Oxford, 1899), pp. 267–71.

A solemn league and covenant for reformation and defence of religion, the honour and happiness of the king, and the peace and safety of the three kingdoms of England, Scotland, and Ireland.

We noblemen, barons, knights, gentlemen, citizens, burgesses, ministers of the gospel, and commons of all sorts in the kingdoms of England, Scotland and Ireland, by the providence of God living under one king, and being of one reformed religion; having before our eyes the glory of God, and the advancement of the kingdom of Our Lord and Saviour Jesus Christ, the honour and happiness of the king's majesty and his posterity, and the true public liberty, safety and peace of the kingdoms, wherein every one's private condition is included; and calling to mind the treacherous and bloody plots, conspiracies, attempts and practices of the enemies of God against the true religion and professors thereof in all places, especially in these three kingdoms, ever since the reformation of religion; and how much their rage, power and presumption are of late, and at this time increased and exercised, whereof the deplorable estate of the church and kingdom of Ireland, the distressed estate of the church and kingdom of England, and the dangerous estate of the church and kingdom of Scotland, are present and public testimonies: we have (now at last) after other means of supplication, remonstrance, protestation and sufferings, for the preservation of ourselves and our religion from utter ruin and destruction, according to the commendable practice of these kingdoms in former times, and the example of God's people in other nations, after mature deliberation, resolved and determined to enter into a mutual and solemn league and covenant, wherein we all subscribe, and each one of us for himself, with our hands lifted up to the most high God, do swear,

1. That we shall sincerely, really and constantly, through the grace of God, endeavour in our several places and callings, the preservation of the reformed religion in the church of Scotland, in doctrine, worship, discipline and government, against our common enemies; the reformation of religion in the kingdoms of England and Ireland, in doctrine, worship, discipline and government, according to the word of God, and the example of the best reformed churches; and we shall endeavour to bring the churches of God in the three kingdoms to the nearest conjunction and uniformity in religion, confession of faith, form of church government, directory for worship and catechizing, that we, and our posterity after us, may, as brethren, live in faith and love, and the Lord may delight to dwell in the midst of us.

2. That we shall in like manner, without respect of persons, endeavour the extirpation of popery, prelacy (that is, church government by

archbishops, bishops, their chancellors and commissaries, deans, deans and chapters, archdeacons, and all other ecclesiastical officers depending on that hierarchy), superstition, heresy, schism, profaneness, and whatsoever shall be found to be contrary to sound doctrine and the power of godliness, lest we partake in other men's sins, and thereby be in danger to receive of their plagues; and that the Lord may be one, and his name one in the three kingdoms.

3. We shall with the same sincerity, reality and constancy, in our several vocations, endeavour with our estates and lives mutually to preserve the rights and privileges of the parliaments, and the liberties of the kingdoms, and to preserve and defend the king's majesty's person and authority, in the preservation and defence of the true religion and liberties of the kingdoms, that the world may bear witness with our consciences of our loyalty, and that we have no thoughts or intentions to diminish his majesty's just power and greatness.

4. We shall also with all faithfulness endeavour the discovery of all such as have been or shall be incendiaries, malignants or evil instruments, by hindering the reformation of religion, dividing the king from his people, or one of the kingdoms from another, or making any faction or parties amongst the people, contrary to the league and covenant, that they may be brought to public trial and receive condign punishment, as the degree of their offences shall require or deserve, or the supreme judicatories of both kingdoms respectively, or others having power from them for that effect, shall judge convenient.

5. And whereas the happiness of a blessed peace between these kingdoms, denied in former times to our progenitors, is by the good providence of God granted to us, and hath been lately concluded and settled by both parliaments: we shall each one of us, according to our places and interest, endeavour that they may remain conjoined in a firm peace and union to all posterity, and that justice may be done upon the willful opposers thereof, in manner expressed in the precedent articles.

6. We shall also, according to our places and callings, in this common cause of religion, liberty and peace of the kingdoms, assist and defend all those that enter into this league and covenant, in the maintaining and pursuing thereof; and shall not suffer ourselves, directly or indirectly, by whatsoever combination, persuasion or terror, to be divided and withdrawn from this blessed union and conjunction, whether to make defection to the contrary part, or give ourselves to a detestable indifference or neutrality in this cause, which so much concerneth the glory of God, the good of the kingdoms, and the honour of the king; but shall all the days of our lives zealously and constantly continue therein, against all opposition, and promote the same according to our power, against all lets and impediments whatsoever; and what we are not able ourselves to suppress or overcome we shall reveal and make known, that it may be timely prevented or removed: all which we shall do as in the sight of God.

And because these kingdoms are guilty of many sins and provocations against God, and his Son Jesus Christ, as is too manifest by our present distresses and dangers, the fruits thereof: we profess and declare, before God and the world, our unfeigned desire to be humbled for our own sins, and for the sins of these kingdoms; especially that we have not as we ought valued the inestimable benefit of the gospel; that we have not laboured for the purity and power thereof; and that we have not endeavoured to receive Christ in our hearts, nor to walk worthy of him in our lives, which are the causes of other sins and transgressions so much abounding amongst us, and our true and unfeigned purpose, desire and endeavour, for ourselves and all others under our power and charge, both in public and in private, in all duties we owe to God and man, to amend our lives, and each one to go before another in the example of a real reformation, that the Lord may turn away his wrath and heavy indignation, and establish these churches and kingdoms in truth and peace. And this covenant we make in the presence of Almighty God, the searcher of all hearts, with a true intention to perform the same, as we shall answer at that great day when the secrets of all hearts shall be disclosed: most humbly beseeching the Lord to strengthen us by his holy spirit for this end, and to bless our desires and proceedings with such success as may be a deliverance and safety to his people, and encouragement to the Christian churches groaning under or in danger of the yoke of antichristian tyranny, to join in the same or like association and covenant, to the glory of God, the enlargement of the kingdom of Jesus Christ, and the peace and tranquillity of Christian kingdoms and commonwealths.

WILLIAM DOWSING'S DESTRUCTIONS IN EAST ANGLIA, 1643–4

Armed with a parliamentary commission and backed by men with hammers, William Dowsing (1596–1668) set off to destroy all 'monuments of idolatry and superstition' in East Anglian parish churches. He was especially concerned to remove any steps that offset the chancel from the main body of the church. Unlike the occasional desecration of churches that accompanied the Civil War, this was an orderly campaign of official iconoclasm. These extracts from Dowsing's report of his work in Cambridgeshire and Suffolk reveal the variety of sacred images still found in seventeenth-century churches. Many more images, pictures and statues survived Dowsing's onslaught because the iconoclast was in too much of a hurry, or because the offending items were beyond the reach of his ladders, or because local officials refused to follow his instructions.

Source: J. G. Cheshire (ed.), 'William Dowsing's Destructions', *Transactions of the Cambridgeshire and Huntingdonshire Archaeological Society*, vol. 3 (1914), pp. 77–91; E. H. Evelyn White (ed.), *The Journal of William Dowsing* (Ipswich, 1885), pp. 26–7.

Cambridge

At Peter's parish, December 30, 1643. We brake down ten popish pictures, we brake off three popish inscriptions of prayers to be made for their souls and burnt the eagles, digged up the steps and they are to be levelled by Wednesday.

Giles parish, December 30, 1643. We brake down twelve superstitious pictures, and took two popish inscriptions, four cherubims, and a holy water font at the porch door.

At Little Mary's, December 29–30, 1643. We brake down sixty superstitious pictures, some popes and crucifixes, and God the Father sitting in a chair and holding a glass in his hand.

At Botolph parish, January, 1643/4. We digged up the steps and brake down twelve popish inscriptions and pictures.

Edward's parish, January 1, 1643/4. We digged up the steps and brake down forty pictures and took off ten superstitious pictures.

All Hallows, January 1643/4. We brake down divers superstitious pictures and eight cherubims . . .

Cambridgeshire

Ditton, January 3, 1643/4. We beat down two crucifixes, and the twelve apostles, and many other superstitious pictures.

At Little Swaffham, we brake down a great many pictures superstitious, twenty cherubims, and the rails we brake in pieces and digged down the steps.

Burwell, January 2, 1643/4. We brake down a great many superstitious pictures.

Wratting, March 21. We brake down six superstitious pictures, and a crucifix, and gave order to level the steps, and take down a cross off the church.

Balsham, March 21. We brake divers superstitious pictures, one crucifix, and gave order to take down a cross on the church, and to take down another on the steeple, and to level the chancel, within a month.

Weston Colville, March 22–3. Superstitious pictures *cuius animae propitietur Deus,*[1] and one 'Pray for the soul', and the twelve apostles, and superstitious pictures and a cross on the porch, and steps to be levelled in the chancel.

Carlton cum Willingham, March 22. A cross on the steeple promised to be taken down, and we brake divers superstitious pictures.

Burrough Green, March 22. We brake down sixty four superstitious [pictures], one crucifix, and Joseph and Mary stood together in the glass,

184

as they were espoused, and a cross on the steeple, we gave order to the churchwardens to take down.

Westley, March 22. We brake down eight superstitious pictures, and gave order to take down a cross at the porch, and gave order for the minister to level the steps.

Dullingham, March 22. We brake down thirty superstitious pictures, two of them crucifixes, and gave order to break down a cross off the church, and to level the steps.

Stetchworth. We brake divers superstitious pictures . . .

Wood Ditton. We brake down thirty superstitious pictures, and a crucifix, and the Virgin Mary, written: oh mother of God, have mercy upon us.

Kirtling. Three superstitious [pictures] and fourteen angels in the chancel, on the roof, which the Lord North's man promised to take off, and the windows broken down, were new made . . .

Suffolk

Sotterly. There were divers superstitious pictures painted, which they promised to take down; and I gave order to level the steps, and to break in pieces the rails, which I have seen done, and to take off a cross on the church.

Benacre, April 6. There was six superstitious pictures, one crucifix, and the Virgin Mary twice, with Christ in her arms, and Christ lying in the manger, and the Three Kings coming to Christ with their presents, and St Catherine twice pictured . . . O Christ govern me by thy Mother's Prayers! and three bishops with their mitres, and the steps to be levelled within six weeks. And eighteen JESUS's written in capital letters on the roof, which we gave order to do out; and the story of Nebuchadnezzar; and *orate pro animabus*,[2] in a glass window.

Covehithe, April 6. We brake down two hundred pictures; one pope with divers cardinals, Christ and the Virgin Mary; a picture of God the Father, and many other, which I remember not. There was four steps, with a vault underneath, but the two first might be levelled, which we gave order to the churchwardens to do. There was many inscriptions of JESUS in capital letters, on the roof of the church, and cherubims with crosses on their breasts; and a cross in the chancel; all which with divers pictures in the windows, which we could not reach, neither would they help us to raise the ladders; all which we left a warrant with the constable to do in fourteen days.

Rushmere, April 8. We brake ten superstitious pictures, and gave order to level the steps in twenty days, to make their windows, and we brake down a pot for holy water.

Mutford, April 8. We brake down nine superstitious pictures, and gave order to take nine superstitious inscriptions of Jesus, two crosses on the steeple, and the steps to be levelled.

Frostenden, April 8. Twenty superstitious pictures, one crucifix, and a picture of God the Father, and St Andrew with his cross, and St Catherine with her wheel, four cherubims on the pulpit, two crosses on the steeple, and one on the chancel. And Mr Ellis, an high constable of the town, told me he saw an Irish man, within two months, bow to the cross on the steeple, and put off his hat to it. The steps were there to level, which they promised to do.

Cove, April 8. We took down forty-two superstitious pictures in glass, and about twenty cherubims, and the steps we have digged down.

Reydon, April 8. We brake down ten superstitious pictures and gave order to take down two crosses, one on the chancel, and another on the porch. Steps we digged up.

Southwold, April 8. We brake down one hundred and thirty superstitious pictures, St Andrew, and four crosses on the four corners of the vestry, and gave order to take down thirteen cherubims, and take down twenty angels, and to take down the cover of the font.

Walberswick. Brake down forty superstitious pictures, and to take off five crosses on the steeple and the porch, and we had eight superstitious inscriptions on the gravestones.

Blyford, April 9. There was thirty superstitious pictures, a crucifix, and the four evangelists, and the steps promised to be levelled, and begun to be digged down. A cross on the chancel they promised to take down, and a triangle on the porch, for the Trinity, and two whips and etc., Christ and a cross, all over the porch.

DIRECTORY FOR PUBLIC WORSHIP, 1645

Under the influence of Presbyterian leaders, the Long Parliament appointed the Westminster Assembly to develop a Directory for Public Worship as a replacement for The Book of Common Prayer. Two ordinances passed in 1645, the first (in January) enjoining the use of the *Directory*, and the second (in August) banning the use of the Prayer Book. While it is easy to see the differences between the old liturgy and its radical successor, it is also possible to discern an underlying similarity in the concern that worship be conducted 'decently and with order', especially in their treatment of baptism, marriage and burial. The authors of the *Directory* envisioned a reformed national church, but sectarians immediately rejected it as confining and intolerable. Source: *The Directory for the Publique Worship of God Throughout the Three Kingdomes* (London, 1646).

Preface

In the beginning of the blessed reformation, our wise and pious ancestors took care to set forth an order for redress of many things which they, then, by the word discovered to be vain, erroneous, superstitious, and idolatrous in the public worship of God. This occasioned many godly and learned men to rejoice much in the Book of Common Prayer at that time set forth, because the mass and the rest of the Latin service being removed, the public worship was celebrated in our own tongue. Many of the common people also receive benefit by hearing the scriptures read in their own language which formerly were unto them as a book that is sealed.

Howbeit, long and sad experience hath made it manifest that the liturgy used in the Church of England (notwithstanding all the pains and religious intentions of the compilers of it) hath proved an offence, not only to many of the godly at home; but also to the reformed churches abroad. For not to speak of urging the reading of all the prayers which very greatly increased the burden of it, the many unprofitable and burdensome ceremonies contained in it have occasioned much mischief, as well by disquieting the consciences of many godly ministers and people who could not yield unto them, as by depriving them of the ordinances of God, which they might not enjoy without conforming or subscribing to those ceremonies. Sundry good Christians have been by means thereof kept from the Lord's table, and divers able and faithful ministers debarred from the exercise of their ministry (to the endangering of many thousand souls in a time of such scarcity of faithful pastors) and spoiled of their livelihood, to the undoing of them and their families. Prelates and their faction have laboured to raise the estimation of it to such an height, as if there were no other worship, or way of worship of God amongst us, but only the service book, to the great hindrance of the preaching of the word, and (in some places, especially of late) to the jostling of it out as unnecessary; or (at best) as far inferior to the reading of common prayer, which was made no better than an idol by many ignorant and superstitious people, who pleasing themselves in their presence at that service, and their lip-labour in being a part in it, have thereby hardened themselves in their ignorance and carelessness of saving knowledge and true piety.

In the meantime, Papists boasted that the book was a compliance with them in a great part of their service, and so were not a little confirmed in their superstition and idolatry, expecting rather our return to them, than endeavouring the reformation of themselves: in which expectation they were of late very much encouraged, when upon the pretended

187

warrantableness of imposing of the former ceremonies, new ones were daily obtruded upon the church.

Add hereunto (which was not foreseen, but since hath come to pass) that the liturgy hath been a great means, as on the one hand to make and increase an idle and unedifying ministry, which contented itself with set forms made to their hands by others, without putting forth themselves to exercise the gift of prayer, with which Our Lord Jesus Christ pleaseth to furnish all his servants whom he calls to that office: so on the other side it hath been (and ever would be, if continued) a matter of endless strife and contention in the church, and a snare both to many godly and faithful ministers, who have been persecuted and silenced upon that occasion, and to others of hopeful parts, many of which have been, and more still would be, diverted from all thoughts of the ministry to other studies; especially in these latter times, wherein God vouchsafeth to his people more and better means for the discovery of error and superstition, and for attaining of knowledge in the mysteries of godliness, and gifts in preaching and prayer.

Upon these, and many the like weighty considerations, in reference to the whole book in general, and because of divers particulars contained in it; not from any love to novelty or intention to disparage our first reformers (of whom we are persuaded that, were they now alive, they would join with us in this work, and whom we acknowledge as excellent instruments raised by God to begin the purging and building of his house, and desire they may be had of us and posterity in everlasting remembrance, with thankfulness and honour), but that we may in some measure answer the gracious providence of God, which at this time calleth upon us for further reformation, and may satisfy our own consciences, and answer the expectation of other reformed churches, and the desires of many of the godly among ourselves, and withal give some public testimony of our endeavours for uniformity in divine worship, which we have promised in our Solemn League and Covenant. We have, after earnest and frequent calling upon the name of God, and after much consultation, not with flesh and blood, but with his holy word, resolved to lay aside the former liturgy, with the many rites and ceremonies formerly used in the worship of God, and have agreed upon this following Directory for all the parts of public worship, at ordinary and extraordinary times.

Wherein our care hath been to hold forth such things as are of divine institution in every ordinance, and other things we have endeavoured to set forth according to the rules of Christian prudence, agreeable to the general rules of the word of God. Our meaning therein being only that the general heads, the sense and scope of the prayers and other parts of public worship being known to all, there may be a consent of all the churches in those things that contain the substance of the service and worship of God; and the ministers may be hereby directed in their administrations to keep like soundness in doctrine and prayer, and may, if need be, have some help and furniture. And yet so, as they become not hereby slothful and negligent in stirring up the gifts of Christ in them, but that each one, by meditation, by taking heed to himself and the flock of God committed to him, and by wise observing the ways of divine providence, may be careful to furnish his heart and tongue with further, or other materials of prayer and exhortation, as shall be needful upon all occasions.

The sacrament of baptism

Baptism, as it is not unnecessarily to be delayed, so is it not to be administered in any case by any private person; but by a minister of Christ, called to be the steward of the mysteries of God. Nor is it to be administered in private places, or privately, but in the place of public worship, and in the face of the congregation, where the people may most conveniently see and hear; and not in the places where fonts in the time of popery were unfitly and superstitiously placed. The child to be baptized, after notice given to the minister the day before, is to be presented by the father, or (in case of his necessary absence) by some Christian friend in his place, professing his earnest desire that the child may be baptized.

Before baptism, the minister is to use some words of instruction, touching the institution, nature, use and ends of this sacrament, showing:

That it is instituted by Our Lord Jesus Christ; that it is a seal of the covenant of grace, of our engrafting into Christ, and of our union with him, of remission of sins, regeneration, adoption, and life eternal; that the water in baptism, representeth and signifieth both the blood of Christ, which taketh away all guilt of sin, original and actual, and the sanctifying virtue of the spirit of Christ against the dominion of sin, and the corruption of our sinful nature; that baptizing, or sprinkling and washing with water signifieth the cleansing from sin by the blood, and for the merit of Christ, together with the mortification of sin, and rising from sin to newness of life, by virtue of the death and resurrection of Christ; that the promise is made to believers and their seed and that the seed and posterity of the faithful, born within the church, have by their birth, interest in the covenant, and right to the seal of it, and to the outward privileges of the church, under the gospel, no less than the children of Abraham in the time of the Old Testament, the covenant of grace, for substance, being the same and the grace of God and consolation of believers, more plentiful than before; that the Son of God

189

admitted little children into his presence, embracing and blessing them, saying, For of such is the kingdom of God; that children by baptism are solemnly received into the bosom of the visible church, distinguished from the world, and them that are without, and united with believers, and that all who are baptized in the name of Christ do renounce and by their baptism are bound to fight against the Devil, the world and the flesh; that they are Christians, and federally holy before baptism, and therefore are they baptized; that the inward grace and virtue of baptism is not tied to that very moment of time wherein it is administered, and that the fruit and power thereof reacheth to the whole course of our life; and that outward baptism is not so necessary, that through the want thereof the infant is in danger of damnation, or the parents guilty, if they do not contemn or neglect the ordinance of Christ when and where it may be had.

In these or the like instructions, the minister is to use his own liberty, and godly wisdom, as the ignorance or errors in the doctrine of baptism and the edification of the people shall require . . .

Then the minister is to demand the name of the child, which being told him, he is to say (calling the child by his name), I baptize thee in the name of the Father, of the Son, and of the Holy Ghost. *As he pronounceth these words, he is to baptize the child with water, which for the manner of doing of it, is not only lawful but sufficient and most expedient to be by pouring or sprinkling of the water on the face of the child, without adding any other ceremony.*

The solemnization of marriage

Although marriage be no sacrament, nor peculiar to the church of God, but common to mankind, and of public interest in every commonwealth, yet because such as marry are to marry in the Lord, and have special need of instruction, direction and exhortation from the word of God, at their entering into such a new condition, and of the blessing of God upon them therein, we judge it expedient that marriage be solemnized by a lawful minister of the word, that he may accordingly counsel them, and pray for a blessing upon them.

Marriage is to be betwixt one man and one woman only, and they, such as are not within the degrees of consanguinity or affinity prohibited by the word of God. And the parties are to be of years of discretion, fit to make their own choice, or upon good grounds to give their mutual consent.

Before the solemnizing of marriage between any persons, their purpose of marriage shall be published by the minister three several Sabbath days in the congregation, at the place or places of their most usual and constant abode respectively. And of this publication, the minister who is to join them in marriage, shall have sufficient testimony, before he proceed to solemnize the marriage. Before that publication, of such their purpose (if the parties be under age) the consent of the parents, or other, under whose power they are (in case the parents be dead) is to be made known to the church officers of that congregation, to be recorded. The like is to be observed in the proceedings of all others, although of age, whose parents are living, for their first marriage. And in after marriages of either of those parties, they shall be exhorted not to contract marriage without first acquainting their parents with it (if with convenience it may be done), endeavouring to obtain their consent. Parents ought not to force their children to marry without their free consent, nor deny their own consent without just cause.

After the purpose or contract of marriage hath been thus published, the marriage is not to be long deferred. Therefore, the minister, having had convenient warning, and nothing being objected to hinder it, is publicly to solemnize it in the place appointed by Authority for public worship, before a competent number of credible witnesses, at some convenient hour of the day, at any time of year, except on a day of public humiliation. And we advise that it be not on the Lord's day . . .

After solemn charging of the person to be married, before the great God, who searcheth all hearts, and to whom they must give a strict account at the last day, that if either of them know any cause, by precontract or otherwise, why they may not lawfully proceed to marriage, that they now discover it: *The minister (if no impediment be acknowledged) shall cause, first the man to take the woman by the right hand, saying these words*: I, *N.* do take thee *N.* to be my married wife, and do, in the presence of God, and before this congregation, promise and covenant to be a loving and faithful husband unto thee, until God shall separate us by death.

Then the woman shall take the man by his right hand, and say these words: I, *N.* do take thee *N.* to be my married husband, and I do, in the presence of God, and before this congregation, promise and covenant to be a loving, faithful, and obedient wife unto thee, until God shall separate us by death. *Then, without any further ceremony, the minister shall in the face of the congregation, pronounce them to be husband and wife, according to God's ordinance, and so conclude the action with prayer to this effect.*

Concerning burial of the dead

When any person departeth this life, let the dead body, upon the day of burial, be decently attended from the house to the place appointed for public burial, and there immediately interred without any ceremony. And because the customs of kneeling down and praying by, or towards the dead corpse, and other such usages in the place where it lies before it be carried to burial, are superstitious; and for that praying, reading and singing both in going to, and at the grave have been grossly abused, are no way beneficial to the dead, and have proved many ways hurtful to the living, therefore let all such things be laid aside. Howbeit, we judge it very convenient, that the Christian friends which accompany the dead body to the place appointed for public burial do apply themselves to meditations and conferences suitable to the occasion: and that the minister, as upon other occasions, so at this time, if he be present, may put them in remembrance of their duty. That this shall not extend to deny any civil respects or differences at the burial, suitable to the rank and condition of the party deceased whilst he was living.

Of singing of psalms

It is the duty of Christians to praise God publicly by singing of psalms together in the congregation, and also privately in the family. In singing of psalms the voice is to be tunably and gravely ordered: but the chief care must be to sing with understanding, and with grace in the heart, making melody unto the Lord. That the whole congregation may join herein, every one that can read is to have a psalm-book, and all others, not disabled by age or otherwise, are to be exhorted to learn to read. But for the present, where many in the congregation cannot read, it is convenient that the minister or some other fit person appointed by him and the other ruling officers, do read the psalm line by line, before the singing thereof.

NICHOLAS PROFFET, *ENGLANDS IMPENITENCIE UNDER SMITING*, 1645

Preaching to the embattled Long Parliament in 1645, Nicholas Proffet ascribed England's troubles to the judgements and punishments of God who was angered by contumacious and unrepentant sin. Proffet's outraged account reads like a roll-call of manifold transgressions: neglect of prayer and fasting, public swearing and drunkenness, women's luxurious apparel, and neglectful profanation of the Sabbath. His call for the magistrate to undertake the correction of these sins aligns him with those forces for godly social reformation that found eloquent expression amidst the disorders of civil war and revolution.
Source: Nicholas Proffet, *Englands Impenitencie under Smiting*, (London, 1645), pp. 44–8.

For all this his anger is not turned away, but his hand is stretched out still. For the people turn not unto him that smiteth them, neither do they seek the Lord of Hosts. Isaiah 9:13.

Now in the last place, this doctrine may be applied for exhortation and special direction to our parliament worthies, upon whom it layeth a double charge, particularly for themselves, and generally for the whole kingdom. If impenitency and continuance in sin cause the continuance of anger, and doth pull down more and heavier strokes upon our nation, then it must be their endeavour to remove this cause of anger, that the anger may be diverted, and this heavy judgement removed from the kingdom; this is the way for them to become repairers of the breach, and restorers of paths to dwell in; for if men will return, anger will cease, and the quarrel would soon be at an end; but if the cause of wrath still continue, we cannot expect that the destroying hand should be drawn in, but that it should be stretched out still. Upon you therefore honourable and beloved the use falleth with a double weight, the doctrine requireth for the removing of the strokes with which the land is smitten, and preventing of heavier ready to fall upon it, that you see that none of your own sins under smiting; that your not turning from them, do not cause the anger of God to continue, and that (being physicians of the state, such as are in places of power) you endeavour by all possible means to cause the people to turn to him that smiteth them; that removing the cause wheresoever you find it, this miserable effect may cease; turning yourselves from whatsoever may be found to be a part of the cause, and endeavouring, as much as in you lieth, to cause the whole kingdom to turn from their sins also, that anger may be appeased, and smiting stayed and cease.

It is not to be doubted, it hath been your desire and care; and is your endeavour to make others to return, you have used means to that end, and have therefore sent ministers into many places, where they were wanting, to call upon men to return; and to remove such as have been idle, unfaithful, and scandalous . . . Compassion is to be used towards some, and severity towards others, that (if it be possible) they may be pulled out of the fire; men must be dealt with for the saving of their souls, as surgeons are wont to deal with their patients for the saving their lives, if lenitives, and more gentle means will not serve, corrosives, cauterizings, and the like must be used. God himself doth take the rod into his hand, when the word is contemned; and if lighter strokes will not serve, he hath heavier blows for those that be impenitent. That the people may be brought to return, instruction and corrections must be used; magistrate and minister, the word and sword must be joined. There are many grievous sins among us, which have provoked the wrath of God against the land, and from which the people should turn, that his anger may be turned away, and his destroying hand taken off from the nation. Many that have been complained of by others, that I have no time nor intention to name, I shall only represent some few, which are more common and obvious, and withal more impudent and scandalous, humbly intreating that some course, which seemeth best to your wisdoms, may be used to suppress them, and to cause the people, if it be possible, to turn from them, as:

First, the great neglect of the duty of these days of humiliation, which many (especially in the country) do not only slight and disregard, but abuse and profane, spending the day, or a great part of it in alehouses and taverns, or about their worldly employment, as if it were different to come or not to come to the public assemblies, to seek or to provoke the Lord of Hosts.

Secondly, the horrible profanation of the glorious, and dreadful name of God, by execrations, blasphemies, and bloody oaths, a sin that doth exceedingly abound, and under which the land doth grievously mourn.

Thirdly, the sottish, and swinish sin of drunkenness, by which men and women make themselves like beasts rather than Christians, and yet in these times of smiting it doth so abound, as hardly can men walk the streets, but to their grief they shall see of both sexes, reel and vomit in a brutish manner without control.

Fourthly, the hateful sin of pride, especially of women, against whom our prophet hath spent a good part of a chapter[3] and elegantly set forth the levity and vanity of the women of his time, and withal how this sin did provoke God, and pull down such a judgement as this land is under; for he doth threaten war, and declare that these men should fall by the sword, and their mighty men in the war, yet some among us (as if they durst out-dare heaven itself) do come into the presence of an angry God in the days of humiliation with naked breasts and such vain attire as do openly discover that lightness and wantonness which is shameful and unsufferable.

Fifthly, there are many other sins, such as Sabbath-breaking, oppression, etc., of which I thought to have spoke something, if the time would have given leave; but I shall only name one thing more, which might much further this work, and that is, that some course may be taken for the purging of the magistracy, that as scandalous ministers so ill justices and scandalous magistrates may be removed, and those that be zealous and pious put in their places: for there will be little hope (if sin be set up to correct vice, and they that turn from God themselves, shall stand in the places of those that should cause others to turn) that the work of reformation will ever go forward, the former or other sins be suppressed and the land purged of them.

A faithful magistracy, and a painful ministry may do much more together, than either of them can do apart. I beseech you, that some course may be taken, such as to your wisdoms may seem best, to put life into laws and ordinances, that they may not be suffered to sleep, and wicked men to sin, but that they may be constrained to break off these sins which do so highly provoke God, and so much hinder our peace. It is noted of King Josiah, that having made a covenant to walk before the Lord, and to keep his commandments, etc., he caused all that were present or were found in Jerusalem and Benjamin to stand to it, i.e. (as some read and expound it) he constrained them by royal power and authority etc. This is the way to remove the cause of our misery, and to save yourselves and the nation, at least, to discharge your own duty, to perform a most acceptable service to your God, and therefore in the words of David unto Solomon (when he had showed his care and preparation for the building the house of the Lord, and the work that was before him) let me make bold to exhort you to this duty, and sue to God for success, *Arise therefore, and be doing, and the Lord be with you.*[4]

THOMAS EDWARDS ON THE PRACTICES AND ERRORS OF THE SECTARIES, 1646

The collapse of episcopal discipline in the early 1640s permitted the rise of sectaries, radical religious splinter groups who rejected any uniform national church. Anabaptists, Antinomians, Congregational Independents, Fifth Monarchists and Seekers, joined soon by Muggletonians, Ranters and Quakers, created a ferment of religious experimentation. Shocked by this sectarian explosion, many former Puritans became spokesmen for religious conservatism. Thomas Edwards (1599–1647), a zealous Presbyterian, exposed the worst excesses of the sectaries and warned of the consequences of religious toleration.
Source: Thomas Edwards, *Gangraena: or A Catalogue and Discovery of many of the Errours, Heresies, Blasphemies and Pernicious Practices of the Sectaries of this time* (London, 1646), pp. 62–7.

Now for the particular practices of the sectaries. I had drawn up many, to the number of seventy, and provided for every practice instances for proof, and upon some of them I could write a large discourse, even a book upon several of them; as of their behaviour and carriage towards the parliament, the kingdom of Scotland, the assembly of divines, the city of London, the ministry of England, yea of all the reformed churches, as of their seeking and getting into all sorts of offices and places . . . their plotting and labouring from the first year of the wars, to get into their hands the sword and power of arms, by having a considerable army, which they might look upon more particularly as theirs and of their way, by attempting to remove and heave at many gallant commanders, to get the command of the strongest garrisons and places . . .

They use to ascribe and attribute all the success of things, all that's done in field, at leaguers, all victories, brave actions to their party, crying them up

195

in pulpits, news-books, conferences, calling them the saviours of the kingdoms; and for this purpose they have certain men that are criers and trumpeters between the army, city and country, who trumpet forth their praises, giving them the titles of terrible, etc. A large book would not contain the relation of all the victories, glorious actions, exploits having been given to the army called Independent.

They give out and boast their party to be more and greater than they are; some of them will speak in all places as if all were theirs, all for them; they have given out as if parliament, armies, city of London, country, all the godly, wise, judicious understanding men, were theirs, and will be theirs: yea, that the assembly, the French churches, the commissioners of the church of Scotland thought well of their way; and so of particular persons that are prime men they have given out, as if they were, or are coming over to them . . . they use to boast of their friends in the House of Commons, and they will acquaint their friends in the House of Commons; and they brag of a toleration, giving out their friends in the House of Commons have said they shall have a toleration; and they boast thus to awe persons, and to make men afraid to speak against them, or to oppose them, but rather to adhere to them who are so powerful, and have so many on their side.

They appropriate to themselves the name of the godly and well-affected party, the title of saints, calling themselves the saints, that they only preach Jesus Christ, and though they be Anabaptists, Seekers, etc. yet they are the saints: this is common in printed books, petitions, sermons, discourses; what, speak against the saints? Be against a toleration for the saints? meaning themselves only.

They pretend one thing, when they intend quite another, and 'tis usual for them to pretend the public good, the benefit of the state, when 'tis evident they intend their own interest, and strengthen of their party; they will pretend peace, love, forbearing of all names of difference, to make the Presbyterians secure, negligent, and to forbear all means of settling things, and yet at the same time go quite contrary, using all means and ways for promoting their own party . . .

What themselves are most faulty in, that they will charge upon others, the Presbyterian ministers and people, as making divisions, and wanting love, as breaking the peace, and causing misrules, tumults, as be guilty of persecution, when as 'tis evident to all the world they are most faulty in all these particulars, and in many more, and for the proof of it I could demonstrate it in a hundred instances.

They do on purpose (having got churches void) keep many churches without ministers, seek out for none, stop (all they can) orthodox ministers from coming in, which they do for two reasons: (1) that so they may pay no tithes; (2) that so they may have the liberty of the pulpits for all kinds of sectaries and mechanic preachers, who come from London, the armies, and other places to preach in and corrupt the people, and that the people being as sheep without a shepherd, may be more easily now drawn away to error and schism; and of this practice there are many sad examples in Hertfordshire, Buckinghamshire, Essex, and that in some great market towns, as Chesham, where thousands of souls are.

They have laboured and do by all ways to have no church government at all settled in this kingdom, but to keep it out. Or secondly, if there must be any, yet to have a defective, imperfect loose government and reformation, that may not be able to do the work, that so others may fall off to their way the more; and for proof of this, they have refused to join for a pure full reformation in points according to their own principles, that so one good might not hinder a greater good (as was expressed) and have opposed to the utmost a thorough presbyterial reformation. (3) They have laboured to get a toleration granted before the government be settled, to get an exception before the rule was made, and if once they had gotten that, let the Presbyterians get the government then when they could, and this they stirred in, and sought to effect last winter. (4) Seeing they could not do this, but this policy was espied, they labour for a toleration together with the reformation, that the church government and a toleration might be borne and brought forth together as twins in one day, and so go hand in hand; and this they are labouring for now, the monster of toleration conceived in the womb of the sectaries long ago, they having grown big with it ever since, are now in travail to bring it forth, and till they could be ready and get things fitted for a toleration, they bestirred themselves so against the London petitions, that of September, those of November, lest government should be settled before a toleration, and therefore one of them said to some citizens, Why should you be so hasty for government, cannot you stay awhile? How long, said they? To spring, said this sectary, hoping their toleration business would be ready by that.

In some parish churches where the sectaries are put in, they have put down all singing of psalms, as at Eltisley in Cambridgeshire, Albery in Hertfordshire, and will not suffer the parishes to enjoy any singing of psalms; and in other places they begin to put down all prayer in the public assemblies, and to say there must be only discoursing and preaching; and in places where they cannot prevail to shut out singing of psalms, they in a contemptuous manner clap on their hats in the time of singing psalms, and having been pulled off, put them on again; yea, in prayer also many of them keep on hats.

They send forth into several counties of this kingdom from their churches in London, as church acts, several emissaries members of their churches, to preach and spread their errors, to dip, to gather and settle churches; they are not content with their own meetings on Lord's days, week days, keeping constant lectures in set places for all to come to that will, thereby poisoning many in the city, but they endeavour the leavening of all the counties, as I might give instance of Lamb, Kiffin, Denne, Oates, with many others sent abroad, yea of some sent into the north as far as York.

They have appointed and kept disputations from town to town in the country, giving out the time, places and questions they will dispute of, as of paedobaptism, the ministry of the church of England, etc., and agree among themselves that some of them shall seem to be for paedobaptism, and in the disputation 'tis maintained at first eagerly by some of their own party against others of them who oppose it; but then after long and great disputation at last they confess they are by the evidence of truth convinced, and before all the people give glory to God that now they see the truth; whereby the people seeing them who pleaded for paedobaptism confessing their error and yielding (they knowing nothing of this precontract and deceit) they also stumble, question and fall; yea, and to spread their errors the more in some great town where some of the sectaries being soldiers have been quartered, they have desired the use of several houses of persons well affected, that in the afternoon some Christians might meet to confer together of some points, not contenting themselves to reason in the house where quartered, nor in any one house that might be larger to hold many, but to get a new house every day, the more to infect and possess the people with their ways and tenets.

All things that have fallen out and do in the kingdoms, of victories, losses, ordinances, petitions, actions, death of particular persons, of all matter in church, state, parliament, assembly, city, they make use of it one way or other to further their design, and turn it for the furthering of their way, and against the presbyterial government, as the business of Dunnington Castle, as the loss of Leicester, upon that framing a petition to adjourn the assembly, with other particulars which I cannot now mention.

Some of the sectaries plead miracles, revelations, visions for their way, and to confirm their doctrine, as some anabaptists at York for their rebaptization, that being baptized in the winter in the River Ouse the water was as hot as if it had been in the midst of summer; as healing the sick with the anointing of oil; as giving out, Christ appeared to an Anabaptist, and forbad her to baptize her child . . .

They have done and practised many strange things in reference to baptism of children, dressing up a cat like a child for to be baptized, inviting many people both men and women as to baptizing of a child, and then when neighbours were come, having one to preach against baptizing of children; they have baptized many weakly ancient women naked in rivers in winter, whereupon some have sickened and died; they have baptized young maids, citizens' daughters, about one and two a clock in the morning, tempting them out of their fathers' houses at midnight to be baptized, the parents being asleep and knowing nothing.

They use to give great and glorious names, and swelling titles to their books they set forth, as *Innocency and Truth Triumphing Together*, as *Truth Gloriously Appearing*, etc., as also to their erroneous doctrines laid down in their books, casting upon truths of God odious names, as *The Storming of Antichrist, Discovery of the man of sin*, etc., their books being just like the Egyptian temples, whose outsides were beautiful and glorious, having the inscription of a deity upon them, but within nothing but a crocodile, a cat, an onion, or some such vile mean creature.

RICHARD BAXTER'S MINISTRY AT KIDDERMINSTER, 1647–60

In his autobiography Richard Baxter (1615–91) chronicles his successful ministry to the hand-loom weavers of Kidderminster, Worcestershire, during the troubled years of the Interregnum. In the following extract he presents a picture of the daily labours and diverse responsibilities of his curacy, which included, in addition to the usual pastoral duties, private teaching and catechizing, doctoring and family counselling. A moderate Presbyterian under Cromwell and a dissenter under Charles II, Baxter became known as a shrewd advisor on spiritual and disciplinary matters. His massive *Christian Directory* (1673) distils several decades of pastoral practice and practical divinity.
Source: J. M. Lloyd-Thomas (ed.), *The Autobiography of Richard Baxter* (London, 1931), pp. 76–84.

In my labours at Kidderminster after my return I did all under languishing weakness, being seldom an hour free of pain . . .

Many a time have I been brought very low and received the sentence of death in myself, when my poor, honest, praying neighbours have met, and upon their fasting and earnest prayers I have been recovered. Once when I had continued weak three weeks, and was unable to go abroad, the very day they prayed for me, being Good Friday, I recovered and was able to preach and administer the sacrament the next Lord's day, and was better after it (it being the first time that ever I administered it). And ever after that, whatever weakness was upon me, when I had (after preaching)

199

administered that sacrament to many hundred people I was much revived and eased of my infirmities . . .

I shall next record, to the praise of my redeemer, the comfortable employment and successes which he vouchsafed me during my abode at Kidderminster, under all these weaknesses. And (1) I will mention my employment, (2) my successes, and (3) those advantages by which under God it was procured, in order.

(1) I preached before the wars twice each Lord's day; but after the war but once, and once every Thursday, besides occasional sermons. Every Thursday evening my neighbours that were most desirous and had opportunity met at my house, and there one of them repeated the sermon, and afterwards they proposed what doubts any of them had about the sermon, or any other case of conscience, and I resolved their doubts; and last of all I caused sometimes one and sometimes another of them to pray (to exercise them); and sometimes I prayed with them myself, which (beside singing a psalm) was all they did. And once a week also some of the younger sort, who were not fit to pray in so great an assembly, met among a few, more privately, where they spent three hours in prayer together; every Saturday night they met at some of their houses to repeat the sermon of the last Lord's day, and to pray and prepare themselves for the following day . . . Two days every week my assistant and I myself took fourteen families between us for private catechizing and conference (he going through the parish, and the town coming to me) . . .

Besides all this I was forced five or six years, by the people's necessity, to practise physic. A common pleurisy happening one year, and no physician being near, I was forced to advise them, to save their lives; and I could not afterwards avoid the importunity of the town and country round about. And because I never once took a penny of anyone, I was crowded with patients, so that almost twenty would be at my door at once; and though God by more success than I expected so long encouraged me, yet at last I could endure it no longer, partly because it hindered my other studies, and partly because the very fear of miscarrying and doing anyone harm did make it an intolerable burden to me. So that after some years' practice I procured a godly, diligent physician to come and live in the town, and bound myself by promise to practise no more (unless in consultation with him in case of any seeming necessity). And so with that answer I turned them all off and never meddled with it more.

But all these my labours (except my private conferences with the families), even preaching and preparing for it, were but my recreations and, as it were, the work of my spare hours. For my writings were my chiefest daily labour, which yet went the more slowly on that I never one hour had an amanuensis to dictate to, and specially because my weakness took up so much of my time . . . All which, besides times of family duties, and prayer, and eating, etc., leaveth me but little time to study, which hath been the greatest external personal affliction of all my life . . .

(2) I have mentioned my sweet and acceptable employment; let me, to the praise of my gracious Lord, acquaint you with some of my success. And I will not suppress it, though I foreknow that the malignant will impute the mention of it to pride and ostentation. For it is the sacrifice of thanksgiving which I owe to my most gracious God, which I will not deny him for fear of being censured as proud, lest I prove myself proud indeed, while I cannot undergo the imputation of pride in the performance of my thanks for such undeserved mercies.

My public preaching met with an attentive diligent auditory . . .

The congregation was usually full, so that we were fain to build five galleries after my coming thither, the church itself being very capacious, and the most commodious and convenient that ever I was in. Our private meetings also were full. On the Lord's days there was no disorder to be seen in the streets, but you might hear an hundred families singing psalms and repeating sermons as you passed through the streets. In a word, when I came thither first there was about one family in a street that worshipped God and called on his name, and when I came away there were some streets where there was not passed one family in the side of a street that did not so, and that did not, by professing serious godliness, give us hopes of their sincerity. And those families which were the worst, being inns and alehouses, usually some persons in each house did seem to be religious . . .

And in my poor endeavours with my brethren in the ministry my labours were not lost . . . Yea, the mercy was yet greater in that it was of farther public benefit. For some Independents and Anabaptists that had before conceited that parish churches were the great obstruction of all true church order and discipline, and that it was impossible to bring them to any good consistency, did quite change their mind when they saw what was done at Kidderminster . . .

(3) Having related my comfortable successes in this place, I shall next tell you by what and how many advantages this much was effected . . .

One advantage was that I came to a people that never had any awakening ministry before (but a few formal cold sermons of the curate); for if they had been hardened under a powerful ministry and been sermon-proof I should have expected less.

Another advantage was that at first I was in the vigour of my spirits and had naturally a familiar moving voice (which is a great matter with the common hearers); and doing all in bodily weakness, as a dying man, my soul was the more easily brought to seriousness, and to preach as a dying man to dying men . . . Another, and the greatest advantage, was the change that was made in the public affairs by the success of the wars . . .

For my part, I bless God who gave me, even under an usurper whom I opposed, such liberty and advantage to preach his gospel with success, which I cannot have under a king to whom I have sworn and performed true subjection and obedience; yea, which no age since the gospel came into this land did before possess, as far as I can learn from history. Sure I am that when it became a matter of reputation and honour to be godly it abundantly furthered the successes of the ministry. Yea, and I shall add this much more for the sake of posterity, that as much as I have said and written against licentiousness in religion, and for the magistrates' power in it, and though I think that land most happy whose rulers use their authority for Christ as well as for the civil peace, yet in comparison of the rest of the world I shall think that land happy that hath but bare liberty to be as good as they are willing to be; and if countenance and maintenance be but added to liberty, and tolerated errors and sects be but forced to keep the peace and not to oppose the substantials of Christianity, I shall not hereafter fear such toleration, nor despair that truth will bear down adversaries.

And our unity and concord was a great advantage to us, and our freedom from those sects and heresies which many other places were infected with. We had no private church, though we had private meetings; we had not pastor against pastor, nor church against church, nor sect against sect, nor Christian against Christian . . . But we were all of one mind, and mouth and way. Not a Separatist, Anabaptist, Antinomian, etc., in the town! . . .

And it was a great advantage to me that my neighbours were of such a trade as allowed them time enough to read or talk of holy things; for the town liveth upon the weaving of Kidderminster stuffs, and as they stand in their loom they can set a book before them or edify one another . . .

And I found that my single life afforded me much advantage; for I could the easilier take my people for my children, and think all that I had too little for them, in that I had no children of my own to tempt me to another way of using it. And being discharged from the most of family cares (keeping but one servant) I had the greater vacancy and liberty for the labours of my calling . . .

Another advantage to me was the quality of the sinners of the place. There were two drunkards almost at the next doors to me, who (one by night and the other by day) did constantly, every week if not twice or thrice a week, roar and rave in the streets like stark madmen; and when they have been laid in the stocks or gaol they have been as bad as soon as ever they came out. And these were so beastly and ridiculous that they made that sin (of which we were in most danger) the more abhorred . . .

And the exercise of church discipline was no small furtherance of the people's good; for I found plainly that without it I could not have kept the religious sort from separations and divisions . . .

Another advantage which I found to my success was by ordering my doctrine to them in a suitableness to the main end, and yet so as might suit their dispositions and diseases . . . And yet I did usually put in something in my sermon which was above their own discovery, and which they had not known before; and this I did that they might be kept humble and still perceive their ignorance and be willing to keep in a learning state. (For when preachers tell their people of no more than they know, and do not show that they excel them in knowledge, and easily overtop them in abilities, the people will be tempted to turn preachers themselves, and think that they have learned all that the ministers can teach them, and are as wise as they; and they will be apt to contemn their teachers and wrangle with all their doctrines, and set their wits against them, and hear them as censurers and not as disciples, to their own undoing and to the disturbance of the church; and they will easily draw disciples after them. The bare authority of the clergy will not serve the turn without overtopping ministerial abilities.) And this I did also to increase their knowledge and also to make religion pleasant to them, by a daily addition to their former light, and to draw them on with desire and delight.

NOTES

1 TRADITION AND CHANGE: THE OLD RELIGION AND THE NEW

1   Behold your king comes.
2   The sons of this age (Luke 16:8).
3   The opening words to the Athanasian creed, which begins, 'Whosoever will be saved, before all things it is necessary that he hold the Catholic faith'.
4   'Impious kings are the ruin of men' (Proverbs 28:15,16).
5   In the Spanish Netherlands.
6   Nicholas Ridley (Bishop of London) and Hugh Latimer (Bishop of Worcester), burned at Oxford in 1555.
7   I Corinthians 13:3.

2 THE ESTABLISHED CHURCH

1   Psalm 121 (Psalms 116 or 127 substituted in 1662).
2   Ephesians 6.
3   Colossians 3.
4   Genesis 9.
5   Eccl. 3.
6   Acts 5.
7   Deut. 21.

3 RELIGIOUS CULTURE AND RELIGIOUS CONTEST IN ELIZABETHAN ENGLAND

1   Nursing mother.
2   I write with my own hand which you alone read.
3   Watchmen, not flatterers.
4   I know your piety.
5   A faithful and wise servant who knoweth how to give his master's family their portion of food in season.
6   To the discipline of the clergy.
7   II Corinthians 10,13.
8   What a fearful thing it is to fall into the hands of the living God.
9   He who acts upon his conscience, resting upon divine law, builds to Hell.

10 Matthew 16.
11 As if from authority.
12 Thus I desire, thus I command, my will stands for the reason.
13 Before the fearful tribunal of he who was crucified, there to receive according to what you did in the flesh, whether good or evil.
14 He is terrible, and he who takes away the spirit of rulers is terrible above all earthly kings.
15 In the bowels of Christ.
16 Not mine but your will be done.
17 Small point.
18 You know not what you ask. Matthew 20:22.
19 We speak after the manner of men because of [our] infirmity. An indirect translation of Romans 6:19.
20 The 1600 text here has 'men', most certainly a misprint.
21 Or 'verily'–here the 1600 edition has 'verely'.
22 A day set aside for exercises in Aristotle's *Posterior Analytics*.

4 THE JACOBEAN CHURCH

1 Greetings in Christ.
2 In writing.
3 Of the arrest of excommunicated persons.
4 That which is first is true.
5 Literally, 'from what comes after'.
6 Garments.
7 Jeremiah 31:3.
8 John 13:1.
9 Literally, 'from what is before'.
10 Paul, in Ephesians 1:4.
11 In ancient geography, a channel known for violent and uncertain currents.
12 Psalm 101:7.
13 Jesus saith unto her, touch me not.
14 Psalm 105:15.
15 Great and wonderful, above him, Psalm 131:1.
16 Above us.
17 Psalm 36:7.
18 Romans 11:33.
19 II Corinthians 12:2.

5 CEREMONIALISM AND ITS DISCONTENTS

1 Young men.
2 Table covering.
3 The word is added to element, and becomes sacrament.
4 Literally, 'provision for a journey'; refers to the holy communion given to those in danger of dying.
5 To celebrate the Lord.
6 Thomas Cartwright (1535-1603), a leading Puritan controversialist.
7 Henry Burton (1578–1648), author of *A Divine Tragedy* (1636) and other controversial works.

6 RELIGIOUS REVOLUTION

1 On whose soul may God have mercy.
2 Pray for the souls.
3 Isaiah 3:16,17,18.
4 I Chronicles 22: 16.

CHRONOLOGY

HENRY VIII (1509–47)

1525	Henry VIII 'Defender of the Faith'
1529	Fall of Cardinal Wolsey
1533	Act in Restraint of Appeals
1534	Act of Supremacy
1535	Execution of John Fisher and Thomas More
1536	Ten Articles
1536	Dissolution of lesser monasteries
1536	Pilgrimage of Grace
1539	Six Articles
1539	Dissolution of greater monasteries

EDWARD VI (1547–53)

1547	Dissolution of Chantries
1547	Homilies published
1549	First Book of Common Prayer
1552	Revised Book of Common Prayer

MARY I (1553–58)

1554	Catholic restoration
1555	Hugh Latimer and Nicholas Ridley burned
1556	Thomas Cranmer burned

ELIZABETH I (1558–1603)

1559	Act of Uniformity
1563	Thirty Nine Articles

207

1563	John Foxe's *Acts and Monuments*
1570	Pope excommunicates Queen Elizabeth
1572	*Admonition to the Parliament*
1577	Archbishop Grindal suspended
1588	Deliverance from the Spanish Armada

JAMES I (1603–25)

1603	Millenary Petition
1604	Hampton Court Conference
1604	Ecclesiastical Canons
1605	Gunpowder treason
1611	Authorized Bible
1618	Declaration of Sports in Lancashire
1618–19	Synod of Dort
1622	Directions for preachers

CHARLES I (1625–49)

1633	William Laud, Archbishop of Canterbury
1633	Declaration of Sports
1637	John Bastwick, Henry Burton and William Prynne mutilated
1640	Parliament meets
1640	Roots and Branches Petition
1641	Protestation Oath
1641	Grand Remonstrance
1642	Civil War begins
1643	Solemn League and Covenant
1645	Directory of Public Worship
1645	William Laud executed
1646	Episcopacy abolished
1649	Charles I executed

CHARLES II (1649/1660–85)

| 1660 | Crown and church restored |
| 1662 | Act of Uniformity |

208

GLOSSARY

adiaphora things theologically indifferent

Advent the season before Christmas

alb a long, white linen vestment worn by priests at mass

All Hallows' day All Saints' day, November 1st

All Souls' day November 2nd, removed from the Protestant calendar

Anabaptists radical Protestants who rejected infant baptism

Annunciation Annunciation of the Virgin Mary, Lady Day, February 25th

antiphoner a book of chants and music for traditional choir services

Arminians anti-Calvinist Protestants, named for the Dutch theologian Arminius

assoil to absolve or acquit

baldrick leather strap attaching the clapper to a bell

bede roll a list of persons to be prayed for

benefice an ecclesiastical living, or position providing a minister with income

Candlemas the Feast of the Purification of the Virgin Mary, February 2nd

censer ceremonial vessel for burning and wafting incense

chalice ornate cup for communion wine

chancel eastern part of the church, where the priest officiates at the altar or communion table, sometimes known as the choir, sometimes divided from the nave by steps, a rail, or a screen

chantry endowment, often with chapel, for masses for the dead; abolished 1547

chasuble principal vestment worn by the priest at the Catholic mass

Christmas feast of Christ's nativity, December 25th, often lasting twelve days

Christmatory a vessel containing chrism, or consecrated oil

churchwardens lay parishioners, chosen or elected to manage the goods of the church

Convocation major assembly of the clergy, in the provinces of Canterbury and York

cope ritual clerical robe, often elaborately ornamented

Corpus Christi medieval feast of the body of Christ, suppressed under Edward VI

cruet altar vessels holding wine and water

curate any priest with the cure of souls; often a junior or assistant minister

dress to keep tidy, arrange

Easter moveable springtime feast celebrating the death and resurrection of Christ

episcopacy church government by bishops and archbishops

Evangelicals based religious doctrines upon the gospel rather than catholic tradition

fanons an embroidered band, resembling a napkin, attached to the left wrist of celebrants at mass

font stone structure used to hold the water at baptism

gemmels a type of hinge

glebe land used to provide extra income for the parish priest

Good Friday commemorates the crucifixion of Christ, before Easter

hedge-priest a clandestine priest

Hocktide after Easter, a time of parish fund-raising

impropriations lay proprietorship of ecclesiastical benefices

Jesus mass votive mass in honour of the festival of the name of Jesus, celebrated on August 7th

jure divino Latin phrase meaning 'by divine right' or 'law'

kneeling oil holy oil

Lady day the Feast of the Annunciation, March 25th, often a day when rents or servants' contracts fell due

Lent the forty days before Easter, supposedly a time of abstinence

liturgy a set form of worship

mass traditional name for the Eucharist or holy communion

Maundy Thursday commemorates Christ's washing of the disciples' feet, before Easter

May day May 1st, a pagan holiday, Christianised as the feast of Sts Philip and James

maypole focus for social dancing, erected on May 1st, thought to be pre-Christian

Michaelmas Feast of St Michael the Archangel, September 29th., another rent or contract day

missal the Roman Catholic mass book

monstrance device to display the consecrated host, especially on Corpus Christi day

morris dance ritual secular dance, associated with Maytide and midsummer festivities

nave the main body of the church, where parishioners sit

Ordinary the unchanging sections of the mass, as distinguished from the Proper, which varies with the ecclesiastical calendar

paedobaptism infant baptism

Palm Sunday Sunday before Easter

paschal referring to Easter

pass to care for

paten the plate that holds communion bread

pax engraved tablet, kissed by the priest at mass and circulated among the people

Pelagians heretic Christians who denied original sin and emphasized free will

Pentecost Whitsunday, the seventh Sunday after Easter, commemorating the descent of the Holy Ghost

pew a long fixed seat in church

prebendary a priest maintained by cathedral revenues

Presbyterians opposed to episcopacy, supported church government by ministers

psalter traditional book of psalms and liturgies

pyx altar vessel reserved for the holy sacrament

rector minister entitled to the tithes of a parish

rochets surplice-like linen vestment, worn by bishops and abbots

Rogationtide season of parish processions and perambulations, usually before Whitsun

rood a carved crucifixion scene, often supported by a rood-beam, screening the choir and chancel from the nave

rushbearing ceremonial garlanding and covering the floor of the church with rushes

sabbatarianism strict observance of the Lord's day

sacring-bells rung at the moment of elevation of the mass

St Catherine's day November 25th, removed from the Protestant calendar

St Edmund's day November 16th, removed from the Protestant calendar

211

St James's day July 25th

St Lawrence's day August 10th, removed from the Protestant calendar

St Mark's day April 25th

St Nicholas's day December 6th, removed from the Protestant calendar

St Paul's day June 30th, removed from the Protestant calendar

St Peter's day June 29th

St Stephen's day December 26th

St Thomas's day December 21st (for the apostle); July 7th (for the martyr), removed

Septuagesima the third Sunday before Lent

Sheer Thursday Maundy Thursday in Holy Week, before Easter

singing-cakes wafer used in celebration of mass

surplice the standard white vestment worn by a priest

trental a series of thirty masses for the dead

tyning (or tynel) a small vessel used to hold holy water

vicar a salaried minister, often a substitute for rector

Whitsuntide late spring or early summer festivities, associated with Pentecost

INDEX

Abbot, George, Archbishop: 137–9, 173

Act of Supremacy, Royal Supremacy: 2, 7, 24, 25, 69, 163

Act in Restraint of Appeals (1533): 2

Act of Uniformity (1559): 5, 40, 56–9

Allen, William: 9, 110–13

altar: *see* communion altar

altar rails: 9, 78, 80, 162

Anabaptists: 32, 70, 138, 195–9, 202

Andrewes, Lancelot, Bishop: 142–3

Anti-Calvinists, Anti-Calvinism, Arminians, Arminianism: 8–9, 142–3, 158, 176, 179, 180

Antwerp: 31–2

Armada, Spanish (1588): 7

Articles of Religion (1563): 5, 48, 59–70, 90, 125, 139, 174, 180

Askew, Anne, martyr: 3, 32–4

Bancroft, Richard, Archbishop: 132–5

baptism: 2, 3, 18, 31, 32, 48–51, 62, 63, 66, 83, 85–6, 124–5, 128–30, 160–1, 165–6, 171, 172, 189–90, 198–9

Baxter, Richard: 10, 199–203

Becon, Thomas: 73–8

Bible, Scripture: 7, 18, 21, 30, 33, 40–2, 60–1, 80, 91, 123, 125, 161, 176

'Black Rubric' (1552): 4, 47–8

Boleyn, Anne, Queen: 24, 25

Bonner, Edmund, Bishop: 4

bonfires: 13

Book of Common Prayer, Prayer Book: 3–4, 5, 6, 7, 9, 24, 40–56, 56–9, 80, 82–7, 91, 92, 97, 124, 125, 162–4, 170, 186–9

Book of Sports, Declaration of Sports (1618; reissued 1633): 7, 9, 145–8, 151–5

Bradshaw, William: 135–7

Buckeridge, John, Bishop: 141–2, 142

burial: 10, 55–6, 86, 92, 159–60, 191–2

Burton, Henry: 8, 151–5

Calvinists, Calvinism: 5–6, 7–8, 9, 111, 114, 137, 142, 169, 173

Canons, Ecclesiastical (1604): 48, 127–32

Catechism: 73–8, 139, 156–7, 164, 199–200

Catholics, Catholicism, Roman Catholicism, Recusants, Recusancy: 1, 2, 4, 6, 7, 11, 82–90, 110–13, 132–5, 137, 143–4, 146, 147, 156, 163, 174, 176, 177, 179, 180, 181

Cecil, Robert: 126

Cecil, William: 110

ceremonies: 8, 9, 22–3, 26, 29, 42–5, 65, 68, 127, 136–7, 163, 169–70, 187–8

Charles I, King: 8, 9, 108, 145–8, 180

Charles II, King: 10, 199

church ales: 148–50

Church courts, Ecclesiastical courts: 5, 87–9, 107–110, 132, 155–7, 177–9

churching of women: 54–5, 83, 87, 166

churchwardens, churchwardens' accounts: 35–9, 78–81, 90–3, 107–10, 155–7, 178

churchyards: 55, 159–60

civil wars, British: 9, 145, 158, 180, 183, 200

communion altar: 8, 11, 20, 33, 37, 38, 91, 158, 161–2, 167–8, 177

communion table: 8, 37, 45, 47, 79, 80,

81, 91, 108, 131–2, 155, 157, 162, 177
confession: 19, 33, 46
confirmation: 2, 124–5
convocation: 13–17, 17
Corpus Christi: 12–13, 36, 38
Cranmer, Thomas, Archbishop: 3, 4, 40
Creed: 18, 46, 51, 61
Cromwell, Oliver, Lord Protector: 9, 199, 202
Cromwell, Thomas: 25

Directory of Public Worship: 9, 180, 186–92
Dissolution of Monasteries: 2, 24–5
Dow, Christopher: 9, 168–72
Dowsing, William: 183–6

Edward VI, King: 3, 4, 13, 24, 25, 40, 56, 57, 59, 70, 124, 169
Edward, Thomas: 10, 195–9
election: *see* predestination
Elizabeth I, Queen: 4, 5, 8, 11, 56–9, 69, 70, 93–9, 110, 124
episcopacy: 6, 7, 9, 82, 128, 163, 174–9, 181–2
Eucharist, Communion, Lord's Supper: 2, 4, 8, 20, 26, 27, 33, 45–8, 57, 66, 67, 83, 84, 91, 131–2, 155, 157, 161–2, 167–8, 172, 173, 177
excommunication: 88, 124–5, 178
extreme unction (last rites): 2

Foxe, John, martyrologist: 4, 9, 13, 32–5

games, sports, and plays: 7, 92–3, 105, 109–10, 132, 145–8, 148–50, 151–5, 176
Gardiner, Samuel: 139–40
Gifford, George: 99–105, 174
Gowrie conspiracy: 79
Grindal, Edmund, Archbishop: 6, 90–3, 93–9, 173
Gunpowder Plot, Fifth of November (1605): 7, 79–80

Hampton Court Conference (1604): 7, 123–7, 170
Henry VIII, King: 2, 3, 13, 24, 25, 30, 32, 33, 124
Hickman, Rose: 4, 29–32, 169
Holy Orders, Consecration: 2, 69, 89

images: 21, 23, 26, 183–6
Ireland: 126, 180, 181

James VI and I, King: 7, 8, 123–7, 143, 145–8, 170
Jewel, John, Bishop: 45
Justification: 20–1, 62, 63

Katherine of Aragon, Queen: 2, 24
Kidderminster (Worcestershire): 199–203
kneeling: 8, 63, 64, 65–6, 115, 117, 121, 123, 169, 173, 193–4, 212, 223, 229
Knox, John: 48, 169

Latimer, Hugh, Bishop: 3, 4, 13–17, 31, 32, 34–5
Laud, William, Archbishop: 8, 9, 148, 151, 155–7
Laudians, Laudianism: 8–9, 142, 169, 174
Leicestershire: 155–7
Long Melford (Suffolk): 11–13

Magistrates: 69, 70, 175, 192–5
Martyn, Roger: 2, 4, 9, 11–13
Mary I, Queen: 4, 11, 13, 24, 28, 29, 30, 31, 169
mass: 27, 28–9, 30, 33, 36, 37, 83, 84, 177
matrimony, marriage: 2, 51–4, 66, 68, 86, 166, 190–1
Matthew, Tobie, Archbishop: 123–7
Montague, Richard: 157–68
More, Thomas: 24

original sin: 18–9, 62, 117, 175
ornaments, church: 59

Papacy, the Pope, the Bishop of Rome: 24, 69
Parkyn, Robert: 2, 24–9, 169
Parliament: 9, 27, 28, 82, 83, 174–9, 180, 182, 192
penance: 2, 19–20, 66, 107–8, 124–5, 164
Perkins, William: 114–20, 139
Piers, William, Bishop: 148–50
Pilgrimage of Grace (1536): 3
Pole, Reginald, Cardinal: 4
preachers, preaching: 13–14, 84, 95–7, 99–105, 105–6, 108, 137–9, 163, 164, 199–203

predestination: 5–6, 8, 59, 63–4, 114–20, 139–40, 164, 175
Presbyterians, presbyterianism: 6, 9, 82, 180, 186, 195, 199
Proffet, Nicholas: 192–5
prophesyings: 93, 97–8
protectorate: 9–10, 199, 202
Protestation Oath (1641): 180
Purgatory: 2, 16, 23–4, 65
Puritans, puritanism: 6–9, 114, 135–7, 146, 147, 155, 157, 163, 195

Reprobation: 6, 117–8, 119–20
Restoration: 10
Ridley, Nicholas, Bishop: 4, 31, 32, 34–5
rood loft, rood screen: 4, 12, 13, 91
'Roots and Branches' (Root and Branch) Petition: 9, 174–9
rubrics: 124

Saints: 2, 3, 13, 21–2, 83, 84, 178
St. Edmund's parish, Salisbury (Wiltshire): 35–9, 78–81
Scotland: 9, 126, 179, 180–3, 195

Sheldon, Richard: 105–7
sign of the cross: 85, 125, 128–30
Six Articles ('King's Book,' 1539): 3, 33
Solemn League and Covenant (1643): 180–3
Stubbes, Philip: 105–7
synod of Dort (1618–9): 7, 142–3

Ten Articles (1536): 2, 17–24
Thirty-Nine Articles: see Articles of Religion (1563)
transubstantiation: 18, 48, 67

vestments: 26, 36–8, 59, 79–81, 86, 89, 125, 130–1, 156–7, 161, 164, 169, 175
visitation, visitation articles: 155–7, 157–68

Ward, Samuel: 120–22

York province: 90–3

Zwingli, Ulrich: 4